Cambridge with Kids

The Essential Guide for Families

Includes Ely, Huntingdon, Newmarket, Peterborough and St Ives

1st Edition

By
Katie Higney

Red Cherry Books

Cambridge with Kids: The Essential Guide for Families 1st Edition

www.cambridgewithkids.com

Published by Red Cherry Books
December 2013
www.redcherrybooks.com

Cover Design & Photography by Red Cherry Books
ISBN 978-0-9928010-2-1

The information is up to date at the time of printing, but occasionally contact details or organisations can change. It is up to parents to decide whether the information given in 'Cambridge with Kids' is suitable or appropriate for their children.

Disclaimer

Copyright

Maps

RED CHERRY BOOKS
81 Fernwalk, Ballincollig,
Cork, Ireland

Contents

Quick Reference Things to Do

INTRODUCTION

Ever wondered where you could find a class for your child on archery, drama, music or sports? Would you like inspiration on things to do locally, such as cinemas, theatres, museums, wildlife parks, or kid friendly places to eat? Where is your nearest antenatal class, playgroup or indoor soft play centre?

I spent several years in Cambridge with young children and I thought it would be great to have all the information in one place. After all, being a parent is a busy job and who wants to spend hours finding the nearest dance class or nursery?

I hope that this book will help you to get the most out of where you live, whether in Cambridge or the surrounding area.
www.cambridgewithkids.com

The City of Cambridge and the Surrounding Area

Cambridge is compact and easy to get around if you have children. The city is best known for its colleges entertwined with tourists, students and bikes. However it is not merely a city with a historic past, or just a town with a famous University. There are world class museums like the Fitzwilliam and unique events such as the Science Festival for kids. And most of these are free!

Nearby Ely, Huntingdon, St Neots, St Ives, Newmarket and Peterborough in the low lying fens have lots of family activities, country parks and historic buildings. From fishing to fen and river walks, country parks to castles there is something for all the family.

Top 10 Family Favourites

1. **Museums:** Find the Knights in Armour in the Fitzwilliam Museum in Cambridge (p21); the stained glass at Ely Cathedral (p61);or explore the Horse Museum in Newmarket (p65).
2. **Summer swims:** Splash about in an outdoor pool in the summer (p68, 83).
3. **Country parks:** Explore the wildlife in Wandlebury Country Park; Milton Country Park; Paxton Pits and Ferry Meadows (p55-56, 70).
4. **Visit an air show:** Watch the magnificent World War Planes zoom across the sky at the Imperial War Museum, Duxford. (p70).
5. **Seasonal fun:** Visit the Lambs at Easter in Wimpole Hall (p55); a summer picnic in Grantchester Meadows (p16) or get lost in Autumn at the Milton Maize Maze (p58).
6. **Saturday Movies:** Many cinemas have a low cost Kids Saturday club (p19).
7. **Take a train or bus for an adventure:** Train to Ely (p61); Guided bus to St Ives (p64) or bus Newmarket (p65); Huntingdon (p63) or a steam train in the Nene Valley (p66).
8. **Play tennis or football** outside on the many open green spaces (p4).
9. **Find objects** left behind on a trail with geocache or go on a treasure hunt (p18).
10. **Indoor Fun:** Swimming, indoor soft play, go karting, ice skating, trampoline and more (p66-69, 83-92).

CAMBRIDGE CITY

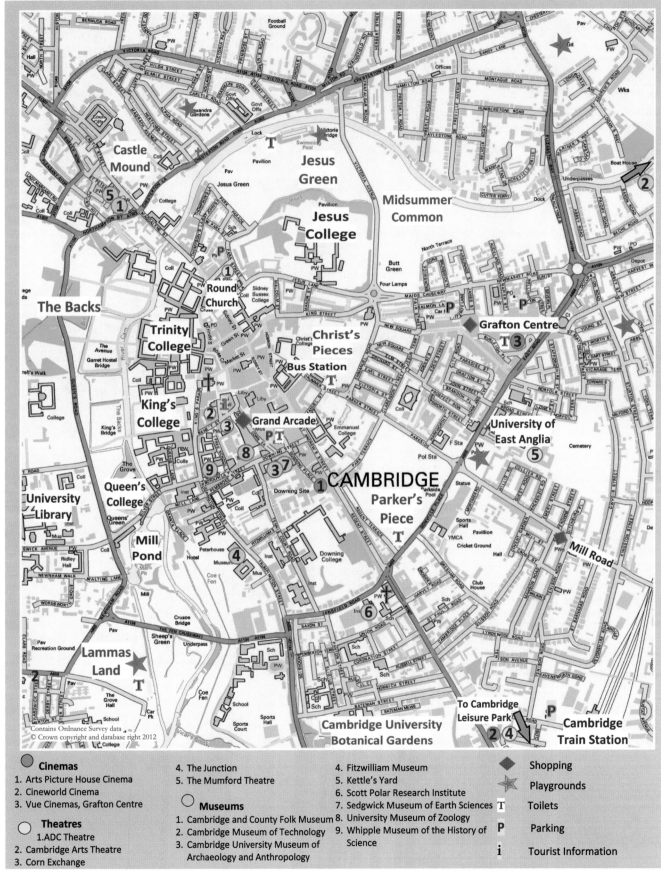

Cinemas
1. Arts Picture House Cinema
2. Cineworld Cinema
3. Vue Cinemas, Grafton Centre

Theatres
1. ADC Theatre
2. Cambridge Arts Theatre
3. Corn Exchange
4. The Junction
5. The Mumford Theatre

Museums
1. Cambridge and County Folk Museum
2. Cambridge Museum of Technology
3. Cambridge University Museum of Archaeology and Anthropology
4. Fitzwilliam Museum
5. Kettle's Yard
6. Scott Polar Research Institute
7. Sedgwick Museum of Earth Sciences
8. University Museum of Zoology
9. Whipple Museum of the History of Science

Shopping

Playgrounds

T   Toilets

P   Parking

i   Tourist Information

CAMBRIDGE CITY

The first section is about the kid friendly places to go in Cambridge. The city is a great place for children, with fantastic parks, interesting museums, cinemas and events.

Most locals get around by bike. There is a brief look at types of child carriers, safety and training. You can even cycle to the centre of town and borrow a buggy for the day. Alternatively, buses are frequent, have low floors and buggy access Local shops cater for every need from maternity, toys, sports, comics and pets.

It is a beautiful city to walk around. If you live in the town it can be easy to forget how pleasant the backs of the colleges are in spring, Midsummer Common in the snow, or just the simple pleasure of having an ice cream with the kids on a hot day by the river.

There are playgrounds in most areas but also right in town at Christ's Pieces or Jesus Green. If it's raining, you could get a kids activity pack to explore the Fitzwilliam Museum, or see a movie at the reduced price Saturday morning cinemas. There are five theatres, three cinemas and plenty of indoor play centres so there is always something to do. There are also many child friendly places to eat out. Or have a picnic on Jesus Green and watch the swans, ducks and boats sail by.

3

PARKS, PLAYGROUNDS & GREEN SPACES

Parker's Piece

Cambridge has a naturally flat, fen landscape and is fortunate in having many green spaces that are great for walking and playing games. Parkers Piece, Midsummer Common and Jesus Green are large greens in the city. These also hold some great children friendly events in the summer. Christ's Pieces have pretty flower beds, a playground and are a throughfare between the Grafton Centre and the Grand Arcade Shopping Centre. The University Botanic Gardens are full of interest for a child to explore.

The river running through the city is flanked by green open spaces. It clings to the side of Midsummer Common, along Jesus Green and the backs of the beautifully kept University Colleges. Eventually it flows out of the city again, through Lammas Land, with cows grazing and weeping willows before winding its way on to Grantchester.

There are plenty of nature reserves including Milton Country Park formed with lakes from old pits, (page 56), and large parks such as Cherry Hinton Hall (page 53). Smaller but just as pleasant are areas such as Logan's Meadow (Abbey) and Nine Wells (Addenbrookes Hospital).

Recreation and Playgrounds

Cambridge City Council has an excellent map and list of playgrounds on it's website www.cambridge.gov.uk

Arbury Court play area
Older and younger children's play area.

Brooks Rd play area
Springy's, a slide and swings suitable for all ages.

Cherry Hinton Rec
Two football pitches, a skateboard ramp and playground.

Chesterton Rec
Two football pitches, skate ramp and under 6's area.

Chestnut Grove Rec
All ages playground.

Coleridge Rec
Football, tennis and children's play-ground.

Dudly Rd Rec
Skate ramp and playground.

Flower Street
Swing and slide.

Green End Rec
Youth shelter, playground.

Gunhild Close
Playground. Timber goals.

Histon Rd Rec
Good children's play area with slide and swings.

Holbrook Rd Rec
Goal end, climber, and springy's.

Kings Hedges Rec
Children's playground and a learner pool.

Riverside and Newmarket Rd
Large open space that leads you right out into the country following the river. Good children's playground near Stanley Road entrance. Cows and horses graze on the land here.

Stourbridge Common Playground

Mill Rd/ East Rd Playground

Jesus Green

Petersfield play area

Peverel Rd

Ravensworth Gardens

Riley Way

Mill Rd/East Rd corner Playground

Romsey Rec

Scotland Rd

Shelly Row

St Albans Rd
Football pitch, skateboard ramp and playground.

St Matthew's Piece

St Thomas Square

Tenby Close

Tennison Rd/Ravensworth Gardens This is located on a roof garden.

Thorpe Way/Fison Rd
Trim trail for small children and fitness zones for older children.

Trumpington Rec
Football pitch and playground.

Woodhead Drive

Parks with Playgrounds

Alexander Gardens
Carlyle Road
This has a climb net for older children, and a play area for under 6s.

Cherry Hinton Hall Park
Cherry Hinton Road
The park has a lake, two paddling pools, and play equipment for older and young children. Also a bird sanctuary.

Christ's Pieces
Emmanuel Road
A very central park with four free tennis courts, a refreshment kiosk and a popular play area for the under 6s. It is a good rest stop between shops and is right by the bus station. It has pretty flower beds and is also a popular hang out for teenagers. There is a Princess Diana Memorial Garden in the centre.

Lammas Land/Coe Fen

Jesus Green
Chesterton Road/Victoria Avenue

This is adjacent to the River Cam, and a great place to watch the ducks and swans. It has a playground for smaller children, a small picnic area and also a skateboard ramp, tennis courts and an open air swimming pool open in the summer. There is also a small kiosk for food or ice creams. It has a beautiful avenue of London Planes and horse chestnut trees. It's a great place to have a picnic.

Lammas Land, Sheep's Green
The Fen Causeway

This is a lovely place to take the kids. It is by the river, with a playground, and a paddling pool. There is a kiosk in the summer. On the wilder parts across the river from the playground are cows. There are some small streams and weeping willows, one side leads to Grantchester, the other the Mill Pond. It also has a free tennis court.

Stourbridge Common
Riverside to Fen Road

This is quite scrub like and not good for playing on, but it has a children's playground near the Riverside entrance. You could take a long walk along the River Cam where you can see swans, ducks, houseboats and rowers.

Green Spaces

Arbury Town Park
Campkin Road

Found behind the Arbury Community Centre. Nearby are the two Kings Hedges Recreation grounds.

Coe Fen
(See also Lammas Land and Sheep's Green)
The Fen Causeway

Meadow land from the Mill Pond to Lammas Land. It often has cows grazing and follows an old wall at the back of the Fitzwilliam Museum. It has small criss cross paths leading to small bridges over the river.

Coldham's Common
Barnwell Road

This is a very large green in the east of Cambridge, Romsey Town area. It is near Abbey Pool and Coldham's Lane playground. Coldham's Brook runs through it.

Midsummer Common
Chesterton/Newmarket Road

A lovely large, ancient grassland by the river. The grass is rougher and not as good for picnics or football. These are busy and well used footpaths, so keep to the left to let bikes pass. Sometimes it contains a herd of cows, recently Red Poll Bullocks. The University boathouses line one side, and you can watch the rowers train for races. In the past few years, the river has also filled with houseboats. The Fort St. George pub serves food.

Midsummer Common

Parker's Piece
East Road
A popular large, flat green great for playing football and other games. In summer you can watch cricket. It has a public toilet and refreshment kiosk in the corner by the Catholic Church.

The Backs
Queen's Road
The 'Backs' of the riverside colleges have well maintained lawns and in spring are full of daffodils and crocuses beneath the trees. More of a walk than a playing space.

Nature Reserves
(See also Animals and Wildlife Section)
Cambridge City has a useful web site with news and events on local nature reserves. There are several in and around Cambridge.
lnr.cambridge.gov.uk

Barnwell East & West
This used to be a piggery, but is now grassland, scrub and a small pond.

Bramblefields Chesterton
Scrub, grassland and a small pond.

Byron's Pool
Grantchester
This is on the road from Grantchester to Trumpington. It has several pools and woodland. Lord Byron the poet used to like swimming here.

Limekiln Close & West Pitt
Cherry Hinton
These were chalk quarries, it is now woodland and grassland.

Logan's Meadow Abbey
On the banks of the River Cam, with mature willows and temporary ponds.

Nine Wells
Near Addenbrooks Hospital
This is a pretty beech copse with springs, which are the source for Hobson's Conduit.

Paradise Meadow Newnham
On the beginning of the path to Grantchester from Cambridge, this has woodland, willows and a marsh.

University of Cambridge Botanic Garden

1 Brookside, Cambridge CB2 1JE
Tel: 01223 336265
www.botanic.cam.ac.uk
The garden was established as a University teaching and research resource by Professor John Stevens Henslow on land acquired in 1831, and finally opened to the public in 1846. It has a cafe and picnic area, a lake and woods. It is great for younger kids to run around by the trees, look at the ducks and explore the meandering paths.

Admission: £4.50 for Adults, 0-16 yrs Free.
Open:
10am-6pm Apr to Sep;
10 am-5pm Feb, Mar, Oct;
10 am-4 pm Nov to Jan.

Annual Events on Cambridge Greens

JUNE
Strawberry Fair
Midsummer Common
Popular free music and arts event., with craft and food stalls. It is completely run by volunteers. It is best for kids earlier in the day, with a parade, as it gets very busy with music acts in the evening.

Midsummer Fair
Midsummer Common

This is one of the oldest fairs in the UK. Today it has modern fairground rides, candy floss and carousels.

JULY
Cambridge Folk Festival
Cherry Hinton Hall
This three day event is one of the most famous folk festivals in the world. It has children's events and a crèche for a limited number at Cherry Hinton Hall. It is a paying festival, but Cambridge City Residents get a discount.

The Big Weekend
Parker's Piece
A great free music event in recent years. With live acts on a main stage, dance and kids activities, fair rides and stalls.

SEPTEMBER
Cherry Hinton Festival
A free community festival held in the park, with music and activities for kids.

NOVEMBER 5th
Bonfire Night
Midsummer Common
A firework and bonfire display to mark Guy Fawkes night.

Map of Cambridge Parks & Green Spaces

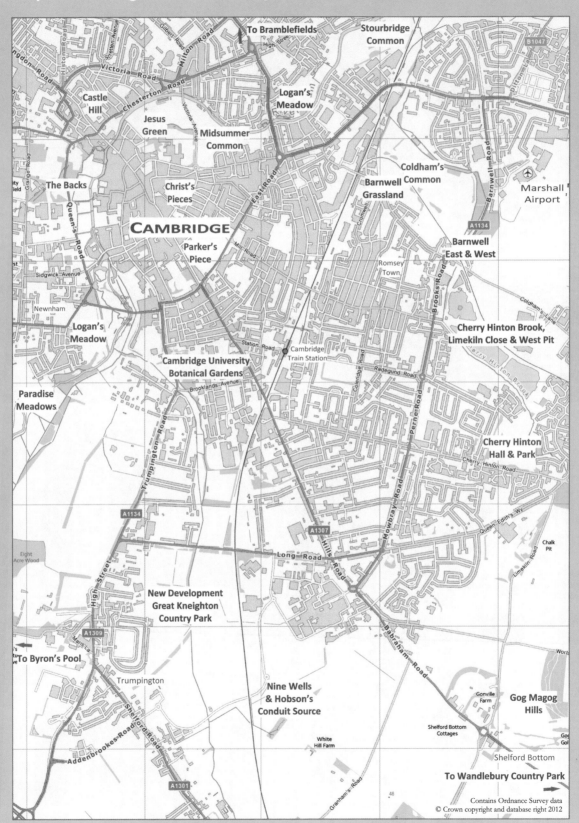

Contains Ordnance Survey data
© Crown copyright and database right 2012

CAMBRIDGE WALKS

Cambridge has a variety of walks that suit children, because it has so many open green spaces around the centre. If you have visitors who want to look around the colleges, then there are very short walks around the river and in the ancient and historic buildings, with the added bonus of being near cafes, public transport and shops if you need them.

To make walks more interesting, children of all ages can be inspired by a bit of knowledge about an areas social and geological history. For example did you know there is an ancient water course running underneath Jesus Green? Or that Castle Hill was where the earliest Cambridge people lived? Walk to see nature, like the autumn leaves, ducks, insects or even bats.

And there are also some fantastic ways to make a mini detective out of your kids, with treasure walks or 'geocaching'. These are a fun way to make an adventure out of exploring.

Facts about Cambridgeshire
- It has over 240 state schools - that is a lot of children!
- The area has less rain than anywhere in the country.
- The population of Cambridge is 125,000 and Cambridgeshire is 600,000.
- The University of Cambridge was founded in 1209. The library has 29 million books.
- The whole town north of the river was almost wiped out by the Black Death in 1349.
- The University of Cambridge has its own constabulary.
- There are around 30,000 students in Cambridge.

City College Walk

Short: 1.3 miles, 30 minutes
Long: 2 miles, 1 hour

This is good for visiting relatives or as a short jaunt around town.

1. Start in **Christ's Pieces** by the main bus station and walk around the corner to **Emmanuelle College**. This has a pond with fishes. Notice the mother and child sculpture on the corner of John Lewis.

2. Then head across to **Downing Street**, past the **University Archeological and Zoology Museums.** Look up to your left at the carvings of the Mammoth, Iguanadon and the Giant Sloth. There is also a

carving of a green man, with leaves coming from his mouth. Carry on down Pembroke Street, and then turn right into Free School Lane. This takes you past the **Whipple Museum.** Turn left after St. Benets Parish Church and turn right into King's Parade.

Stop at the gold plated **Corpus Clock,** with the grasshopper on top showing time being eaten up. At odd times, the eyes blink. It is conceived and funded by John Taylor. The inscription is in Latin, and means 'The world passeth away, and the lust thereof'.

3. If you want a shorter walk, carry on walking towards King's College and Great St. Mary's Church, up Trinity Street to the Round Church (98.

4. If little legs can take it, go for the longer walk by the backs. Cross the road to walk down the lane to Granta Place and the **Mill Pond.** This is a nice place to stop, on a summers day to have a picnic.

5. Walk over the bridge and across to Queens College. The next right is a path across a green that will take you on to **the backs of Kings and other colleges**. In the spring it is full of crocuses and daffodils.

The Round Church

6. The **Garrett Hostel Lane** takes you over a bridge with a lovely view of Trinity Hall and Clare College. The cobbled street bends around into Trinity Lane past Gonville and Caius College.

7. Then you can either choose to walk into town for the shops, the market, or a cafe (Tatties is closest on Trinity Street).

8. Or you can go left past **Trinity College** and the tempting Old Sweet Shop. Over the road is the medieval **Round Church** (or Church of the Holy Spechulcre).

9 Look out in the pavement for the **brass flower studding.** They were 'planted' by the Council to encourage people to walk over Magdalene Street and beyond. If you follow them, past Kettles Yard Art Gallery you'll see Castle Hill, on the right with views of all of Cambridge. It is a short steep climb.

Brass Flowers

River Walk to Stourbridge Common

1. Starting in **Magdalene Bridge**, take the wooden river walk to Jesus Green, past the ducks by the Weir, past the playground and under the Victoria Avenue Bridge coming out in **Midsummer Common.**

2. Carry on past the Fort St. George Pub, and past **Ferry Cutter's Bridge,** underneath the Elizabeth Way dual carriageway to follow Riverside. If you want a shorter walk or a diversion, take the New Bridge to **Logan's Meadow.**

3. Carrying on up Riverside, past the tall chimney of the **Museum of Technology.** Soon after you come to the entrance of Stourbridge Common. It feels wilder, with rough grass and often grazing cows. There is a playground to the right.

Riverside Bridge

4. **Stourbridge Common** used to hold Stourbridge Fair, It was a Medieval Fair that was once the largest one of its kind in Europe. The **Leper Chapel** was granted permission to hold the 3 day fair to raise funds by King John in 1199. The **Green Dragon Bridge** used to be, like most Cambridge bridges, a ferry pulled by a Horse Grind.

Museum of Technology

The River Cam

Mini Walks for Tired Little Feet

Lammas Land to Coe Fen - ½ mile

This is a nice area of meadowland to roam around with plenty to explore. It has the addition of a playground and in summer a free outdoor pool There are a few pathways cutting through the flat fen scrubland, around the Mill Pond and following the wall at the back of the Fitzwilliam Museums.

Vicars Brook - ½ mile
This is a charming river path under trees at the back of allotments. Starts at the corner of Brooklands Avenue, and Trumpington Road, opposite the back of the Botanic Gardens. Follow the sign that says 'Public Footpath to Long Road'.
BUS: Citi 4 runs from the centre to the start and finish every 20 minutes.

Midsummer Common to Jesus Green - ½ mile

There is lots to see just by following the river looking at the boats, the swans and the weir by the bridge in Jesus Green. There is plenty of grass to run around and you can stop off at the playground or kiosk by Jesus Lock.

Midsummer Common

Jesus Green

Nature

River Wildlife

The river has swans and ducks, pike and perch, you may even spot kingfishers. You might be lucky enough to see more exotic species such as black swans, Egyptian geese, wood ducks and

mandarin ducks which have escaped from bird collections. You can also see seagulls. The odd cow has even fallen in the river! (It has been rescued safely).

Bats

As you look at the river in the evening, you might be lucky enough to spot a bat. The bat flies over the water to feed on insects. Bats are the world's only flying mammal. They emit their own sonar used to find their prey. They need to eat 3000 insects a night just to stay alive and are very important for our ecosystem. (There are punt tours for bat watching scudamores.com). There is even a Cambridgeshire Bat group www.facebook.com/CambridgeshireBatGroup

The Backs

These are full of daffodils and crocuses in the spring. Mead-owsweet grows near ditches, bogs and on river banks. The greens look natural but are totally man made.

Cambridge Geology Trail

www.sedgwickmuseum.org

The Sedgwick Museum of Earth Sciences has a great guide to looking at rock types and geological features in our every day environment. You

can purchase it at The Sedgewick Museum. For example, did you know that the outside of the Marks & Spencer Store is made from different types of magma (formed from hot rock), white granite, red granite and black gabbro. Grand Arcade is clad in Jaumont Limestone from France, and Jura Yellow Marble limestone. Look

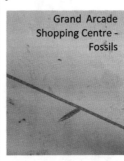
Grand Arcade Shopping Centre - Fossils

closely at the floor where you can see fossils of shell and cuttle fish.

Cambridge City Football Ground

This used to be called Swan's Pit. It was a sand gravel quarry, and most of the buildings are made from this material. Fossils of giant deer, mammoth, woolly rhino and horse were found here, dated 180,000 years ago, in the Ice Age.

Jesus Green

At the entrance to Jesus Green Swimming Pool you would have been under water thousands of years ago. There is a buried channel 10-15 metres deep. It runs beneath Jesus College, past Cambridge City football ground and north towards the Histon Road.

Grafton Centre

There is an old ridge of gravel starting from behind the old Leper Chapel on Newmarket Road to the Grafton Centre, which is the course of an old eastern tributary of the River Cam. The source of the present Cam joined the river at the site of the Grafton Centre. We know this because of ancient river deposits of mud, gravel and sand.

Newmarket Road

The remains of reindeer, mammoths, woolly rhino and horse were found in Newmarket Road and have been dated to about 20,000 years old. At this time in the last Ice Age, ice sheets had ramped up on the North Norfolk coast, making the Cambridge area a very chilly ice-bound, high arctic environment. You can see the remains of these animals in the Sedgwick Museum.

History

Castle Hill

Cambridge originally started at the site of Castle Hill. The river used to be known as the Granta and the Saxons named it 'Grantabrycge' (bridge of the Granta) and built St Benet's Church. The area grew as a Scandinavian trading centre and as an inland port.

Castle Hill

The Norman's built a Castle on the hill in 1068, but now just the mound remains. Climb up and you can see for miles. If you look at the city coat of arms you'll see ships, sea horses and bridges.

Cambridge Train Station

The railway arrived in 1845, and placed outside the town centre following pressure from the University who restricted travel of undergraduates.

Elizabeth Way Bridge

In the 19th century, because of drops in wages and more mechanisation in the countryside, many people flocked to nearby towns like Cambridge to work on the pits, building colleges and the railway. Most of the housing was in East Road and Newmarket Road, which was cramped and in a poor state, lived in by manual labourers. Most of these houses have now been pulled down. The roundabout was where the village of Barnwell existed. Part of Barnwell Priory still exists on Beche Rd.

Hobson's Conduit

After disease and plague from unsanitary conditions, early in the 1600s the town and the University joined to fund Hobson's Conduit. It's a watercourse that brings fresh water into the city.

The water is from Nine Wells, which are springs at the foot of the Gog Magog hills near Great Shelford. This water is naturally filtered through the chalk rock, into Vicar's Brook. The Conduit sent to the bottom of

Pembroke Street to flush out the ditch and keep the water moving. It flows to Market Square.

The octagonal monument shown, once formed part of the Market Square Fountain, and was moved to Lensfield Road corner after a fire in the Market in 1856.

The original courseway still functions along Trumpington Street, where it is known as Pem (east side) and Pot (west side).

Thomas Hobson made lots of money on horse traffic between Cambridge and London. The expression 'Hobson's Choice' means that you've got 'no choice'. It was because he rented horses to students who had no choice about which horse they got.

Walk to Grantchester

This is a 3 mile walk following the river in the south of the city, and is one of the best walks around Cambridge. A round trip on a straighter road back makes 5 miles in total.

1. You can start from **Lammas Land** or Grantchester Street. As you walk down the street there is a little Co-op shop where you can get supplies for the journey, especially drinks on a hot day.
BUS: The 18 bus goes from Drummer Street, Cambridge every hour, to Grantchester Street and Grantchester village.

2. Turn right onto Eltisley Avenue, past a chemist shop and then onto **Grantchester Meadows.** The houses gradually make way for grassy fenland. This is the start of the walk.

3. There are two options, to keep on the more marked, higher path, or one closer to the river. In the summer, many people picnic by the banks of the river. The path continues on to Grantchester High Street.

4. The **Orchard Tea Rooms,** once the place of poets, has deckchairs under the apple trees for a tea and scone break.
Return Jouney: You can retrace your steps or go on the shorter route along Trumpington Road. After you reach Grantchester, keep left on Grantchester Road. Past the Mill Pond .The pavements can be narrow and winding.

5. After 50m take a right to Byron's Pool. Then back to Grantchester Road and turn right.

5. Follow the road as it forks, onto Church Lane and then left to Trumpington Road.. Follow the pedestrian and cycle path back to Cambridge. It

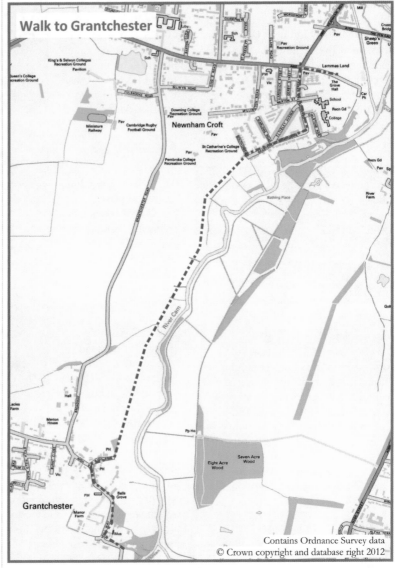

Walk to Grantchester

is a busy road but more direct than the Grantchester Meadows path.
BUS: To take the bus back, there are several along Trumpington Road. The 88 park and ride bus goes every 10 minutes from a stop near Waitrose or opposite Porson Road.

Grantchester Village

This ia a really pretty little village, with thatched cottages, a 14th century church. For refreshments try the local pubs the Blue Ball or Green Man, or sit outside in deck chairs under apple trees at the Orchard Tea Gardens.

Grantchester is said to have the highest concentration of Nobel Prize winners in the world. It is also a song by Pink Floyd, whose band members were from Cambridge. There is a legend that there is a two mile old underground passage from the Old Manor House in Grantchester to King's College Chapel. A fiddler was said to have volunteered to follow the passage, and set off until his music became fainter and fainter, and he was never seen again.

Sculpture and Carvings

There are several sculptures, carvings and engravings around Cambridge, as well as interesting emblems of animals. They can be nice to look out for with kids when you are out and about.

Some of my favourites are: Mammoth, Iguanadon, Bears, skeleton of Whale, wooden Mother and Child and Earthbound, (the 'upside down' feet - which is a whole statue of a man upside down). And that is just Downing Street!

Look out for the three Cambridge Sculpture Trail Guides, available free at the Tourist Office or online - www.cambridgesculpturetrails.co.uk

The Swimmers - Betty Rea
Parkside Pool

The Ploughman

Bears
unknown

Bison

Confucius - Wu Wei Shan
Clare College

Earthbound - Antony Gormley

CAMBRIDGE WALKS

Longer Walks Around Cambridgeshire

DEFRA – Rural Affairs
Tel: 08459 335577
helpline@defra.gsi.gov.uk
www.countrywalks.defra.gov.uk
This lists more than 1800 walks in the United Kingdom. Select your destination and the website provides mini guides and map references to help explore the countryside.

Cherry Hinton Brook
www.friendsofcherryhintonbrook.org.uk
Follows a route past Coldham's Common to join the Cam north west of Cherry Hinton Hall. It rises near Lime Kiln Hill. It is a busy route for walkers and cyclists. Kingfishers can be seen along this path

Fen Drove and Bishop Manor
A 5 mile circular walk in Fen Ditton and Horningsea. Interesting history and quiet fenland.

Hobson's Brook and Nine Wells
A 3 mile straight walk in Trumpington and Great Shelford following Hobson's Brook from Cambridge City to its spring source at Nine Wells.

Ouse Valley Way
Northamptonshire to King's Lynn
At 150 miles the Ouse Valley Way is one of the longest river valley walks in Britain. The route takes in Godmanchester, the picturesque Houghton Mill, St Ives & the Cambridgeshire Fens.

Shepreth and Barrington
A 6 mile circular walk in Shepreth and Barrington. Includes two nature reserves and a picnic area.

Wilbrahem Fen
A 4.5 mile circular walk through the fen drove roads and reed beds.

Looking for Treasure

Treasure Trails - Cambridgeshire
www.treasuretrails.co.uk
A commercial website where you can buy trail maps and explore on a treasure hunt. In Cambridge there is a Riverside Walk, two College trails, a Ghost Story Trail and one from the train station to the city. Also Grantchester, Ely, Huntingdon.

Geocaching
www.geocaching.com
This is a modern day treasure hunt, using a GPS device to find hidden containers or 'caches'. It is a nice, simple idea set up by volunteers worldwide. And it's free. You can put in your postcode and search for nearby caches. You can also find out how to hide your own cache using the guidelines online. They will contain a log book to sign, and a small number of items of low monetary value that you can trade e.g. Key rings, small toys.

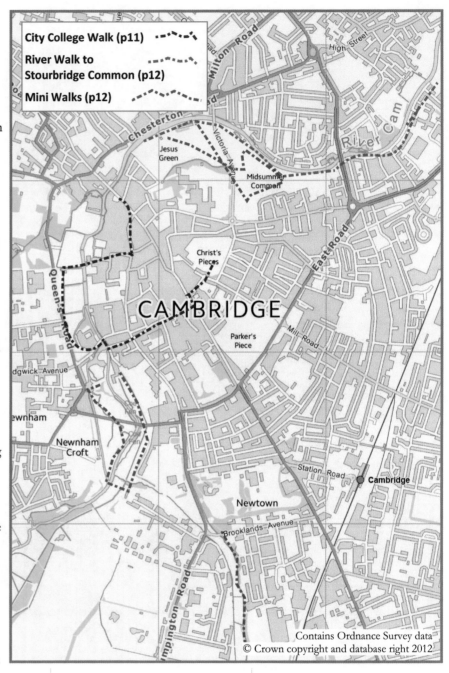

City College Walk (p11)

River Walk to Stourbridge Common (p12)

Mini Walks (p12)

Contains Ordnance Survey data © Crown copyright and database right 2012

RAINY DAYS

What to do When it's Pouring Outside

It's raining outside but the little ones are getting restless. What is there to do?

There are some great museums in Cambridge, most of them free. My personal favourites are the **Fitzwilliam Museum** and the **University of Cambridge Museum of Zoology**, but there are many others.

There are three good local cinemas; **Cineworld**, **Vue** and the **Arts Picture House** which all have special children showings. And if you fancy letting the kids run around and let off steam, there are soft play areas like the **Funky Fun House**, **Cheeky Monkeys Play Barn,** swimming pools and leisure centres.

Or you can put on the raincoats and wellies and let the kids splash in puddles! The section contains ideas of what to do inside if you really don't want to venture out.

Cinemas

Arts Picture House Cinema
38-39 St Andrew's St, Cambridge CB2 3AR
Tel: 0871 902 5720
www.picturehouses.co.uk/cinema/Arts_Picturehouse_Cambridge
This 3 screen arts cinema shows a wide variety of films. There is a Kid's Club on Saturdays suitable for 3–10 year olds. On Wednesday morning is Big Scream, a club for new parents and their babies (under 1 year). Toddler time is 30 minute shows for pre-school children to introduce them to the big screen, £3 per child (adults free). Autism friendly screenings have low lights left on and the volume reduced, cost £3.

Cineworld Cinema
Cambridge Leisure Park, Clifton Way, Cambridge CB1 7DY
Tel: 0871 200 2000
www.cineworld.co.uk/cinemas/7
Multi 9 screen cinema complex at Cambridge Leisure Park, showing all the latest block busters. Places to eat nearby.

Has movies for juniors, £1.50 Saturday AM. It also has a kids club every Saturday for £1 for members, £3 non members.

Vue Cinema
The Grafton Centre, East Rd, Cambridge CB1 1PS
Tel: 0871 224 0240
www.myvue.com/home/cinema/cambridge
8 screen cinema within the Grafton Centre. kids AM club screens a selected kids film every Saturday and Sunday and every day in school holidays £1.75 and 3D movies £3.00. Also teen tickets, up to 20% off adult price.

Soft Play Centres

Cheeky Monkeys Activity Centre
Babraham Rd Fulbourn CB21 5HR
Tel: 01223 881658
www.cheekymonkeysltd.co.uk
A farm based playbarn in Fulbourn, 4 miles east of Cambridge. It has plenty of space for kids to let off steam. It has an outdoor play tractors, playhouse, sandpit and indoor soft play. There is a cafe too, and in the summer strawberry and raspberry picking.
Admission: Child £3.80 weekday term time, £4.50 weekends and holidays.
Open: Term time Tue to Fri 10:00-17:00, Sat & Sun 10:00-17:00 (closed Mondays).

Funky Fun House
8 Mercers Row Cambridge, CB5 8HY
Tel: 01223 304705
www.funkyfunhouse.com
Indoor family play centre. Soft play, slides, a sports pitch, special play areas for babies and for toddlers, party rooms and an on-site cafe make this good for rainy days.
Admission: Child £3.70 Mon-Fri, £4.50 Weekends & School Holidays (50p per adult).
Open: Mon to Fri 10:00-18:00, Sat & Sun, School Holidays, 09:00-18:00

Kreepie Krawlies Soft Play
Great Shelford & Fowlmere, Cambridge
Tel: 01763 209174 or 07447 582457
info@kreepiekrawlies.co.uk
www.kreepiekrawlies.co.uk
Mobile soft play company for children aged 0-4 years and a dedicated 'baby

The Fitzwilliam Museum

area' where children and carers can play together. Great Shelford Memorial Hall, Woodlands Lane, Great Shelford.
Admission: Child £3.50
Open: Tues & Fri term time only, 9.40am-12.

Whale of a Time
8 Viking Way, Bar Hill, Cambridge CB3 8EL
Tel: 01954 781018
www.whaleofatime-cambridge.co.uk
Play areas for Crawlers and Toddlers and older soft play and multi adventure.
Admission: £4 to £4.50 per child, £1.50 Crawlers.
Open: Mon to Fri 10:00-17:00; Wkend 10:00-17:30

Story Telling
Available at many libraries in Cambridgeshire, see page 60.

Cambridge Central Library
1st Floor, 7 Lion Yd Cambridge CB2 3QD
Tel: 0345 045 5225
www.cambridgeshire.gov.uk/leisure/libraries/directory/cambridge_central_library
Free 'Rhymetime' for birth - 18 months every Thursday 2.30-3pm and Saturday 10.30-11am.
Storytime for children 18 months to 5 years on Mondays 10:30-11am and Sunday 3-3:30pm. Also a Bookstart Bear Club (free membership, baby and treasure pack).

Good children's section, for younger kids and also older children and teenagers. In the summer, children can take part in the Summer Reading Challenge.

Theatres in Cambridge

ADC Theatre
Park Street, Cambridge CB5 8AS
Tel: 01223 300085
Boxoffice@adctheatre.com
www.adctheatre.com
This is the oldest University playhouse, behind the Round Church. The resident company is the Cambridge University Amateur Dramatic Club whose alumni include Sir Derek Jacobi and Stephen Fry.

Cambridge Arts Theatre
6 St. Edwards Passage, Cambridge CB2 3PJ
Tel: 01223 503333
info@cambridgeartstheatre.com
www.cambridgeartstheatre.com
This is right in the heart of Cambridge, with regular national and local productions.

Corn Exchange Theatre
Wheeler Street, Cambridge CB2 3QB
Tel: 01223 357851
admin.cornex@cambridge.gov.uk
www.cornex.co.uk
This is Cambridge's largest venue, it has regularly scheduled children's theatre and family events. It also has a cafe.

The Junction
Clifton Way, Cambridge CB1 7GX
Tel: 01223 511511
tickets@junction.co.uk
www.junction.co.uk
Off Hills Road near the Railway Bridge. This has a variety of cultural programmes, music, theatre and events, and a youth programme for teenagers. Regular theatre shows for families.

The Mumford Theatre
Anglia Ruskin University, Cambridge, CB1 1PT
Tel: 01223 352932
mumford@anglia.ac.uk
www.anglia.ac.uk/mumfordtheatre
This has a range of touring professional, local community and student theatre, as well as music events including free lunchtime concerts.

Staying Inside
What do you do if you are stuck inside?

Painting and Getting Messy
If you can stand the mess, let their creative streaks run wild with a good paint session, with brushes, fingers or making shapes out of potatoes.

Camping Indoors
Use blankets, chairs and tables or sofas and torches and let them make a den.

Chill Out Time
A good DVD or children's program can help everyone to relax after a busy day.

Make a Box House/Car/Boat
Any huge boxes are worth saving. You can cut out windows and doors or eye holes.

Dressing Up
A box of odd rags and outfits.

Playing in the Sink
Let them play with their water toys.

Little Chefs
There are lots of great children's cookbooks or ideas online, to make pizzas, cakes, cookies or lemonade.

Making Fairy Cakes

Museums and Galleries

All of those listed below are FREE admission.

Cambridge and County Folk Museum

2/3 Castle Street Cambridge CB3 0AQ
Tel: 01223 355159
www.folkmuseum.org.uk
This interactive museum displays the everyday life of Cambridgeshire people.
Open: Mon - Fri 10:00-13:00, 14:00-17:00

Cambridge Museum of Technology

Cheddars Lane, Cambridge CB5 8LD
Tel: 01223 368650
www.museumoftechnology.com
Sited by the River Cam, the Museum is housed in the Old Pumping Station.
Open: Mon - Fri 10:00-13:00 14:00-17:00

Cambridge University Museum of Archaeology and Anthropology

Downing St, Cambridge CB2 3DZ
Tel: 01223 333516
www.maa.cam.ac.uk
This has artefacts from all of the world.
Open: Mon - Fri 12:30-16:30

Fitzwilliam Museum

Trumpington St Cambridge CB2 1RB
Tel: 01223 332900
www.fitzmuseum.cam.ac.uk
Fantastic place to take kids. The suits of armour, impressive staircase and artefacts from around the world really inspire the imagination.
Open: Mon - Fri 10:00-13:00 14:00-17:00

Kettle's Yard

Castle St Cambridge CB3 0AQ
Tel: 01223 748100
www.kettlesyard.co.uk
Kettle's Yard is a house with a permanent collection of 20th century art. It is the home of HS 'Jim' Ede, a former curator of the Tate Gallery in London. The gallery is a beautifully maintained home and much bigger on the inside. See his collections of Miró, Henry Moore and others.
Open: House 14:00-16:00 Tue-Sun, gallery 11.30-17:00 Tue-Sun

Scott Polar Research Institute

Lensfield Road Cambridge CB2 1EP
Tel: 01223 336540
www.spri.cam.ac.uk
The Institute was established in 1920 by Frank Debenham as a memorial to Scott and his companions.
Open: Mon - Fri 12.30-16:30

Sedgewick Museum of Earth Sciences

Downing St, Cambridge CB2 3EQ
Tel: 01223 333456
www.sedgwickmuseum.org
Look out for the dinosaurs carved above the door, and the world's biggest spider inside.
Open: Mon - Fri 10:00-13:00, 14:00-17:00 Sat 10:00-18:00

University Museum of Zoology

Downing St, Cambridge CB2 3EJ
Tel: 01223 336650
www.museum.zoo.cam.ac.uk
Great museum, with a huge whale skeleton outside and plenty to amuse the kids on a rainy day.
Open: Mon - Fri 10:00-16:45. Sat 11:00-15:45

Whipple Museum of the History of Science

Free School Ln Cambridge CB2 3RH
Tel: 01223 330906
www.hps.cam.ac.uk/whipple
This holds a pre-eminent collection of scientific instruments and models, dating from the Middle Ages to the present.
Open: Mon - Fri 12:30-16:30

FUN FOR FREE

There is much to do in Cambridge for free. Of course there are the parks, playgrounds and open spaces. But there are also free events, fantastic museums, story telling in libraries and free swimming in the summer.

Free Events
Page 57

Cambridge Science Festival - **Mar**
Ely Eel Day - **Apr**
Arbury Carnival - **Jun**
Strawberry Fair - Cambridge - **Jun**
Cherry Hinton Festival - **Sep**
Open Cambridge Weekend - **Sep**
Cambridge Dragon Boat Festival - **Sep**
Bonfire Night - 5th **Nov**
Milll Road Winter Fair - Cambridge -**Dec**

Museums
Page 21

Cambridge and County Folk Museum
Cambridge Museum of Technology
Cambridge University Museum of Archaeology and Anthropology
Fitzwilliam Museum
Kettle's Yard
Scott Polar Research Institute

Sedgewick Museum of Earth Sciences
University Museum of Zoology
Whipple Museum of the History of Science

Story Telling/Rhymetime
Page 60

Various Libraries in Cambridgeshire.
Cambridge Central Library

Swimming
Page 82-3

Some free sessions in indoor pools at certain times with a membership card. Outdoor pools open in the summer, the following are free:
Lammas Land Outdoor Pool
Cherry Hinton Outdoor Pool

Wildlife & Country Parks
Page 51-56

Some of these have a charge to go into the houses, but the grounds or parks are free.

Mole Hall Wildlife Park
Wandlebury Country Park and the Gog Magog Hills
Cherry Hinton Hall Grounds
Wimpole Estate Grounds
Grafham Water
Walpole Water Gardens
Hinchingbrooke Country Park
Milton Country Park
Clare Castle Country Park

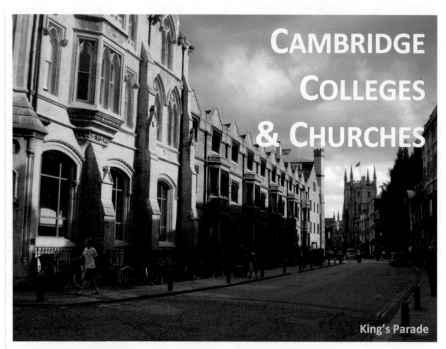

CAMBRIDGE COLLEGES & CHURCHES

King's Parade

A Brief Kid Friendly Guide to the Colleges

The University of Cambridge is the third oldest university in the world (after Bologna and Oxford). It was formed in the 13th Century by a group of students who fled from hostility in Oxford. The earliest college was Peterhouse, founded in 1284. There are now 31 colleges and over 150 departments, faculties and schools. Cambridge graduates have won 61 Nobel Prizes, the most of any university in the world.

It can be a nice change to walk around the colleges, and a good way to combine local highlights with visitors or grandparents who come to visit. Although be warned it gets very busy with tourists in the summer.

Visiting the Colleges

You can visit some for free, others for an admission fee. Walking on the lawns, or games or picnics, exploring stairs or other places is not allowed, so be mindful with children. The colleges are private places where people live, work and study, so it isn't a great place to be noisy or let the kids run riot. But as a Harry Potter type experience, it can be fun to wander through the courts, chapels and halls.

During the examination time from mid-April to late June most colleges are closed to the public. Some colleges do not admit prams, dogs or push-chairs. Information about these restrictions are given on notice boards and at the college gates.

Alternatively, you do not have to go into the colleges to enjoy them. Walking along the backs is a pretty way to break up the day in the city centre. You could start from the Round Church, walk past Trinity College, turn right into Free School Lane, over the bridge and around the back of King's College and finish up by the Mill Pond with an ice cream or a picnic on a summer's day.

King's College and King's College Chapel

King's Parade, Cambridge
This is the most famous and most visited college. There are queues to the televised choir on Christmas Eve, and it's architecture is big and exalting.

Queen's College

Silver Street, Cambridge
Founded by two Queen's in the mid 1400s, the college is linked by the Mathematical Bridge. A magnificent medieval Old Hall.

Trinity College

Trinity Street, Cambridge
This has a library designed by Christopher Wren, and was Isaac Newton's college.

St. John's College and the School of Pythagoras

It has a large number of courtyards, and the School of Pythagoras is the oldest academic building in Cambridge. Wordsworth had a room here. The lovely 'Bridge of Sighs' links the college.

Jesus College

Jesus Lane, Cambridge
This is a large college with attractive grounds and many sculptures.

Churches

Great St. Mary's Church

King's Parade, Cambridge

23

A strongly University Church, built around 1300. In the middle ages it was an official gathering place for meetings and debates for the University. You can climb the steep winding stairs for a spectacular view of Cambridge. Just try not to be on the stairs when the bell rings!

Our Lady and the English Martyrs Church (Roman Catholic)

Hills Road, Cambridge
A beautiful church built in 1890, a neo-gothic style with a 214 foot spire. In 1941 in an air raid, a bomb struck the sacristy. The stained class windows show scenes from the lives of English martyres, such as St John Fisher.

The Round Church

Also 'The Church of the Holy Sepulchre', located opposite the sweet shop on the corner of Rounch Church Street and Bridge Street. It is one of four medieval round churches still in use in England. Built around 1130, by the Fraternity of the Holy Sepulchre. It has dog tooth ornamentation and carved human heads.

Sightseeing and Tours

Bus Tours:
City Sightseeing
www.city-sightseeing.com
Cambridge City Hop On Hop Off Tour

Boat Tours:
Riverboat Georgina
www.georgina.co.uk
One or two-hour cruises

Cambridge Tourist Information Centre

Peas Hill, Cambridge CB2 3AD
All enquiries: 0871 226 8006
info@visitcambridge.org
www.visitcambridge.org
Conducts city tours, has information on local sites.
Open: Summer (Apr-Oct) MonFri 1000-1700, Sat 1000-1700, Sun & Bank Holidays 1100-1500.
Winter (Nov-Mar) Mon-Fri 1000-1700 Sat 1000-1700 Su - closed

The University of Cambridge

The University of Cambridge celebrated its 800th birthday in 2009. It is the second oldest University in the English speaking world. It is particularly renowned for maths and science. Charles Babbage designed the world's first computer in the mid 1800s. It has produced 13 British prime ministers, nine archbishops of Canterbury, and several well known comedians.

People of Cambridge

People who lived or studied in Cambridge include:
Isaac Newton (Trinity College)
Charles Darwin (Christ's College)
Samuel Pepys (Writer)
John Major (Prime Minister)
Stephen Hawking (Scientist)
John Maynard Keynes (Economist)
Douglas Adams (Writer)
Keith Palmer of The Prodigy (Musician)
Richard Attenborough (Actor)
Snowy Farr (Fundraiser)

Snowy Farr

I remember seeing Snowy when I was a child in Cambridge. He used to busk in the city centre and was unmistakable by his eccentric red military coat and top hat which often had white mice sat on it.

He was a colourful character, who raised thousands of pounds for The Guide Dogs of the Blind Association. He received an MBE for his efforts.

He had a long white beard and played a one man band. He took his white pets out with him, such as mice, cats, dogs and occasional goat.

He was formerly a road sweeper, and lived in the village of Westwick. His garden contained flags, dolls and teddy bears. A statue dedicated to Snowy is outside the Guildhall on Market Square.

Snowy Farr - Gary Webb

Sir Isaac Newton

He was an English physicist and mathematician and is most famous for discovering the laws of gravity. His Laws of Motion and Universal Gravitation laid the basis for much of modern science of the universe. He was a fellow of Trinity College, Cambridge.

He was bought up by his grandmother, never married, and was destined to become a farmer but he hated it. Partly out of revenge for a school bully, he became the top ranked student at his school, leading him to Cambridge University.

Newton said that he was partially inspired by watching the fall of an apple from a tree. Although there is no evidence it fell on his head. Reputed descendants of the tree are still at Trinity College and the Botanic Garden.

The River Cam

This slow moving river winds and curls its way around the meadows and colleges of Cambridge. It is like a green lung, preserving the open grasslands around it through the city centre and beyond.

Rowing on the Cam

From Midsummer Common northwards there are several rowing club houses on the west side of the river, and in the mornings you can often see the clubs practising for the various races. The 'May' bumps are in June, where crews aim to get a higher position by catching the boat ahead before getting 'bumped' from behind. The Oxford and Cambridge Boat Race takes place around Easter along the River Thames.

Punting along the River

This is the archetypal romantic view of Cambridge, with slowly gliding punts moving past the historic colleges and past the weeping willows. In reality it does get quite busy in summer. Be aware that sometimes people do fall in! That said, it can be a fun day out, especially for visitors. Many of the punting companies provide life jackets for children on request. You may want to have a 'chauffeur' punt, if you have children. If you punt yourself, sometimes you can get stuck holding on to the pole in mud!

Cambridge Punt Company
www.cambridgepuntcompany.co.uk
Cambridge Chauffer Punts
www.punting-in-cambridge.co.uk
Granta www.puntingincambridge.com
Lets go Punting www.letsgopunting.co.uk
Scudamore's www.scudamores.com
The Cambridge Punting Compnay
www.thecambridgepuntingcompnay.co.uk
The Punting Company
www.traditionalpuntingcompany.com
Trinity Punt Hire www.trin.cam.ac.uk

Top 10 Touristy Things to do in Cambridge with Children

1. Walk up to the top of Great St. Mary's Church. The view over Cambridge is worth the steep climb, but try not to be on the stairs when the bells ring!

2. Visit the Fitzwilliam Museum. A very fine museum with a grand entrance, knight's armour, cafe and plenty for kids to do.

3. Walk along the Backs of King's College in the snow or in the spring.

4. Take a picnic by the Mill Pond and watch people punt by.

5. Visit the Botanical Gardens and run around the trees.

6. Play football in Parker's Piece, where football association rules were created.

7. Trinity College, Chapel and Gardens. Or Clare, Queen's or Downing College. Any of the Colleges is worth seeing to get a taste of academic life and have a peek at the courtyards, the history, and the inspiring work of it's past and current students.

8. Get a cake or a bun from Fitzbillies Cake Shop.

9. Sedgewick Museum of Earth Sciences. Worth seeing for the whale bones alone. Some great examples of huge crabs and strange creatures from the past.

10. Run up the very steep Castle Hill and see the views all over Cambridge.

SHOPPING IN CAMBRIDGE

Great St Mary's Church

Lions Yard Shopping Centre
St. Tibbs Row, Cambridge CB2 3ET
Tel: 01223 350608
info@thelionyard.co.uk
This is the oldest shopping centre in Cambridge.

Grafton Shopping Centre
Between Newmarket Rd and East Rd, Cambridge, CB1 1PS
Tel: 01223 316201
www.graftoncentre.co.uk
Late night shopping every Wednesday. It has Mothercare, several fashion and phone shops, Debenhams, Boots, cafes, Burger King and also houses Vue Cinema. Outisde there are several charity shops in Burleigh Street. They have a kid's club, running craft activities once a month.

Grand Arcade
St Andrew's St Cambridge, CB2 3BJ
Tel: 01223 302601
www.grandarcade.co.uk
The newest indoor shopping area in Cambridge, also open late night shopping every Wednesday. It houses John Lewis, and several more upmarket clothing, shoe, jewellery and beauty stores. It joins on to Lions Yard Shopping Centre.

Mill Road
This is the place to go to find a great variety of independent shops and cafes. There are health food shops, restaurants, take aways and cafes, too many to list, plus some great curry houses and late night convenience stores. The Sally Ann, the furniture and second hand store is the biggest in town.

Cambridge Market
Market Square, Cambridge
This is open seven days a week and is still held in the ancient square where it has been selling fruit, vegetables and wares for hundreds of years. It is right in the middles of town in, of course, Market Square.

All Saints Garden Arts & Craft Market
All Saints Garden, Trinity St, Cambridge
Usually held on Saturdays, this is the place for local stalls selling art and crafts.

Cambridge City Centre
There is an impressive amount and variety of shops in a compact and mostly traffic free centre. Rose Crescent, Trinity Street and Green Street have some lovely boutique stores. There is a Marks and Spencer (Market Square) and Sainsburies (Sidney Street) for food shopping.

Public Toilets and Baby Changing
Chesterton Road
Drummer Street Bus Station
Gonville Place/Parker's Piece
Grafton Centre
Jesus Green
Lammas Land
Lion Yard Shopping Centre
Park Street Car Park
Quayside
Silver Street
Victoria Avenue (Midsummer Common)

Toys, Clothes & Equipment

There are lots of shops in Cambridge to cater for your maternity, baby and child needs. As an alternative to shops for toys, for a one off fee, the Toy Library lends toys for two weeks at a small cost.

Toy Libraries in Cambridge, Histon & Sawston

Jumbo Toy Library Under 5's Playgroup

St Lukes Barn, Frenchs Rd, Cambridge CB4 3JZ
Tel: 07939222774
sbailey@sjcs.co.uk
www.jumbotoylibrary.org.uk
Toys and puzzles for 0-5yrs available to borrow on a 2 week basis at a small cost. Once only £2.50 membership fee. For hire are a ride-on train and an airflow adventure centre.

Histon Toy Library

Histon Early Years Centre, New School Road, Histon Cambs CB24 9LL
Tel: 01223 712075
office@histon.cambs.sch.uk

Merry Go Round Toy Library

Ross Street Community Centre, Ross Street, Cambridge CB1
Tel: 01223 242072
Over 150 toys to borrow from 50p for two/three weeks. Toys for indoors and outdoors (slide/trampoline etc). Lifetime mebership only £1 per family.

Sawston Toy Library

St Mary's Church Hall, Church Lane, Sawston, Cambs CB22 3JR
Tel: 01223 833684
toylibrary@thehillclan.org

Toys for hire, refreshments available, a play area and video, DVD, CD ROM hire.

Buying Online

Amazon

www.amazon.co.uk
As well as books, amazon is now a huge list of products.

Cambridge Freecycle Network

groups.freecycle.org/cambridgefreecycle
Recycling of your unwanted items, including children's equipment/toys.

Shopping for Kids

Build A Bear Workshop

Unit 19, Grand Arcade, Andrew's St, Cambridge
Tel: 01223 309922
www.buildabear.co.uk

Boots

28 Petty Cury, Cambridge
Tel: 01223 350213
www.boots.com
Good for essentials.

Cambridge Baby

48 Hemingford Rd, Cambridge
Tel: 01223 572228
www.cambridgebaby.co.uk

Cuckoo Kids

Burwash Manor Barns, New Rd, Cambridge CB23 7EY
Tel: 01223 264152
www.cuckooclothing.co.uk
Boutique clothes in a restored farmhouse.

Clarks Shoes

13-14 Petty Cury, Cambridge
Tel: 01223 368486
25, Grafton Centre, Fitzroy St, Cambridge
Tel: 01223 314374
John Lewis, 10 Downing St, Cambridge
Tel: 01223 361292
www.clarks.co.uk
Provide a good fitting service.

Debenhams

36-40 Grafton Centre, Cambridge
Tel: 844 561 6161
www.debenhams.com
This also is handy for kids clothes.

Gap Kids

2 Market Hill, Cambridge CB2 3NJ
Tel: 01223 324101
www.gap.eu
Classic, wearable kids clothes.

Jelly Baby

8 High St, Cambridge CB22 6SP
Tel: 01223 870530
www.jelly-babe.com
Cute clothes.

John Lewis

Grand Arcade, 10 Downing Street, Cambridge CB2 3DS
Tel: 0844 693 1709
www.johnlewis.com/our-shops/cambridge
Good selection of childrens clothes.

Kids Classics

152-154 High St, Cambridge CB4 1NS
Tel: 01223 301236

Polarn O. Pyret

Unit SU45, 51, Grand Arcade Shopping Centre
14 St Andrew's St, Cambridge
Tel: 01223 306514
www.polarnopyret.co.uk

Good stripy range.

Mothercare Grafton Centre

26 Grafton Centre, Cambridge
Tel: 01223 460325
www.mothercare.com

Primark

62-74 Burleigh St Cambridge CB1 1DJ, United Kingdom
Tel: 01223 300026
www.primark.co.uk
Budget ranges.

Grand Arcade

Rosie in Stitches

111 Hillcrest, Bar Hill, Cambridge CB23 3TH
Tel: 01954 782431
www.rosieinstitches.org.uk
Friends of Rosie Hospital, many hand made baby and children's stuff.

The Cambridge Toy Shop

15-16 Sussex St, Cambridge
Tel: 01223 309010
www.cambridgetoyshop.co.uk
A huge range of toys.

The White Company

SU 53 Upper Mall, Grand Arcade, Cambridge CB2 3BJ
www.thewhitecompany.com/help/uk-stores/cambridge
White classic range.

Toys 'R' Us

Coldhams Ln, Cambridge
Tel: 01223 460045
www.toysrus.co.uk

Bookshops (with Childrens Section)

Heffers Bookshop

20 Trinity St, Cambridge
Tel: 01223 463200
www.bookshop.blackwell.co.uk

Waterstones

22-24 Sidney St, Cambridge
Tel: 01223 351688
www.waterstones.com

WHSmith

14-15 Market St, Cambridge
Tel: 01223 311313
www.whsmith.co.uk

Computing, Games and Comics

Forbidden Planet Ltd
60 Burleigh St, Cambridge CB1 1DJ
Tel: 01223 301666
www.forbiddenplanet.com
Comic shop and sci-fi items.

Game Stores Ltd
47-48 Lion Yard Shopping Centre, Cambridge CB2 3NA
Tel: 0871 5940066
7 Fitzroy St, Cambridge CB1 1ER
Tel: 0871 5940066
www.game.co.uk
Computer games.

Games Workshop Ltd
54 Regent St, Cambridge CB2 1DP
Tel: 01223 313350
www.games-workshop.com
Games Workshop selling a wide range of models and accessories for fantasy role-play and war gaming.

Inner Sanctum Collectibles Ltd
6 Homerton St, Cambridge CB2 8NX
Tel: 01223 240333
www.innersanctumcollectibles.co.uk
Gaming, role playing and collectables.

Dancewear

Attitude Dancerwear
25 Hills Rd, Cambridge
Tel:01223 322227
www.attitudedancewear.co.uk

Kelly Marie's Dancewear
Unit 2 Fishers Yard, Market Square, St Neots, Cambs PE19 2AG
Tel: 01480 477212
www.kellymariesdancewear.co.uk

Fancy Dress

Aladdin's Cave
Hungry Hall Farm, Oldhurst Road, Wyton,78- Huntingdon PE28 2DU

Tel: 01480 451914
www.fancydresshuntingdon.co.uk

Classworks Costumes
2a Rock Road, Cambridge CB1 7UF
Tel: 01223 210883
www.classworkscostumes.co.uk

Party Mania Cambridge
34 Burleigh St, Cambridge
Tel: 01223 313000
www.partymania.co.uk

Wardrobe Costume
27 Cromwell Road, Cambridge CB1 3EB
Tel: 01223 518303
www.wardrobecostume.co.uk

Nappy Information and Laundry Services

Cambourne Baby
Cambourne Cambridgeshire CB23 6DQ
Tel: 07980 003437
am@cambournebaby.co.uk
www.cambournebaby.co.uk
Reusable cloth nappies and biodegradable disposable nappies to parents in Cambourne and the surrounding villages to your door.

Go Real! - National web site
Tel: 845 850 0606.
info@goreal.org.uk
www.goreal.org.uk
Independent source of information.

Real Nappies - Huntingdonshire & Fenland Cambridgeshire
Tel: 07794 506478
huntingdonrealnappies@gmail.com
www.huntingdonrealnappies.co.uk
Free advice and demonstrations of a range of real nappy systems within Huntingdonshire & Fenland either on 1:1 basis or to groups.

Mother's Little Helper - Cambridge
motherslittlehelpers.co.uk
Nappy laundry costs £11 a week.

Organic and Specialist Food Shops

Arjuna Wholefoods
12 Mill Rd, Cambridge CB1 2AD
Tel: 01223 364845
www.arjunawholefoods.co.uk

CobsBakery.com
14-15 Robert Davies Court, Nuffield Rd, Cambridge CB4 1TP
www.runningshoes.org.uk

Tel: 01223 241207
www.cobsbakery.com
Organic and specialist breads.

Green Bay Harvest Ltd
62 Hills Rd, Cambridge CB2 1LA
Tel: 01223 967920
www.greenbayharvest.co.uk

Organic food boxes

Cambridge Organic Food Co.Ltd
Penn Farm Studios 7 Harston Rd, Haslingfield, Cambridge CB23 1JZ
Tel: 01223 873300
www.cofco.co.uk

Waterland Organics
Willow Farm Lode Fen, Lode, Cambridge CB25 9HF
Tel: 01223 812912
www.waterlandorganics.co.uk

Pet Shops and Services

Abington Boarding Kennels Ltd
Haydn Bourne Bridge, Abington, Cambridge, Cambridgeshire, CB21 6AN
Tel: 01223 832311

Cambridge Reptiles
175 St. Neots Rd, Hardwick, Cambridge, Cambridgeshire, CB23 7QJ
Tel: 01954 212187
www.cambridgereptiles.co.uk

Camelot Creature Comforts
3 Hale Fen, Littleport, Ely, Cambs CB6 1EN
Tel: 01353 864538

www.camelotcreaturecomforts.com

Coral Cave Aquatic Centre & Pet-Paks Superstore
175 St. Neots Road, Hardwick, CAMBRIDGE, Cambridgeshire, CB23 7QJ
Tel: 01954 776224
www.petpaks.com

Frog End Pet Supplies
Phillimore Garden Centre Cambridge Rd, Melbourn, Royston, Hertfordshire, SG8 6EY
Tel: 01763 293463
www.frogendpetsupplies.com

Grumpy Pets
150a Scotland Rd, Cambridge CB4 1QQ
Tel: 01223 566488
www.grumpypets.co.uk

Just for Pets
253 Barnwell Rd, Cambridge CB5 8SL
Tel: 01223 568162
www.justforpets.uk.com

Little Paddocks
Cow Lane, Great Chesterford, Saffron Walden, Essex, CB10 1RJ
Tel: 01799 6110071
little-paddocks.co.uk
Dog boarding.

Pets at Home Ltd
Unit 7b Beehive Centre, Coldhams Lane, Cambridge CB1 3ET
Tel: 01223 329589
www.petsathome.com

Pets Corner UK Ltd
Country Gardens A10 (Between Cambridge & Royston), Royston, SG8 6RD
Tel: 01403 332577
www.petscorner.co.uk

Pet-Paks Superstore
175 St. Neots Rd, Hardwick, Cambs CB23 7QJ
Tel: 01954 776619
www.petpaks.com

Poochie Parlour
44 Arbury Court, Cambridge CB4 2JQ
Tel: 01223 309829
www.poochieparlour.co.uk
Dog grooming.

The Country Store
Unit 12a Sawston Park, London Rd, Pampisford, Cambridge, Cambridgeshire, CB22 3EE
Tel: 01223 837977
www.thecountrystore.co.uk

Skateboard Shops

Billys
15 Burleigh St, Cambridge CB1 1DG
Tel: 01223 568368
www.billys.co.uk

Sportswear and Equipment

DW Sports Shop
Beehive Centre Coldhams Lane, Cambridge CB1 3ET
Tel: 0844 3725353
www.dwsports.com

Hire Fitness (Cambridgeshire)
96 Greenfields, Earith, Huntingdon,
Cambs PE28 3QY
Tel: 0845 8641380
www.hirefitness.co.uk

Hobbs Sports
36 Sidney St, Cambridge CB2 3HX
Tel: 01223 362428
www.hobbssports.co.uk

J.D Sports
32 Lion Yard, Cambridge CB2 3NA

Tel: 01223 356855
Unit 3 The Guineas, Newmarket, Suffolk, CB8 8EQ
Tel: 01638 662913
www.jdsports.com

Kentbridge Sports
The Barn Main Street, Caldecote Cambs CB23 7NU
Mob: 07896 252337
www.kentbridgesports.co.uk

Newmarket Sports & Leisurewear Ltd
12 The Guineas, Newmarket, Suffolk CB8 8EQ
Tel: 01638 661888
www.newmarketsports.co.uk

SportsDirect.com
Unit 34-37 Lion Yard, Cambridge CB2 3NA
Tel: 0870 3339599
Unit 5, Cambridge Retail Park Newmarket Rd, Cambridge CB5 8WR
Tel: 0870 3339677
www.sportsdirect.com

Sweatshop
21-25 Coldhams Business Park, Cambridge, CB1 3LH
Tel: 0844 332 5635
www.sweatshop.co.uk

The Football Store
South Stand Cambridge United Football Club, Cambridge CB5 8LN
Tel: 01223 413718
www.prokituk.com

Top Spin Tennis
Hills Rd Sports & Tennis Centre Purbeck Rd, Cambridge CB2 8PF
Tel: 01223 241956
www.topspintennis.co.uk

Two Seasons
Unit 5 Christ's Lane, Cambridge CB1 1NP
Tel: 01223 362832
www.twoseasons.co.uk

Vitas Cricket
Unit 8 Vitas Business Centre, Dodson Way, Peterborough, Cambs PE1 5XJ
Tel: 01733 305541
www.vitascricket.co.uk

Up & Running
36 Trinity St, Cambridge CB2 1TB

Tel: 01223 311843

Photographic Services

Specialising in children's photography.

Ashworth Photography
44 Isaacson Rd, Burwell,Cambs CB25 0AF
Tel: 01638 601571
www.ashworthphotography.co.uk

Cambridge Portraits
Tel: 007515 353404
www.cambridgeportraits.co.uk

CI Photography
23 Harlestones Road, Cottenham, Cambs CB4 8TR
Tel: 01954 776575
www.ciphotography.co.uk

Debbie Wallwork Photography
Tele: 01954 205640
Mobile: 07968 623249
info@debbiewallwork.com
www.debbiewallwork.com

Dumbletons Studio
4 Milton Rd, Cambridge CB4 1JY
Tel: 01223 358007
www.dumbletons.com

Francesca. DB Photography
67 The Oaks, Milton, Cambridge CB24 6ZG
Tel: 0778 7397755
info@francescadb.com
www.francescadb.com

Granta Photography
9 Malletts Road, Cambridge CB1 9EZ
Tel: 01223 658106
www.grantaphotography.co.uk

Helen Bartlett
Tel: 0845 603 1373
info@helenbartlett.co.uk
www.helenbartlett.co.uk

Helen Traherne Photography
21 Pound Road, Hemingford Grey, Cambs PE28 9EF
Tel: 01480 374988
Mob: 07714 213558
helen@trahernephotography.co.uk
trahernephotography.co.uk

Idyllic Imagery
43 Meadowsweet Close, Haverhill, Suffolk, CB9 9DN
Tel: 01440 842566
www.IdyllicImagery.co.uk

Inkwell Photographic
4 Cross Lane Close, Orwell, Royston, Hertfordshire, SG8 5QW
Tel: 01223 208699www.inkwellphotographic.com

Lime Green Dreams
Unit 10 Saxon Way, Melbourn, Royston, Hertfordshire, SG8 6DN
Tel: 01763 293426
www.limegreendreams.com

Mary King Photography
48 Ainsworth St, Cambridge CB1 2PD
Tel: 07850 691273
www.marykingphotography.co.uk

Memories Photography
54 High Street, Over, Cambs CB24 5ND
Tel: 01954 776371
www.memoriesimages.co.uk

Matthew Power Photography
58 Mill Hill Rd, Eaton Ford, St. Neots, Cambs PE19 7AJ
Tel: 07969 088655
www.matthewpowerphotography.co.uk

Ros Stephens Photography
Tel: 07769 727634
hello@rosstephensphotography.com
www.rosstephensphotography.com

Sara Noel Photography
Tel: 01223 862178
Mobile: 07979 714562Snoel@saranoelphotography.co.uk
www.saranoelphotography.co.uk

St. Ives Photographic Studio
55 Russett Avenue, Needingworth, St. Ives, Cambs PE27 4UE
Tel: 01480 469717
www.st-ives-studio.co.uk

EATING OUT

There are some great places to eat in Cambridge, from breakfast cafes to upmarket restaurants. For eating out in other areas, such as Peterborough or Ely, see under each area. These are just some of the eating places in Cambridge that I have found to be reliable and welcoming of children, but there are many more.

Bella Italia

The Watermill, Newnham Road, Cambridge CB3 9EY
Tel: 01223 367507
www.bellaitalia.co.uk
Good value children's menu, three courses and drink for £5.25, with an activity book. There are also two other restaurants in the Grafton Centre and Cambridge Leisure Park.
Hours: Mon - Thu: 09:00-23:00
Fri - Sat: 09:00 - 00:00 Sun: 09:00 - 22:30

Browns (Classic)

23 Trumpington Street, Cambridge CB2 1QA
Tel: 01223 461655
www.browns-restaurants.co.uk/locations/cambridge
This is a large restaurant directly opposite the Fitzwilliam Museum, and serves classic food. It has a more adventurous children's menu than most, including crab & tiger prawn linguine, steak pie, as well as burgers and chicken. Two courses (children) £7.
Hours: Mon-Thu: 09:30-23:00, Fri & Sat 12:00-23:00, Sun 12:00-22:30

Byron Burgers

12 Bridge Street, Cambridge CB2 1UF
Tel: 01223 462927
www.byronhamburgers.com
Described as 'proper' burgers, using Scottish beef. It has a simple but tasty kids menu, with macaroni cheese and mini burgers. Two courses are £6.50. For adults remember to order your burger well done if you don't like it pink medium.
Hours: Mon-Sat 11.00-23.00. Sun 11.00-22.30

Charlie Chan (Chinese)

14 Regent St Cambridge CB2 1DB
Tel: 01223 902293
This is one of the oldest restaurants in Cambridge. Downstairs is more casual, for family dinners or lunches.
Hours: Sun - Sat: 12:00-17:00, 18:00-23:00

Clowns (Italian)

54 Kings Street, Cambridge CB1 1LN
Tel: 01223 355711
This is a great laid back, warm, family run place, and has good reasonably priced Italian dishes. It is decorated with paintings of clowns.
Hours: Mon-Sun: 8:00-23:00

Frankie & Benny's (New York Italian)

Cambridge Leisure Park, Clifton Way, Cambridge CB1 7DY
Tel: 01223 412430
www.frankieandbennys.com
It has a varied kids and juniors menu and organic baby food. All the main kid staples are catered for like spaghetti bolognaise, bananas and custard, burgers and ice-cream. Birthday parties can be pre-booked.
Hours: Mon - Sat:: 09:00-23:00, Sun: 09:00-22.30

Lalbagh Bangladeshi & Indian Diner

49 Alms Hill Bourn, Cambridge CB23 2SH
Tel: 01954 719131
www.lalbaghrestaurant.com
A very good eat in and take away, not central but nice food. Lunchtime offers are two courses for £12.50. It doesn't have a children's menu.
Hours: Mon to Sun 12:00-14:00, 17:30-22:30.

Marks & Spencer Cafe

5 Market Hill, Cambridge CB2 3NJ
Tel: 01223 355219
www.marksandspencer.com
Upstairs at the store. This has a good children's meal deal that includes fruit, a drink and a snack.

Pizza Express

7a Jesus Lane, Cambridge CB5 8BA
Tel: 01223 324033
www.pizzaexpress.com
It doesn't have the pizza express sign on the outside, as it is located in the historic Pitt club building near Jesus College. It has a 'piccolo' children's menu, with activity pack. Kids I know love the Banbinoccino (a little cappuccino without the coffee).
Hours: Mon-Sun 11.30-23:00

Pizza Hut

19-21 Regent Street, Cambridge CB2 1AB
Tel: 01223 323737
www.pizzahut.co.uk

The kids menu includes an all you can eat salad, and it has an ice cream factory. There are also restaurants on Newmarket Road and Cambridge Leisure Park.
Hours: Sun-Thu: 12:00-22:00 Fri-Sat: 11:00-23:00

Rainbow Cafe (Vegetarian)

9a King's Parade, Cambridge CB2 1SJ
Tel: 01223 902138
www.rainbowcafe.co.uk
This popular cafe has been serving vegetarian food for 20 years. Tasty soups and cakes and healthy main dishes. Closed on Mondays at time of going to press. They provide free organic baby food and have a children's menu of pasta or half portions of mains.
Sun: 10:00-16:00, Mon: Closed. Tue - Sat: 10:00-22:00

Sticky Beaks (Home Baking Cafe)

42 Hobson St, Cambridge CB1 3NL
Tel: 01223 359397
www.stickybeakscafe.co.uk
Lovely cakes, like butterscotch layer cake. Lunch salads include chickpea, butternut squash and feta cheese.
Mon-Fri 08:00-17:30, Sat 09:00-17:30 Sun 10:00-17:00

Tatties (Cafe)

11 Sussex Street, Cambridge CB2 1TB
Tel: 01223 323399
This is a budget choice, and great for hungry kids if you are shopping in town. It gets very busy, but service is fast. I find most kids will eat a baked potato with a choice of several different toppings.
Hours: Mon-Sat:: 08:30-19:00, Sun: 10:00-17:00

The Blue Lion (Classic Pub Fare)

74 Main Street, Hardwick, Cambridge CB23 7QU
Tel: 01954 210328
www.bluelionhardwick.co.uk

Good classic cooking, using locally sourced ingredients. It does a children's menu and gluten free menu. For kids there are fish and chips, burgers and corned beef hash for £6.50 plus drink.
Hours: Mon to Fri: 12:00-14:30, 18:00-21:00
Sat: 12:00-21:00, Sun: 12:00-20:00

The Missing Sock

Finders Corner, Newmarket Road, A1103, Stow Cum Quy, CB25 9AQ
Tel: 01223 902136
www.themissingsock.co.uk

Main courses £13 - £21. A unique restaurant, that offers four 'dining experiences', including a lounge area where you can play music, and a dining area where you can self cook. It is a bit out of town but has some fun events such as the kids Sunday club 1.30-2.30 where kids can make a sock puppet and see a puppet show.
Sun: 11:00-00:00, Mon - Tue: Closed
Wed - Fri: 12:00-15:00, 18:00-00:00
Sat: 11:00-15:00, 18:00-00:00

The Orchard Tea Gardens

45-47 Mill Way, Grantchester, Cambridge CB3 9ND
Tel: 01223 845788
www.orchard-grantchester.com

This historic place sells lovely scones and tea, and on a summer's day you can sit on one of the deckchairs in the orchard. Great for a treat after a walk or cycle to Grantchester with the kids.
Hours: Mon-Sun: 10:00-16:00

Scones at the Orchard Tea Gardens

The Sea Tree

13-14 The Broadway, Mill Rd, Cambridge CB1 3AH
Tel: 01223 414349
www.theseatree.co.uk

Really good fish bar, where you can get traditional fish and chips, as well as different dishes of mackerel, calamari or fish stew. It has an eat-in and take-away menu. Kids can have handmade fishfingers and chips.
Mon 17:00-22:00, Tue to Fri 12:00-14:00, 17:00-22:00, Sat 12:00-22:00. Sun 17:00-21:00

Urban Larder

No. 9 The Broadway, Mill Rd, Cambridge CB1 3AH
Tel: 01223 212462
www.urbanlarder.co.uk

Good locally sourced food, such as local honey, cheeses from the Wobbly Bottom Farm and jams from the W.I. Ladies. It has a large range of gluten and wheat free food. Known for its pies, pasties and baked goods.

Zhonghua Traditional Snacks

13 Norfolk Street, Cambridge CB1 2LD
Tel: 01223 354573
Zhonghuatraditionalsnacks.com

It's a small, cosy restaurant serving Chinese handmade dumplings and noodle dishes. Reasonable prices and good service.

Shopping for Food

Some children need encouragement to eat fruit and vegetables, and trying to juggle busy lives with meals and shopping can be tricky. There are now plenty of online supermarkets that deliver to your door, also organic vegetable boxes and smaller suppliers of meat and other foods. Market Square has good fruit sellers, and there are food shops in town and ethnic food shops on Mill Road.

For great baking, try Norfolk Street Bakery, for fresh meat try Northrop's Butcher's on Mill Road, and for organic health foods try Arjuna Wholefoods on Mill Road.

There are big supermarkets around the city, on Newmarket Road, Hills Road Leisure Park, Trumpington, Histon Road and Milton. In addition, there are Cooperative Stores, Tesco Express and a Sainsburies in and around the city centre.

Picnics

Cambridge has many green lawned, grassy spaces that can be a perfect spot for picnics. Here are a few ideas:

- Only take what you can carry easily if you are going on foot or cycling. It sounds obvious but it's easy to be weighed down.
- Sandwich fillings: marmite & cheese, tuna, ham, jam. Crackers, carrot sticks, dips, crisps, small slices of pizza. Fruit juice in cartons and water.
- Children can get dehydrated in the sun so make sure you have plenty to drink.
- Wipes, plastic bags for rubbish, sun hats & cream, picnic blanket.
- Games like frisbee, football, or exploring with a magnifying glass to look at insects.
- Check the weather. Bring waterproofs in case.

Top picnic spots in Cambridge

- Grantchester Meadows
- Jesus Green
- Christ's Pieces
- Lammas Land
- The Backs
- Cambridge University Botanic Gardens

CYCLING

Cambridge is a fantastic place to cycle around. It is flat, relatively small and there are several cycle ways and off-road cycling paths. It has the highest levels of cycling in the UK. Cycling with children can be great fun. Cycle shops in the city can give advice on what to buy, safety and practicalities.

Cycle Training

www.dft.gov.uk/bikeability

It's a good idea to take a course in cycle training. For children the bikeability training can be taken on three levels, starting when they have learned to ride a bike. There are levels to progress through. They recommend that children do levels 1 and 2 before cycling on their own to school.

Safety

In terms of life-years gained and lost, the health benefits of cycling outweigh the risks, according to information provided by CTC, the UK's national cyclists organisation. But there are ways that you can make it as safe as possible.

- In child carriers - never let go of your bike when your child is in the seat.
- Watch out for hanging straps, clothes, anything that could get caught in the wheels or mechanisms.
- Always wear a helmet, lights at night, and reflective gear.
- Be especially careful on the roads. There is some debate about the safety of trailers on the roads. Cambridge

has plenty of cycle lanes and off road paths.

- Put your bike in for a service with a cycle shop regularly.
- Take cycle training.
- Do not overtake at left hand turns near large vehicles at junctions. They have a blind spot which could have fatal consequences.
- Do not sound the bell at cows or animals, as they may startle.

Cycle assertively so that other traffic can see you, and with children who are learning to cycle, keep off the road on cycle paths until they are much older.

Child Cycling Safety Website

www.talesoftheroad.direct.gov.uk

The governments **child cycling safety website** has some really useful tips, as well as a highway code facts road safety leaflet, magazines and quizzes.

Types of child carriers

It is worth spending a bit of time choosing which option will be best for you, through websites or advice from a cycle shop.

It isn't recommended that a baby ride on a bike until they can support their own head and wear a cycle helmet, at least 1 year or older. You will also need to keep your child warm, and a waterproof jacket when it rains, they will get colder than you on the seat. And in the summer remember the sun factor cream.

Cambridge City Council Pushchair Scheme

This is such a handy idea for parents who want to cycle into town but then need to push a young child around on a buggy. You can borrow a pushchair for free from the two covered parks (see below) at **Station Cycles** and the **Bicycle Ambulance** shop.

Cycle Parks in Cambridge

There are two covered parks in the city (as well as many outdoor rails).

Park St car park - space for 200 cycles in basement. Cycle lockers available at £10 per month. Tel: 01223 458515. Bicycle Ambulance Shop (see page 56).

Grand Arcade car park - space for 200 cycles. Closes 23:30. The Shop run by Station cycles (see page 56) has luggage lockers available at £2 per day.

Make sure all equipment reaches British safety standards, and check with the cycle shop how to fit the child seat properly. Make sure you are comfortable with the balance of the bike. Some recommend trying the seat out with a bag of potatoes first.

Use a good bike lock and register your bike at immobilise. There are several cycle racks all around the city, and outside the main shopping centres.

Child Trailers

These fit on to the back of the bike usually and are suitable for younger children. Some trailers can take two children, and are most suitable for off-road cycling. Occasionally they fit on to the front of the bike.

Helmets
Ensure that helmets are the right size, fitted correctly, and changed as the child grows older.

Child Seats
These can be rear or front mounted. Front-mounted seats can make it easier to get on and off the bike, but can be more difficult to balance whilst cycling. Rear mounted seats will also need some careful balancing too, but are widely available.

Make sure to buy ones with cushioning, straps and headrests as children often go to sleep in them.

Tag-a-long bikes
These can be used for older children, where they can enjoy cycling too. They are smaller bikes that fit onto the bag of your own bike with a bar.

Cycle Routes
www.cambridge.cyclestreets.net/
www.cambridgeshire.gov.uk/transport/around/cycling

You can buy good maps in any local book or stationery shop. There are very useful maps online with Cambridgeshire Council and Cyclestreets which also has photos of cycle routes.

Keep on the left and sound the bell on shared pedestrian paths when overtaking people.

Teaching your child to ride a bike

Balance bikes, where your child's feet can 'scoot' along are good starts, as are three wheeled trikes, which provide stability, and stabilisers attached to their first bike.

It is a scary but exciting experience for both of you, and you will be teaching them a skill for life. Choose a quiet, green, flat spot and build up your childs confidence at their pace. It can take some time, depending on your child, and patience. If they really don't want to, wait a little while and then try again when they are more amenable to the idea.

Remind them to keep pedalling and to look straight ahead. It is tempting to hold the handlebars for them all the time, but that won't teach your child how to balance, at some point you have to let go!

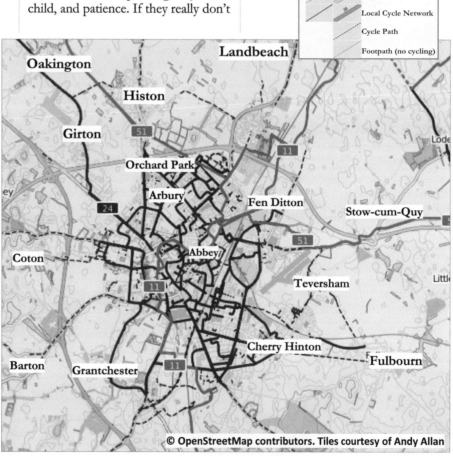

© OpenStreetMap contributors. Tiles courtesy of Andy Allan

Cycle Hire (& Purchase)

Bicycle Ambulance
Park Street, CB5 8AS
07838 162572
bicycleambulance.com

City Cycle Hire
61 Newnham Road, CB3 9EY
01223 365629
www.citycyclehire.com

Cambridge Station Cycles
7 Station Rd, CB1 2TZ
01223 307125
Railstation@stationcycles.co.uk

Cambridge Station Cycles
Grand Arcade Cycle Park,
Corn Exchange St
01223 307655

Cycle Tours

Cambridge Bike Tours
Tel: 01223 366868
Info@cambridgebiketours.co.uk
www.cambridgebiketours.co.uk
Choice of tours, and can combine
lunch, bikes and punting.

Cycle Shops

Avenue Cycles
100 Stretten Ave, CB4 3ER
01223 322716

Ben Hayward Cycles
69 Trumpington St, CB2 1RJ
01223 352294
www.benhaywardcycles.co.uk
Repairs at 15 Laundress Lane 01223 301118)

Billy's Bike & Skate Store
15 Burleigh St, CB1 1DG
01223 568368
www.billys.co.uk

Blazing Saddles
110 Cherry Hinton Rd, CB1 7AJ
01223 415367

Bridge Cycles
22a Magdalene St, CB3 0AF
01223 361411

CAM Cycles
92 Mill Rd, CB1 2BD
01223 500988
www.camcycles.co.uk

Cambridge Cycle Centre
8 Botolph Lane, CB2 3RD
01223 307114

Cambridge Cycle Company
34 Woollards Lane, Great Shelford, CB22 5LZ
01223 847100
www.cambridgecyclecompany.co.uk

Cambridge Station Cycles Superstore
9 High Street, Histon, CB24 9JD
01223 232182
www.stationcycles.co.uk

Chris's Bikes
2 Thornton Way, CB3 0NJ
01223 276004
www.chrisbikes.co.uk

Cycle King
195-197 Mill Rd, CB1 3AN
01223 214999
www.cycleking.co.uk

Cycle Repair Shop
26 Mill Rd, CB1 2AD
01223 360028
www.cyclerepairshop.co.uk

Discount Cycles
171 Mill Rd, CB1 3AN
01223 576545

Giant
144 Hills Road, CB2 8PB
01223 415349
www.giant-bicycles.com

Greg's Cycles
186 Mill Rd, CB1 3LP
01223 210678

Halfords Ltd
442 Newmarket Road, CB5 8JL
01223 454280
www.halfords.com

Howes Cycles
104 Regent St, CB2 1DP
01223 350350
www.howescycles.co.uk

John's Bikes
3 Arbury Court, CB4 2JQ
01223 353373

King St Cycles
82 King St, CB1 1LN
01223 367275

Kingsway Cycles
8 City Road, CB1 1DP
01223 355852

Lensfield Road Cycles
69-71 Lensfield Rd, CB2 1EN
01223 323559
www.lensfieldroadcycles.co.uk

PRIMO Cycles
5-7 Jesus Lane, CB5 8BA

www.primocycles.co.uk

Richardsons Cycles
Cambridge Rd, Histon, CB4 4LQ
01223 518855
www.richardsonsonline.co.uk

Rocco's Bikes
Unit 3A, 23-25 Gwydir St, CB1 2LG
07855 606393
www.roccosbikes.co.uk

The Bike Man
The Market Square, CB2 3QJ
07850 814186
www.thebikeman.co.uk

The Cambridge Bicycle Doctor
07964 427151
www.thecambridgebicycledoctor.com

The Electric Transport Shop
Hope Street Yard, CB1 3NA
01223 247410
www.electricbikesales.co.uk

The Kurser
47 High Street, Cherry Hinton
CB1 9HX
01223 240270
www.thekurser.co.uk

The School Run Centre
Hope Street Year, CB1 3NA
07772 738899
www.schoolruncentre.co.uk

Townsends Light Blue Cycle Centre
72 Chesterton Rd, CB4 1EP
01223 315845
www.townsends-lb.co.uk

Trumpington Cycles
134 Cambridge Rd,
Great Shelford, CB22 5JU
01223 566145

University Cycles
9 Victoria Ave, CB4 1EG
01223 355517

There are many services that can make a parents life a bit easier. This chapter contains a list of essential information on travel, healthcare, money, benefits and more.

Having kids can open up another world. It can start when expecting your first baby, or considering fostering or adoption. This section lists maternity services, antenatal classes, pregnancy yoga and beyond.

Maternity activities include everything from aquanatal swims (a great way of feeling less huge when pregnant), to hypnotherapy and 'mantenatal' workshops (for men) run by the National Childbirth Trust (NCT).

If you have children and need help with birthday parties, did you know that there is a 'Slimy' science party, a spy mission or a pool party on offer?

Teenagers may be worried about exams and futures, or may be attached to that Xbox. There is information on all these issues.

After all that you may wonder if there is any time left for you, so check out the section on Time Out for Parents and Carers.

If you have a problem with your child, need parenting advice or have general concerns, there is a Support and Advice section. Perhaps you are from overseas and adjusting to life in the UK. There are some local play groups in Cambridgeshire, such a Polish, Chinese, French and Spanish groups.

USEFUL INFORMATION

Cambridge Train Station

Healthcare

You should call the NHS 111 service if you need medical help fast, but it's not a 999 emergency.

You will be assessed, given advice and directed straight away to the local service that can help you best. Calls to NHS 111 are free from landlines and mobile phones.

NHS Choices

This is a very useful place to start if you want to locate a doctor, dentist, health service or are just want information. www.nhs.uk

Hospitals

Addenbrooke's Hospital

Cambridge University Hospitals NHS Foundation Trust, Hills Rd, Cambridge CB2 0QQ
General enquiries Telephone: 01223 245151
Accident & Emergency Telephone: 01223 217118
www.addenbrookes.org.uk

Peterborough City Hospital

Edith Cavell Campus, Bretton Gate, Peterborough PE3 9GZ
Tel: 01733 678000
www.peterboroughandstamford.nhs.uk

Cambridgeshire Constabulary

Cambridge Control Room:, Parkside Police Station, Parkside, Cambridge CB3 1JG
Tel: 01223 358966
Type Talk: 0800 515152
www.cambs.police.uk
Manned from 0700 - 0200 (seven days a week)

Headquarters, Hinchingbrooke Park, Huntingdon
Cambridgeshire PE29 6NP
Tel: 01480 456111

General Phone Enquiries (less urgent crime enquiry)
Tel: 101 (24 hours, 7 day a week)
Emergencies: 999

Fire and Rescue Service

For general enquiries and fire prevention advice in Cambridgeshire.
Tel 01480 444 500 (in an Emergency 999)
www.cambsfire.gov.uk

Gas Emergency

Gas emergency: 0800 111 999

Housing

Housing is expensive in the region, but particularly in Cambridge, whether you are looking to buy or to rent. There are several accommodation agencies and estate agents. In recent years new homes have been built, particularly flats.

Cambridge City Council has a Housing Advice service which offers free, confidential advice.Tel: 01223 457918

Money

Money gets tighter with children. There are some good advice organisations if you are getting into debt, such as your local Citizens Advice Centre (on the next page). The website Money Saving Expert is also useful for budgeting and saving money:
www.moneysavingexpert.com

Helpful banks and bureaux de change:
Abbey National, 60 St Andrew's St, Cambridge
Tel: 01223 350495
Cooperative Bank, 75 Burleigh St, Cambridge
Tel: 01223 316289
Lloyds TSB, 3 Sidney St, Cambridge
Tel: 0845 072 3333
Thomas Cook, 8 St Andrew's St, Cambridge
Tel: 01223 543100

Travel

Cambridge is very well served with public transport. There is an excellent website that can give you public transport and/or car journey details. Just type in the start address and finish address or postcode and time and it will give you a detailed breakdown of trains/buses and walking times.
www.transportdirect.info

Google maps is also very useful, in giving you time and directions by car, by foot or by cycling. maps.google.com

Air

Stansted Airport
Tel: 0870 0000303
www.stanstedairport.com
Stansted is London's third-busiest airport, 35 miles northeast of central London and the nearest to Cambridge. Direct trains to Cambridge; fast access to the M11.

Bus

Cambridge Coach Services Ltd Tel 01223 236333
Cambridgeshsire (Cambridge, Huntingdon, Ely, St Ives) Stagecoach Tel 01223 433250
National Express operates from Parker's Piece to London, airports and around the country Tel: 08717 818178
Peterborough Bus Routes (Transit)
www.peterborough.ca/Living/City_Services/Transportation

Bus - Park & Ride

Both Cambridge and Peterborough have excellent park and ride schemes. Cambridge has a 7 day a week service across five sites and parking is free. They are colour coded; GREEN (Milton to Babraham Rd); RED(Madingley Rd to Newmarket Rd);

BLUE(Trumpington). Services run every 10 minutes weekdays and Saturdays.

The Busway
This is the new guided busway service. Frequent buses between Huntingdon, St Ives and Cambridge. Also buses to Trumpington and Addenbrooks Hospital. www.thebusway.info

By Foot
Cambridge and Peterborough are both compact and easy to explore on foot. Try www.walkit.com/cambridge to see your route and even calories burned.

By Bike - See page 54
Cambridge is the cycling capital of the UK and has two large cycle parks in the city centre., Grand Arcade and Park Street.

Car
Cambridge, Peterborough and surrounding area iseasily accessible from the M11, M1/A1 and A14 motorways. **Parking: T**here are five centrally located multi-storey and three surface car parks in Cambridge.

Train
Cambridge Train Station is 20 minutes walk from the city centre. You can hire cycles from Station Cycles, or take the bus.
National Rail Enquiry Service
Tel: 08457 484950
www.nationalrail.co.uk

Traveline - 0871 200 2233
www.traveline.org.uk

Taxis
The two largest cab firms in **Cambridge:**

Panther Taxis Tel: 01223 715715
Cam Cab Ltd Tel: 01223 704704
However there are many taxi ranks, at the train station and in the city centre. Likewise, there are many other taxis firms in the surrounding area, but for convenience there are some listed here.

Peterborough - City Cabs
Tel: 01733 341111
Huntingdon - Steves Taxis
Tel: 01480 412333
Newmarket - 1 Taxis
Tel: 01638 560660
St Ives - A&B Taxis
Tel: 01480 271847

Work
The internet, local newspaper and employment agencies are all good places to start if you are looking for work.

Cambridge Evening News Jobs
cambridge.jobsnow.co.uk

University of Cambridge Jobs
www.jobs.cam.ac.uk

Peterborough Telegraph & Jobs Today
www.peterboroughtoday.co.uk/jobs

Unemployed/Parental Benefits

Cambridge Citizens Advice Bureau
66 Devonshire Rd, Cambridge CB1 2BL
Tel: 0844 848 7979
www.cambridgecab.org.uk
Cambridge & South Cambridgeshire
Tel: 0844 848 7979
www.cambridgecab.org.uk
Peterborough Citizens Advice
Tel: 0844 499 4120
www.peterboroughcab.org.uk

Huntingdon, St Neots, St Ives Areas
www.citizensadvice.org.uk/huntscab-2
For one to one advice and information.

Jobcentre Plus
Freephone 0800 0556688
www.direct.gov.uk.

Statutory Maternity Pay
You can get Statutory Maternity Pay if you have been working for the same employer for at least 26 weeks, by the time you are 15 weeks away from the date your baby is due. This means that you must have worked for the same employer throughout your pregnancy. It is paid by your employer if you are away from work to have a baby. It can be paid for up to 39 weeks

Maternity Allowance
You must have been working for at least 26 weeks in the 66 weeks before you are due to give birth. The rules about the benefits you can claim in pregnancy and early maternity are complicated. It is

worth contacting the Citizens Advice Bureau or Jobcentre Plus.

Statutory Paternity Pay
If you are a working father, or the partner of a woman having a child (including a same-sex partner), you may be able to get Statutory Paternity Pay for two weeks during your paternity leave.

Parental Leave
Men and women both have the right to take unpaid time off work as parental leave if they have worked for their employer for one year.

Child Benefit and Child Tax Credit
Child Benefit is a tax-free benefit paid to most people with children.

Child Tax Credit is a payment for people with children, whether they are in or out of work. It is paid by HM Revenue and Customs. You can get Child Tax Credit if your income is low enough and you are responsible for at least one child.

AT A GLANCE
Emergency fire/police/ambulance
Tel: 999

Cambridge City Council Housing Advice
Tel: 01223 457918

Cambridge Citizens Advice Bureau
Tel: 0844 848 7979
www.cambridgecab.org.uk

Healthcare
NHS 111 service if you need medical help fast, but it's not a 999 emergency.
NHS Choices website
www.nhs.uk

Jobcentre Plus
Freephone 0800 055 6688

Travel
Stansted Airport
Tel: 0870 0000303
Cambridge Coach Services
Tel 01223 236333
Stagecoach
Tel 01223 423554
National Express
Tel: 08717 818178
National Rail Enquiry Service Tel: 08457 484950
Traveline 0871 200 2233
Cambrige - Panther Taxis
Tel: 01223 715715

Parenting

Bad Mothers Club
www.badmothersclub.com
'In the aisle by the chill cabinets, no-one can hear you scream.' This is the tag line of this tongue in cheek look at parenting.

Barnardo's
www.barnardos.org.uk
Parenting support through family centres and work with children.

Family Advice
www.familylives.org.uk
A parenting charity with advice and information.

Mumsnet
www.mumsnet.com
A forum for mothers and parents, including reviews of products for children.

Parenting Support Centre
www.parenting.co.uk

Sticky Fingers Travel
www.stickyfingerstravel.com
Family friendly travel advice.

Single Parents
Cambridge UK Single Parents_____page 45
Gingerbread_____page 45

Support and Advice for Children

Childline
www.childline.org.uk
Tel: 0800 1111
Confidential information and advice for young people themselves on bullying, back to school and other topics.

NSPCC
National Society for the Protection of Children
www.nspcc.org.uk
Tel: 0808 800 5000
Text: 88858
Help@nspcc.org.uk
Help and advice if you are worried about a child, free 24 hour helpline.

Talk to Frank
www.talktofrank.com
Confidential drugs advice.

Young Minds
www.youngminds.org.uk
Parent helpline: 0808 802 5544
Help and advice on young people's mental health and wellbeing.

Teenagers
Exams, Careers, Volunteering

UCAS Progress
www.ucasprogress.com
A website for 14-19 year olds to find courses and training in Cambridgeshire.

Youthoria - the website for 11-19 year olds in Cambridgeshire
www.youthoria.org
This informative website is packed with information for teenagers in Cambridgeshire. It includes job vacancies, news, features, apprenticeships, training, life advice, learning and more.

NHS Choices - Beat Exam Stress
www.nhs.uk/Livewell/childhealth6-15/Pages/Examstress
NHS website that has some handy tips on how to reduce exam stress. Getting good sleep, good food and exercising can help a great deal.

Healthy Teens
Physical Activity
Check out the activities listing in the swimming and sports section. There is a huge variety on offer and it has so many benefits for children and young people, it can improve mental wellbeing and physical fitness as well as reduce obesity.

The NHS recommends at least 1 hour of physical activity every day for children and young people, which should be a mix of moderate activity such as fast walking and vigorous activity like running.

www.nhs.uk/Livewell/fitness/Pages/physical-activity-guidelines-for-young-people

Relationships and Young People
Teenagers are growing, maturing and at some point will take an interest in relationships. Some teens may feel confused about whether they are gay, or what sex is all about. Some may be worried about changes in their bodies. As a parent it's not always easy to support a child growing up. But to be informed is a start.

NHS Live Well - Teen Health
www.nhs.uk/Livewell/Sexandyoungpeople
Teenagers can find out about their health, how to stay safe, common myths about pregnancy, a bodies question and answer page, acne, bereavement, advice on how to avoid peer pressure, 'it's ok to say no' and other support.

Brook Advice Clinic
www.brook.org.uk
Confidential advice on sexual health for the under 25s.

Bullying
www.cambridgeshire.gov.uk/childrenandfamilies/parenting/childsbehaviour/bullying
The Cambridgeshire County Council website has useful information and advice. There are things that can be done to reduce or avoid bullying or being bullied. A child who avoids school, or becomes withdrawn, more anxious or aggressive may be experiencing bullying. You can also contact your child's school directly if you are at all concerned. See the section on computers for advice on online bullying.

General Support & Advice
Samaritans
24 hour telephone line: 08457 909090
www.samaritans.org

Concern about Abuse

If you are concerned or suspect abuse, that a child may be suffering physical, sexual or emotional abuse or neglect, or if as a parent or carer you feel that you may harm your child, then contact the Cambridgeshire Child Protection Team on 0345 045 5203 between 8am to 6pm Monday to Friday. Outside of these hours, the Emergency Duty Team is on 01733 234724 or the police 999. Email:ReferralCentre.Children@cambridgeshire.gov.uk

The Team's website has more information on the signs of harm and what to do if you are at all concerned. www.cambridgeshire.gov.uk/childrenandfamilies/parenting/keepingchildrensafe/childprotection/

You can also contact the NSPCC and young people can contact Childline (details in previous page).

Stop it Now!
Tel: 0808 10000 900
Help@stopitnow.org.uk
www.stopitnow.org.uk
A campaign to prevent child sexual abuse. It has a lot of advice and information.

Domestic Violence

Note: If you are being abused and are using a computer or phone to which your abuser has access, it is strongly recommended that you take measures to cover your activity, for example use a library or internet cafe.

Cambridge Domestic Violence Action Group
cambridgedomesticviolence.weebly.com

National Domestic Violence Helpline
Tel: (Freephone 24hr) 0808 2000 247

Cambridge Women's Aid
Tel: 01223 460 947
refuge@cambridgewa.org.uk
www.womensaid.org.uk

Information, support and temporary accommodation.

Mankind
Tel: 01823 334 244
www.mankind.org.uk
Support for male victims of domestic abuse and domestic violence

Refuge
www.refuge.org.uk
Help for women and children facing domestic violence.

Technology and Kids

Have you ever wondered how much time to let your kids play computer games, watch TV, or whether to get an Ipad? Technology can be incredibly useful.

Kids naturally want to keep up with other kids. So what limits, if any, should you choose? There is also the cost consideration, you can't get your kid the latest phone if you have not got the money.

However there are other concerns, such as bullying online, exposure to inappropriate material, children's lack of exercise from sitting around, and spending excessive hours playing the Xbox.

Generally, the information that I've read recommends that you talk to your child about online dangers, and tell them what to do if they are worried. Explain that anything they put online could be seen by anyone, and it is important not to pass on detailed information such as their name, age or address. Use filtering software to block inappropriate sites and get to know and understand what websites they visit.

Microsoft recommends that up to at leasts the age of 10 years you should sit with your children while they use computers. As they go into the teens, to continue to supervise their activities, educate them about safe use and set clear rules. Keep the computers where you can see them rather than their bedrooms.

Here are some sources of information to help you protect your child and make up your own mind about what limits to set.

Childline - Advice for Children - Online Bullying
Tel: 0800 1111
www.childline.org.uk/Explore/Bullying/Pages/online-bullying

NSPCC Keeping Your Child Safe Online
www.nspcc.org.uk/help-and-advice/for-parents/keeping-your-child-safe

Microsoft Age-based Guidelines for Kids' Internet Use
www.microsoft.com/en-gb/security/family-safety/childsafety-age

Think U Know
www.thinkuknow.co.uk
Website for kids about online safety.

Online Fun and Games for Kids

Cbeebies
www.bbc.co.uk
Toddler TV, education, fun & games from the BBC.

CBBC
www.bbc.co.uk/cbbc
Children's TV, education and fun.

Guinness World Records
www.guinnessworldrecords.com

Haring Kids
www.haringkids.com
Interactive site with online colouring and animation.

How Stuff Works
www.howstuffworks.com
Informative, interesting website that will widen your child's world.

Switch Zoo
www.switchzoo.com
Make new animals by switching bodies and heads.

Travelling with Children

It can help to think ahead when it comes to travelling with children. A baby needs a lot of equipment, a buggy and if bottle fed, formula and bottles. Toddler routines may get upset and teenagers may get bored. But do not be disheartened! It is possible to have a lot of fun with a bit of patience and practical help.

Travel Light - This may seem impossible, but it can really help not to have to lug a lot of bags. Check if hotels have travel cots ahead.

Toys/Games - If possible, try to bring only those that will really get a lot of use. Although pack an extra surprise book or toy in case. Kids can have their own bag.

Pack for Delays - Include extra nappies, snacks, change of clothes, colouring book.

Flying - Be prepared with liquids in a separate clear bag. Baby food/formula is allowed. Take a good, collapsible buggy.

Be Realistic - Allow for the fact that you have kids and don't expect too much out of yourself or them. Sometimes it's the simplest things about travelling that are the best, so enjoy!

Families from Abroad: Adjusting to Life Away From Home

Whether you are coming for a job contract, or have moved to Cambridgeshire permanently, it can be a challenge to adjust to a new environment, and help children to settle in. Children may take a bit of time to settle into a new school.

It may help to get involved in activities in the school if you can, and arrange play dates to help your child socialise. You may want help learning English for you and/or your child. There are several English language teachers in Cambridge. Listed are just some support groups and there may also be support at a local Children's Centre (p169).

123 Soleil
Mill Road Baptist Church, 178, Mill Road, Cambridge CB1 3LP
0-5yrs French culture and language group.

Cambridge Chinese School
Netherhall School (Upper School side) Queen Ediths Way, Cambridge CB1 8NN
ccs-headteacher@srcf.ucam.org
ccs.soc.srcf.net
Established in 1985, with over 100 pupils, to teach chinese language and culture. Runs every Sunday.

Grupo Aquarela
Ross St Community Centre, Cambridge
Tel: 07584138659
Playgroup for Potuguese speakers.

Polish Saturday School
231 Chesterton Rd, Cambridge CB4 1AS
Tel: 07970 153395
5-15yrs. To teach children of Polish descent the language and history.

Polska Soleczna Szkola W Ely
The Foruom, Barton Rd, Ely CB7 4DE
polskaszkola-ely.org.uk

For the local community, to cultivate Polish history and culture.

Semillitas (Spanish Speaking)
Ross Street Community Centre, Ross Street, Cambridge CB1 3UZ
Tel: 01223503385(Eva)

Nicolas Copernicus Polish Saturday School - Peterborough
Tel: 07840 372465
nfo@school-pl.co.uk
www.school-pl.co.uk

English as an Additional Language
Schools will usually be supportive, and you can help your child learn English at home. There are several courses available and teachers in Cambridge. Cambridgeshire **Race and Equality Diversity Services (**CREDS) can support you if you need more help or advice.
Tel: 01223 703882

School Admissions
All children must legally start school in the term following their 5th birthday, although places are offered following your child's 4th birthday. Contact:

Admissions Team
CC1206, Castle Court, Castle Hill, Cambridge CB3 0AP
Tel 0345 045 1370
www.cambridgeshire.gov.uk/childrenandfamilies/education/primary/apply-primary

From thinking about wanting to have a baby, to becoming pregnant and being a first time parent can be quite a journey. Your GP or information from the NHS is the first contact if you are trying to conceive or are pregnant. In addition, in Cambridge there are a huge range of antenatal classes and support. This chapter lists local services and sources of support on every stage of that journey.

Maternity Care

When you first suspect that you are pregnant, visit your local health centre or GP who will then be able to explain your maternity or 'antenatal' care. You will be offered appointments to check your progress and offer advice. You will also be offered antenatal classes and breastfeeding workshops. All hospitals offer at least two ultrasound scans during pregnancy, the first around 8-14 weeks, or 'dating scan', and the second between 18 and 21 weeks 'anomaly scan'.

NHS Choices
NHS Choices has a wealth of information on pregnancy, maternity services, the birth and early years.
www.nhs.uk/Conditions/pregnancy-and-baby/pages/pregnancy-and-baby-care.aspx#close

National Childbirth Trust (NCT)
Main branch contact:
Tel: 0844 243 6071
Chair@NCTCambridge.org
Antenatal and postnatal classes:
bookings5g@nct.org.uk or 0844 243 6896
This has a local branch run by volunteers and offers support for parents and those who are pregnant. It can be a good way of getting to know local parents.
Nearly New Sale enquiries:
0844 243 6071 option 2
www.facebook.com/NCTCambridge
www.nct.org.uk/branches/cambridge

NCT Mantenatal Workshop
Cambridge
Tel: 0844 243 6896
bookings5g@nct.org.uk
www.nct.org.uk/courses
Antenatal course for men.

NCT Twins & Multiples Workshops
Cambridge
Tel: 0844 243 6896
bookings5g@nct.org.uk
www.nct.org.uk/courses

Ante-Natal Classs - Huntingdon & District NCT
Tel: 0844 243 6886
bookings5q@nct.org.uk
www.nctpregnancyandbabycare.com
Classes available in St Ives, Huntingdon & St Neots, Huntingdon Cambs PE28 2HX

Antenatal classes in Cambridge, Saffron Walden and Ely (NCT)
Cambridge
bookings5g@nct.org.uk
www.nct.org.uk

St Neots & District NCT
Ante-natal & Post-Natal Classes, Branch 571, Anglia, St Neots Cambs PE19 1LD
Tel: 0844 243 6886
bookings5q@nct.org.uk
www.nctpregnancyandbabycare.com

Cambridge IVF
www.cambridge-ivf.org.uk
This is a new purpose built conception unit for the region. It offers NHS and self funded treatments. Usually your GP or hospital consultant would write a letter of referral.

BUMP TO BABY

Mother and Child Sculpture - Sophie Dickens - John Lewis -

Cambridge Fetal Care
The Rosie Hospital,
Cambridge University Teaching Hospitals NHS Foundation Trust,
Hills Road, Cambridge
CB2 2QQ
Tel: 01223 217227 (clinic co-ordinator 9:30am-3pm Mon-Friday; answerphone at all other times)
Fax: 01223 216185
admin@fetalcare.co.uk
www.fetalcare.co.uk
Offers a private service for pregnancy scanning, texting and counselling, based at the Rosie Hospital.

Maternity Units

The Rosie Hospital at Addenbrooke's is the main maternity service in Cambridge. You can usually choose to have your baby in a hospital, a midwife-led unit or at home, depending on your health and your pregnancy.

Rosie Hospital
Robinson Way
Cambridge
Cambridgeshire
CB2 0QQ
Tel: 01223 217 617
www.cuh.org.uk/cms/rosie-hospital

Hinchingbrooke Hospital
Hinchingbrooke Park
Hinchingbrooke
Huntingdon
Cambridgeshire

PE29 6NT
Tel: 01480 416416

Hinchingbrooke Hospital - Antenatal Classes

Hinchingbrooke Park, Huntingdon Cambridgeshire PE29 6NT
Contact: ANC Clinic Midwife
Tel: 01480 416416

Antenatal Classes in Cambridge

Ante & Post Natal Pilates Sessions

Activate Pilates, West Solarium, Fulbourn, Cambridge Cambridgeshire CB21 5XE
Tel: 0773 8866771
info@activatepilates.co.uk
www.activatepilates.co.uk

Antenatal HynoBirthing Classes

Cambourne, Cambridge
Tel: 07974 19 47 44
info@birtheasy.co.uk

Antenatal Classes - Cambridge

Lotus Blossom Childbirth Classes, Cambridge
Tel: 07977 921709
doulamaddie@gmail.com
www.cambridgeantenatal.co.uk

Aquanatal Excercise in Water

Bumpercise & Aquatots, Chesterton Sports Centre Pool, Gilbert Rd, Cambridge
Tel: 01223 569067
sarah@bumperciseandaquatots.co.uk
www.bumperciseandaquatots.co.uk

BabyCalm

Cambridge
Tel: 07513 329906
victoria@babycalm.co.uk
www.babycalm.co.uk/teachers/victoria-montgomery

Bumpercise & Aquatots

39 Cambridge Road, Impington, Cambridge Cambridgeshire CB4 9NU
Tel: 01223 569067

sarah@bumperciseandaquatots.co.uk
www.bumperciseandaquatots.co.uk

Pregnancy Pilates Class

The Bodywise Studio, Unite 4 Dales Brewery, Gwydir Street, Cambridge CB1 2LJ
Tel: 07879645964
bethiahope@hotmail.com
www.pilatesformovement.co.uk

Total Toning Pregnancy Class

Cottenham Community Centre, High Street, Cottenham Cambs CB24
Tel: 07854170540
debs_l2bu@hotmail.co.uk

Antenatal Classes outside Cambridge

Active Labour and Pregnancy Yoga Workshops - Ely

The Yoga Studio Ely, Tower Farm, Tower Road, Little Downham, Ely CB6 2TD
Tel: 07763653029
krachanow@gmail.com
www.yogastudioely.co.uk

Antenatal Relax & Breathe - St Neots

St Neots Cambs
jenny@relaxstneots.com
www.relaxstneots.com

Aquanatal - St Ives

St Ivo Leisure Centre, Westwood Road, St. Ives, Cambs PE27 6WU
Tel: 01480 388500
StIvoLeisureCentre@huntsdc.gov.uk
www.huntsleisure.org/LeisureCentres/StIvo

Lazy Daisy - Active Birth, Antental and Pregnancy Classes - Newmarket

Newmarket and Surrounding Area
Tel: 07759685247
karen@lazydaisybirthing.co.uk
www.thelazydaisychain.co.uk

Mother Nurture Doula Antenatal Classes, Ely

Tel: 07712 439637
tara@mothernurturedoula.co.uk
www.mothernurturedoula.co.uk

Mum 2 Be Swim - St Neots

One Leisure St Neots, Barford Road, Eynesbury, St Neots Cambridgeshire PE19 2SA
Tel: 01480 388700
oneleisurestneots@huntingdonshire.gov.uk
www.oneleisure.net

Pilates for Pregnancy

Venues around Great Shelford, Cambridge, CB22
Tel: 01223 841968
enquiries@physiopilates.org.uk
www.physiopilates.org.uk

Pregnancy Aquacise - Huntingdon/Peterborough

Tel: 07857 683291
babybliss@tesco.net
www.mybabybliss.info

Antenatal Yoga for pregnancy, birth and baby

Birthlight Antenatal Yoga

Physic health centre, Oakington rd, Girton Cambs CB3 0QH
Tel: 01223 479658
sallybirthlight@aol.com
www.birthlightcambridge.com

Birthlight Yoga

At various venues in and around Cambridge.
Tel: 07840 523 898
www.joyfulbirthbaby.com

Bumps to Babies Pregnancy & Post-natal Yoga - Ely

Old Dispensary, 13 St Mary's Street, Ely Cambridgeshire CB7 4ER
Tel: 01954 204742
enquiries@bumpstobabies.co.uk
www.bumpstobabies.co.uk

Daisy Birthing, Huntingdon
Equilibrium Yoga Centre, Huntingdon
Tel 01536 744154
steph@bumpbirthandbeyond.co.uk
www.bumpbirthandbeyond.co.uk

Twins Antenatal and Postnatal Class

Daffodil Children's Centre, Godmanchester Community Primary School, Park Lane, Godmanchester Cambridgeshire PE29 2AG
www.cambridgeshirechildrenscentres.org.uk/godmanchester

Waterbirth Workshop
The Meadows Community Centre, 1 St Catharine's Road, Cambridge CB4 3XJ
Telephone: 0844 243 6896
bookings5G@nct.org.uk
www.nct.org.uk/in-your-area/course-finder/view/15302

YogaBirth
Venues in Cambridge
sharon.budworth@virgin.net
Mobile: 07791002064
yogabirthcambridge.co.uk
Classes for pregnancy and couple workshops.

Yoga 4 Pregnancy - Huntingdon
Oak Tree Centre, 1 Oak Drive, Sallowbush Road, Huntingdon Cambs PE29 7HN
Tel: 01480 380307
barbara@yoga4everybody.co.uk
www.yoga4everybody.co.uk

Yoga Class
Trumpington Pavilion, Anstey Way, King George V Playing Field, Trumpington Cambridge CB2 9JF
Tel: 07816 610742
julia.east@hotmail.co.uk
www.trumpingtonresidentsassociation.org/Pavilion_programme.html

YogaBirth - Yoga for Pregnancy and Birth - St Ives
St Ives Health Centre, Armes Corner, London Road, St Ives Cambs PE27 5ES
Tel: 01480 353441
sharon.budworth@birthandmore.co.uk
www.birthandmore.co.uk

Hypnotherapy for Birth

Barefoot Mummy - Natal Hypnotherapy Workshops
Cambridgeshire
Tel: 07779893703
shonakitchener@natalhypnotherapy.co.uk

www.barefootmummy.com

BirthSense HypnoBirthing Classes
Tel: 07941 429691
info@birthsense.co.uk
www.birthsense.co.uk

ComfortableBirth HypnoBirthing
Cambridge, Huntingdon, Newmarket and surrounds
Tel: 07967102059
marie@comfortablebirth.com

HypnoBirth
Ely, Cambridge and surrounding areas Cambridgeshire
Tel: 01353 659341
philippa.featherstone@ntlworld.com
www.hypnaissance.com

Post Natal Classes

Post Natal Exercise Class
The Barn Health and Leisure Gym, Girton, Cambridge CB3 0QH
Tel: 07854170540
debbieprince@bloomingfit.com
www.bloomingfit.com

Mother's Little Helper
motherslittlehelpers.co.uk
Services for parents, particularly back at home after a newborn, such as nappy laundry, dog walking, gardening in Cambridge City.

Adoption & Fostering

Cambridgeshire County Council
Tel; 0800 052 0078
www.cambridgeshire.gov.uk/childrenandfamilies/parenting/becomingaparent/adoption
You can obtain an information pack from Cambridgeshire County Council, which has comprehensive information if you are considering fostering or adopting a child.

Single Parents

Cambridge UK Single Parents
www.meetup.com/Cambridge-UK-Single-Parents
A community of single parents in and around Cambridge, who meet to share ideas and support. It coss £60 for 6 months, but the first meeting is free if you'd like to try it out.

Gingerbread
Tel: (Freephone Helpline) 0800 802 0925
www.gingerbread.org.uk
National support group, for advice and information. There is a Cambridge / Whittlesford friendship group, please check web site for details.

Ramsey Children's Centre
Unit 3, Stocking Fen Rd, Ramsey PE26 1SA
Tel: 01487 814812
Lone Parent Support Group for those with children aged 0-5 yrs.

Home-Start

This voluntary scheme offers friendship, support and practical help to families with children under five years old. Particularly those families struggling to cope. Available in certain areas around Cambridgeshire.

Cambridge & District
Contact: The Fields Children's Centre, Galfrid Road, Cambridge CB5 8ND.
Tel: 01223 210202 or email: office@homestartcambridge.co.uk
Contact: Priors Court Community Room, 14a Priors Court, Ely CB6 3AH
Tel: 01353 663158 or email: office@homestarteastcambs.org.uk

Royston & South Cambridgeshire
Contact: Unit 6 Valley Farm, Station Road, Meldreth, Royston SG8 6JP
Tel: 01763 262262 or email: admin@hsrsc.co.uk www.hsrsc.co.uk
www.homestartcambridge.co.uk

East Cambs and South Fenland
www.home-start.org.uk

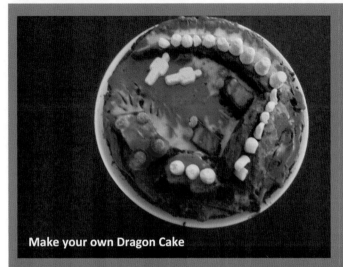

Make your own Dragon Cake

1. **Kelsey Kerridge Sports Parties**
   Archery/football/basketball/trampolining and more. *www.kelseykerridge.co.uk*

2. **Sublime Science** – Provides potions, bubbles and magic tricks *www.sublimescience.com/kids-party-cambridge-entertainer*

3. **David Lloyd Pool Party** or Birthday party *www.davidlloyd.co.uk/home/families*

4. **Chesterton Sports Centre** -Birthday pool or Bouncy Fun party *www.chestertonsportscentre.org.uk/activities/birthday-parties*

5. **Si5 Spymissions,** which includes a meal and a secret spy mission. *www.spymissions.co.uk/parties*

6. **Craft Monkey Paint Your Own Pottery, Build a Bear,** St Neots. Can come to your venue. *www.craftymonkeypotterypainting.com*

7. **Pizza Express** – Make Your Own Pizza Party – with a balloon and certificate to take home. *www.pizzaexpress.com/parties/kidspizzamaking*

8. **Nature Activity Party at Wandlebury** – Based in the Stable Rooms, can be a nature discovery or twilight walk. Bring food, they have plates and beakers. *www.cambridgeppf.org/wandlebury-country-park*

9. **Carluccio's Picnic Punting Party** – Includes Italian Kids Picnic, punting and life vests. *www.puntingincambridge.com/Carluccios-kids*

10. **Cambridge Kung Fu Kids Party** – An hour of activity and Kung Fu moves with a mini ceremony where everyone gets a certificate. *www.cambridgekungfu.com/kids/parties*

Do It Yourself

Alternatively, you can organise your own party, with finger food, treats, fun and games, at your home or outside as a picnic. Smaller children could play traditional games like musical chairs or 'Simon says', and you can rope in help from other parents. Some people hire a local hall or a bouncy castle. Party bags, if you want them, can work out expensive. Instead you could buy a set of books like the Mr Men series or do a lucky dip, or get the kids to decorate their own cup cake to take away.

TIME OUT FOR PARENTS & CARERS

Being a carer of children, particularly young children, can be a demanding job. It can be hard to take time off to take care of yourself. If you are able to get some time off, there are many places in and outside of Cambridge to relax and indulge, such as a spa treatment at 'The Park' at Cambridge Regional College, which offers affordable rates. If you want to keep in shape, there are gyms with an attached crèche.

If you are missing the cinema and have a baby, there are special 'Big Scream' screenings at the Arts Picture House. Longer term, you may be considering your career, retraining or volunteering. If you are a single parent, it can be even harder to get time off, however there are support groups locally (page 45).

Pampering & Relaxation

The Varsity Hotel & Spa
Thompson's Lane (off Bridge street), Cambridge CB5 8AQ
Tel: +44 (0)1223 30 60 30 I
info@thevarsityhotel.co.uk
www.thevarsityhotel.co.uk
Elemis Spa.

The Glassworks Gym
Thompson's Lane (Off Bridge Street), Cambridge CB5 8AQ
Tel: 01223 305060
contact@theglassworksgym.co.uk

Imagine Spa
Best Western Cambridge Quy Mill Hotel, Church Road, Stow-Cum-Quy, Cambridge CB25 9AF
Tel: 01223 294179
imaginespa.co.uk/quymill
quymill@imaginespa.co.uk
Imagine Spa Quy Mill is based at the Best Western Cambridge Quy Mill hotel on the edge of Cambridge.

Lxir Spa Caruso
70 Regent St, Cambridge
Tel: 01223 300777
www.lxirspacaruso.co.uk

Sanctuary Spa Cambridge
Grand Arcade (2nd Floor), Cambridge
Tel: 01223 657054
www.thesanctuary.co.uk

The Park
Beauty Salon and Hairdresser
Cambridge Regional College, Kings Hedges Road, Cambridge CB4 2QT
Tel: 01223 418998
Affordable prices and hairdressing. Different rates if service by students.

Babysitters

It is not easy to find someone that you trust to mind your child If you decide to get a babysitter, whether a friend, family or professional service, consider their experience, whether they have first aid training, how they will play, deal with a tantrum or problem with your child. Ask for references and follow these up. You will need to decide if they are responsible enough to look after your child and handle an emergency. The NSPCC recommends only using registered childminders.
www.nspcc.org.uk/help-and-advice/for-parents/keeping-your-child-safe

Ofsted
www.ofsted.gov.uk
For a list of registered childminders.

Gyms With Crèche's

David Lloyd
Coldham's Business Park Coldham's Lane Cambridge CB1 3LH
www.davidlloyd.co.uk/home/families
Children's gym. Soft play area. Crèche

Spirit Health Club Cambridge
Holiday Inn Cambridge, Lakeview, Bridge Road, Impington, Cambridge CB24 9PH
Tel: 01223 236620
spirit.cambridge@ihg.com
www.spirithealthclubs.co.uk/clubs
Beauty Treatments, Children's Play Area, Crèche on Mon, Tue and Fri mornings.

Movies

Staying in is the new going out! Well, it can be, if you have young children and limited or zero babysitting. However there are DVD rentals, box sets and

satellite TV on demand features so that you can still see the latest movies at home. There is also the 'Big Scream', where you can watch a movie in a cinema if you are a parent with a baby under one.

Arts Picture House Cambridge - Big Scream
www.picturehouses.co.uk/cinema/Arts_Pictur ehouse_Cambridge/Whats_On/Clubs_Group s/Big_Scream/
Low lights are left on and nappy changing facilities for these movies exclusively for parents with babies under one year old. Usually on Wednesday mornings but check website. See page 33.

DVD Rentals & Satellite Options
There are so many options, and special offers these days. Check out www.moneysavingexpert.com for the best deals.

Education and Training

Cambridge Awise
info@camawise.org.uk
camawise.org.uk
The aim is to advance the participation of girls and women in the sciences.

Cambridge Central Library
7 Lion Yard, Grand Arcade,
Cambridge CB2 3QD
Tel: 0345 045 5225
www.cambridgeshire.gov.uk/leisure/libraries/ directory/cambridge_central_library

Access to public computers free to library members, photocopiers and printers. It is also linked to the National Adult Careers Service. The learning centre gives free advice to help with deciding on the right training and employment for you. It is located at the top floor and runs an appointment system. Phone 01223 728512 to enquire.

Cambridge Women's Resource Center
CWRC The Wharf, Hooper Street, Cambridge CB1 2NZ
Tel: 01223 321148
www.cwrc.org.uk
A guidance worker is available to support women who want to move on into employment, training or education. Support with CVs and application forms. It has a creche from 9:15-12:15 and 13:00-15:30, Monday to Friday term time only. Training is available in English, Maths and other subjects. Many are free or very low rates.

National Careers Service
nationalcareersservice.direct.gov.uk
Provides advice and support on careers.

Open University
www.open.ac.uk
Distance learning, with flexible options which can fit around children.

Adult Careers Service Cambridgeshire
www.cambridgeshire.gov.uk/jobs

Tel: 07717 677940
Adult careers advisors for people in Cambridgeshire and Peterborough. Also a useful search engine for local jobs.

Cambridge Evening News Jobs
www.cambridge.jobsnow.co.uk
Jobs in Cambridgeshire.

Centre 33 Young Carers Project
Tel: 01223 307488
youngcarers@centre33.org.uk
www.centre33.org.uk
The Project supports 8 - 18 year old young carers in and around Cambridge who support a family member with a long-term illness, disability, mental health problem or who misuse drugs or alcohol. They also look for volunteers with the centre.

Volunteering

Volunteer Centres Cambridgeshire & Peterborough
www.volunteeringcambsandpboro.org.uk
Six volunteer centres to match people with organisations.

Volunteer Centre Cambridge & District
Tel: 01223 356549
www.cam-volunteer.org.uk
Helps to match people who want to volunteer with organisations needing volunteers.

CAMBRIDGESHIRE

Cambridgeshire has much to offer families. It includes **Peterborough, Newmarket, Huntington, Ely, St Ives** and beyond.

Peterborough has ice skating, go karting and a steam train, or you can feed the ducks in a stroll through pretty Ely. Alternatively, visit **Houghton Mill** in Huntingdon, the Horse Museum in Newmarket or the animals at **Linton Zoo.** The picturesque medieval towns of **Saffron Walden**, **St Ives** and **St Neot's** are lovely. You can even explore a cave in **Royston.**

Anglesey Abbey has beautiful gardens, **Ely and Peterborough Cathedral** are magnificent. **Hinchingbrooke House, Kimbolton Castle, Buckden Towers, Elton Hall** and **Wimpole Hall** are also worth a trip out. Because the area is very flat, many airfields were built here, such as RAF Bomber and Fighter Command in the Second World War. This is also why the only American Second World War burial ground is found outside Cambridge. The sweeping, marsh lands make beautiful country parks, such as Wicken Fen, Nene Park, Flag Fen, Wandlesbury Country Park, Brampton Wood, the Ouse Valley, Wicken Fen, Paxton Pits and Grafham Water.

Tourist Information Centres

Cambridge
Peas Hill, Cambridge CB2 3AD
Tel: 0871 226 8006
info@visitcambridge.org
www.visitcambridge.org

East of England Tourist Board
The Pavilion Gardens, Buxton, Derbyshire, SK17 6BQ.
Tel: 01473 822922
www.eastofenglandtouristboard.com

Ely
Oliver Cromwell's House,
29 St. Mary's Street, Ely
Tel: 01353 662062
tic@eastcambs.gov.uk
www.visitely.org.uk

Huntingdon
38 High Street, Southoe, St. Neots PE19 5YE
Tel: 07505 567614
Ehunts.tic@huntsdc.gov.uk
www.visitcambridge.org/beyond-cambridge/huntingdon
www.huntingdon-accommodation.org

Peterborough
9 Bridge Street, Peterborough PE1 1HJ
Tel: 01733 452336
tic@peterborough.gov.uk
www.visitpeterborough.com

Saffron Walden
1 Market Place, Saffron Walden, Essex CB10 1HR
Tel: 01799 524002
tourism@saffronwalden.gov.uk
www.visitsaffronwalden.gov.uk

St. Neots
St Neots Town Council, Priory Lane, St Neots, Cambridgeshire PE19 2BH
Tel: 01480 388911
mail@stneots-tc.gov.uk
www.stneots-tc.gov.uk

Wisbech and the Fens
2-3 Bridge Street, Wisbech PE13 1AF
Tel: 01945 583263
tourism@fenland.gov.uk
www.visitcambridgeshire.org

Children's Centres & Toy Librarys

www.cambridgeshirechildrenscentres.gov.uk
Children's Centres can offer advice and support for people with young kids. Some also have 'Toy Libraries' where you can lend toys for a small cost.

Education, Schools and Colleges

www.cambridgeshire.gov.uk/childrenandfamilies/education
There are 205 Primary Schools, 31 Secondary Schools and 24 Further Education Colleges state funded in Cambridgeshire.

Websites

BBC News Cambridgeshire
www.bbc.co.uk/news/England/cambridgeshire
Up to date news on the area.

Cambridgeshire County Council
www.cambridgeshire.gov.uk
Information on the County Council, Housing, Environment, Jobs, Families, Policing and Leisure.

Cambridgeshire Net
www.cambridgeshire.net
Online community hub listing the details of thousands of local organisations, courses, events and activities and facilities such as venues for hire in Cambridgeshire.

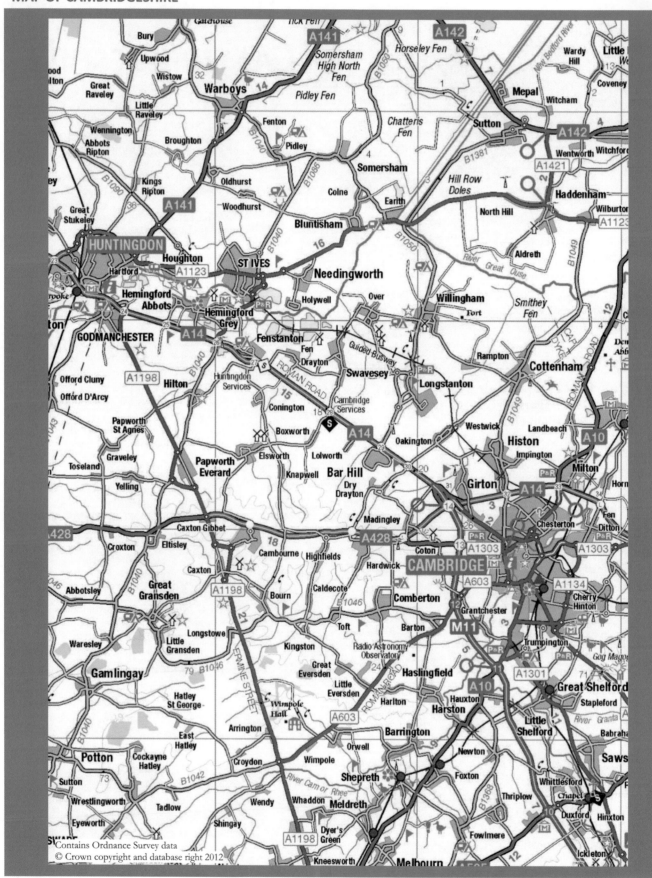

Did you Know?

- A domestic dog is a subspecies of the gray wolf. They have a sense of smell up to 1 million times more sensitive than humans.
- Polar bears share DNA of Irish Brown Bears and are probably descended from Ireland.
- Pigeons can learn to tell the difference between Monet and Picasso.
- A bee must travel the equivalent of 3x around the world to produce one jar of honey. They also have 5 eyes.
- A snail can sleep for 3 years.
- Ants will not cross a chalk line.
- For every person there are about 200 million insects.
- The hedgehog likes to eat slugs, worms and beetles.

Information from wikipaedia.com

Nature web sites for kids

canalrivertrust.org.uk/explorers/families
www.rspb.org.uk
www.wildlifewatch.org.uk
www.naturedetectives.org.uk

Nature Reserves

Ouse Washes Nature Reserve

Welches Dam Manea, March PE15 0NF
Tel: 01354 680212
ouse.washes@rspb.org.uk
www.rspb.org.uk

The Ouse Washes is an excellent introduction to Fenland wildlife. In the winter, the reserve attracts thousands of ducks and swans; and redshanks, lapwings and snipe breed in the summer. Walking behind the banks avoids putting the wildfowl to flight. There are 10 hide's available and a visitor centre.

Getting there: Train - 45 minutes. Change or take a taxi at Ely. Manea Station is 5km from the reserve (no Sunday trains). **Car** - 1 hour 15 minutes (32 miles).

Paxton Pits Nature Reserve See page 70

Wicken Fen Nature Reserve

Lode Lane, Wicken, Ely, CB7 5XP
Tel: 01353 720274
wickenfen@nationaltrust.org.uk
www.wicken.org.uk

Britain's oldest nature reserve. A unique fragment of the wilderness that once covered East Anglia, the Fen is a haven for birds, plants, insects and mammals alike. It can be explored by the traditional wide droves and lush green paths, including a boardwalk nature trailhides. It also has a visitor centre.

Open: 10:00-17:00 daily.
Admission: Adult £5.90, Child £2.95, Family £14.75.
Getting there: Car - 40 minutes (18 miles). **Train** - not really accessible, 9 miles from Ely Station.

Welney Wildfowl Reserve

Hundred Foot Bank, Welney, Nr.Wisbech PE14 9TN
Tel: 01353 860711 (The Warden) for information and a leaflet.
info.welney@wwt.org.uk
www.wwt.org.uk/wetland-centres/welney

A National Trust site, and one of the most important wetlands in Europe. It is also home to the National Dragonfly Centre. Herons, cormorants, many ducks and geese, dragonflies, butterflies and wild flowers. It has a Visitor Centre and Cafe. 850 acre wildfowl reserve including nature trail.

Open: 10am-5pm daily
Admission: Adult £5.70 Child £2.85
Getting there: Train Ely (9 miles). By road 17 miles north-east of Cambridge via A10.

Wildlife Parks And Zoos

Banham Zoo

Kenninghall Road, Banham,
Norfolk NR16 2HE
Tel: 01953 887771
www.banhamzoo.co.uk

Over 2000 animals in nearly 50 acres of park and gardens. Cafe and visitor centre. Zebras, giraffes, Leopards, monkeys, penguins and birds. Also a Skytrek activity.

Open: Daily 9:30-17:00 usually, later opening summer, earlier closing winter, check website.
Admission: Peak days Adult £16.00, Child £11.50
Getting there: Bus/Train -not really accessible, closest Train is Norwich, 1 hour to Norwich, 1 hour by Bus 10A at least from Norwich to Banham. **Car** - 1 hour 30 minutes (50 miles).

Exotic Pet Refuge

102 Station Road, Deeping St. James,
Peterborough PE6 8RH
Tel: 01778 345 923
www.exoticpetrefuge.org.uk

Founded in 1984, the Exotic Pet Refuge is a small charity that gives home to all kinds of animals. Not for general public, open only 6 days a year, check website.

Mole Hall Wildlife Park

Widdington, Saffron Waldon,
Essex, CB11 3SS
Tel: 01799 540400
enquiries@molehall.co.uk
www.molehall.com

25 acres of park and a tropical house in the grounds of Mole Hall, a fully moated historic manor house. There are black Welsh mountain sheep, Alpacas and many birds. Also deer and pigs. No food or drink is allowed in the park.

Open: All year.
Admission: Free.
Getting there: Car - 1 hour (21 miles) - the park is clearly sign posted from the B1383 and junction 8 of the M11 (be careful not to overshoot and take junction 8a). **Bus/Train** - 1 hour. Train to Audley End, Bus 301 to Widdington, Walk 22 minutes.

Linton Zoo

Hadstock Rd, Linton, Cambridge, CB21 4NT
Tel: 01223 891308
enquiries@lintonzoo.co.uk
www.lintonzoo.com

Exotic animals like tarantulas, giant tortoises, hornbills, toucans, parrots and snow leopards, Sumatran tigers and Grevy's zebra. It also has gardens with Tasmanian giant tree ferns.
Open: Check website as this varies, usually 10:30-16:00/17:00or 18:00 in summer holidays.
Admission: Adult £9.00, child £6.50.
Getting there: Bus - 45 minutes. Bus X13 to Linton, walk 15 mins.**Car** - 23 minutes (10 miles).

Shepreth Wildlife Park

Willersmill, Station Road, Shepreth, SG8 6PZ
Tel: 01763 262226
www.sheprethwildlifepark.co.uk

It includes lemurs, meerkats, a tiger, also a waterworld, nocturnal house, a cafe and play barn. Also a cafe and playground.
Open: 10am-6pm in Summer, 10am-5pm Winter (reduced days in winter)
Admission: Wildlife park only - Adults £10.50 Children £8.50 (<2 yrs free)
Getting there: Off A10 between Cambridge and Royston, or the train to Shepreth (it's right by the station).

Animal Centres

Boydells Dairy Farm

Wethersfield, Braintree, Essex CM7 4AQ
Tel: 01371 850481
enquiries@boydellsdairy.co.uk
www.boydellsdairy.co.uk

A small working farm run by the Treadgold family, speicalising in sheep milking. Guided tour, you can try milking a cow or sheep, ride a donkey cart and it has hens and even llamas.
Open: 14:00-17:00 Fri, Sat and Sun and Bank Holidays.
Admission: Adults £5.00, Child £4.00
Getting there: Bus/Train - 3 hours. Train to Stansted Airport, Bus 133 to Braintree, Bus 10 to Shalford, Boydells .
Car - 1 hour (30 miles).

The Raptor Foundation

The Heath, St Ives Road, Woodhurst, Huntingdon, Cambridgeshire, PE28 3BT
Tel: 01487 741140
info@raptorfoundation.org.uk
www.raptorfoundation.org.uk

The foundation provides sanctuary, care and rehabilitation for birds. Many species of raptors, a tea room, pond, shop, exhibition and play area. Runs experience days like Falconry day and Hawk Walk, and photography activities.

Open: 10:00-17:00 in summer, check website for details.
Admission: Adult £5.50, Child £3.30
Getting there: Bus - 1 hour 10 minutes. Busway A to Wytoon Airfield, Bus 30 to Old Hurst, Bus 22 to Woodhurst. **Car** - 45 minutes (20 miles).

The National Stud   See page 108

Wood Green Animal Shelter

London Road, Godmanchester, Cambs. PE29 2NH
Tel: 08701 90 40 90
www.woodgreen.org.uk

Provides Shelter and care for up to 6,000 domestic animals every year. Set in 52 acres of countryside. Some larger breeds such as llamas and deer are permanent residents. Weekends events and a cafe.
Open: 10:00-16:00 daily.
Admission: Free
Getting there: Train - 1 hour, Huntingdon nearest (10 minutes by taxi).
Car - 35 minutes (17 miles).

Swans, Ducks and 'Mr Asbo'

The River Cam and Ouse are home to several species of duck and swans. Most ducks are Mallards, the males having a green head. But sometimes you can see Pintail (brown head with black back), Tufted Duck (black head and body and tufts), Wood Duck (reddish

chest, black top), Wigeon (reddish chest and head), or the exotic looking Mandarin Duck. The swans are still owned by the Queen. In recent years, Cambridge rowers wrote to the Queen about an aggressive swan, nicknamed 'Mr Asbo'. He had attacked people in boats. Mr Asbo has now been moved to a quieter location.

Wildlife and Nature by Season

Spring
This is nest building time for birds, see if you can spot them in the trees. Listen to the bird songs, cuckoos, woodpeckers, pigeons, blackbirds and crows. Find frogspawn in ponds, and see the catkins, blossom, bluebells and daffodils bloom.

Summer
Look out for ants, see how they follow a trail and carry leaves many times bigger than themselves. Bees and cabbage white butterflies are hovering around the flowers. Yellow dandelions, daisies and buttercups are on the meadows. On a hot day in the grass, you may be able to hear grasshoppers. Ladybirds help to eat the green aphids which attack plants.

Autumn
A great time to go on acorn, conker and pine cone hunts, and run through russet red fallen leaves. Squirrels will be collecting for their winter store. Spiders and their webs are comon. There are also mushrooms growing in grasslands and around trees.

Winter
See which trees and bushes have lost their leaves, and which are evergreen, like holly, ivy and pines. Hedgehogs and bats hibernate, other animals have to find shelter.

HOUSES & GARDENS

Cambridge City

Cambridge University Botanic Gardens (see page 14)

Cory Lodge, Bateman Street, Cambridge, CB2 1JF
Tel: 01223 336265
enquiries@botanic.cam.ac.uk
www.botanic.cam.ac.uk

A lovely place to wander and take the kids. It has a rock garden, lake and water garden, tropical rainforest, alpine house and glasshouses. There are historic systematic beds, 1600 different types of plants, a winter garden and beautiful trees. Good for a picnic or it also has a cafe.

Cherry Hinton Hall

Cherry Hinton Road, Cambridge, CB1 8DB
www.cherryhintonhall.com

A Victorian country house set in a beautiful (now public) park, built by John Oakes, who used to be a surgeon at Addenbrooke's Hospital. The grounds are well known for hosting the annual Cambridge Folk Festival. Great childrens play area, paddling pool, large ponds and grass spaces. The island in the pool is known locally as Giants Grave, after the giant Gogmagog. Or it may also have come from some Iron Age burials which were excavated on Lime Kiln Hill, where the skeletons were unusually tall (found in 1854). It is also the site of a spring which provided a major water supply to Cambridge in 19th century. The Hall itself is now owned by Cambridge City Council. It was built in 1839 in Elizabethan style, and includes a Butler's Pantry and spiral staircase.

The Leper Chapel

Barnwell Junction on the Newmarket Road, Cambridge, CB5 8JJ
(opposite Cambridge United Football Ground)
www.en.wikipedia.org/wiki/Leper_Chapel,_C ambridge

Cambridge's oldest complete building, the Chapel of St Mary Magdalene, also known as the Leper Chapel dates back to the 12th century. It was built as part of an isolation hospital for lepers. In 1199 King John granted the Hospital the right to hold a three-day fair on the Vigil of Holy Cross. Rent from the stalls boosted the income, and it grew into Stourbridge Fair, the largest medieval fair in Europe which lasted until 1933. Goods included silk, wool, garlic, cheese and hops, reflected now in the names of the nearby streets (Garlic Row, Oyster Row, Cheddars Lane). Every September the fair is recreated in a smaller way, with medieval dancing, history talks, peddlars, an alchemist and stalls selling similar goods. There is even a University of Cambridge Proctor and Constables to police the event!
Getting there: Bus, Citi 3 and get off at Coldhams common/Ditton Walk stop.

Cambridgeshire

Anglesey Abbey

Garden & Lode Mill, Quy Road, Lode, Cambridgeshire CB25 9EJ
Tel: 01223 810080
angleseyabbey@nationaltrust.org.uk
www.nationaltrust.org.uk/anglesey-abbey
House built in 1600 on the site of a 12th-century priory, with a collection built by Huttleston Broughton, 1st Lord Fairhaven. There is nearly 100 acres of landscape garden and arboretum with over 100 pieces of sculpture. There is a winter walk and snowdrops n January and February, hyacinths in the spring, herbaceous borders and dahlia gardens in the summer and magnificent autumn foliage. A working watermill regularly mills grain for sale. Hip-carrying infant seats for loan (available in the house), a Children's quiz/trail, family adventure packs.
Open: See website, different times for house, gardens and mill. Gardens generally 10:30-17:30.
Admission: Gardens only Adult £6.35, Child £3.35, Family £16.85. Whole Property Adult £10.40, Child £5.40, Family £27.00.
Getting there: Car: - 6 miles north east of Cambridge on B1102. Signposted from A14 (jct. 35). **By Foot** - Harcamlow Way from Cambridge. Cycle - NCN51, 1¼ miles. **Bus** -Stagecoach route 10 from Cambridge Bus Station.

Audley End House & Gardens

Off London Road, Saffron Walden, Essex, CB11 4JF
Tel: 01799 522842
www.english-heritage.org.uk/daysout/properties/audley-end-house-and-gardens

HOUSE & GARDENS

The National Trust

www.nationaltrust.org.uk
Tel: 0844 8001895

Many historic and beautiful sites are protected by the National Trust. If you like visiting National Trust sites often then you may want to be a member to get discounted rates.

Membership gives access to over 350 gardens, historic houses and castles in the UK. Fees vary but as an example annual membership for an individual paying by direct debit is £41.62, Child £19.50, Family £72.75 (introductory rate). Children under 5 go free.

An insight into Victorian life. The house has elaborately decorated rooms and an art collection. Stables with horses and a Victorian groom. Also a service Wing including kitchen, scullery, pantry and laundries, gives you an insight into Victorian life below stairs. Originally adapted from a medieval Benedictine monastery, the house and gardens at Audley End were amongst the largest and most opulent in Jacobean England.

Parkland designed by "Capability" Brown. Fine formal Victorian gardens in process of being restored to their former glory. Walled organic kitchen garden stocked to match the 1800's plants. River Cam dammed to provide artificial lake.

There are two cafes, one with a playground next to it. Extensive grassed areas idea for family activities. Bike stands available by Lion Gates, but please do not ride bikes inside the

Wandlebury in the Autumn

grounds. Kites are welcome. Sling Loan on request

Open: See website as these change. Usually erm time Saturday and Sunday 10-4pm, School Holidays open all week.
Admission: Adult £13.00, Child (5-15 yrs) £7.80, Family (2 Adults, 3 children) £33.80.
Getting there: Bus Burton/Four Counties 59, Stansted Transit 301 from Audley Endrailway station stopping in Saffron Walden. **By Car** 1 mile W of Saffron Walden on B1383 (M11 exit 8 or 10). **By Train,** Audley End 1 1/4 miles. Note: Footpath is beside busy mainroad, 1.5 miles from the station.

Bourne Post Mill

Bourn Post Mill is located off Caxton Road, Bourn CB23 2SU between the villages of Bourn and Caxton.
www.cambridgeppf.org/bourn-post-mill
One of the oldest surviving windmills in the country. Exterior can be visited any time during daylight, the inside on National Mills weekend (second Sunday in May) and last Sunday of the month in Summer. Check website to be sure.
Getting there: Car - On the A428 from Cambridge take the turn after the blue footbridge signed Caldecote then follow Bourn Airfield and then Bourn, and take a right turn into Caxton Road. Alternatively turn off the A1198 at Caxton village. The mill is signed from the centre of the village.

Denny Abbey and Farmland Museum

Ely Road, Waterbeach, Cambridge CB25 9PQ
Tel: 01223 860988
Info@farmlandmuseum.org.uk
www.dennyfarmlandmuseum.org.uk
The Abbey is a 12th century building lived in by Benedictine monks, Franciscan nuns and Knights Templers. The farmland musem has a programme of events such as basket making, family history and children's activity days on school holidays on Tuesdays and Thursdays, 12:00-16:00 (50p per child). It has a cafe, picnic area, childrens play area and shop.
Open: In the summer, April-October Weekends and bank holiday Mondays 10.30-17.00, weekdays 12.00-17.00 Closed November to March.
Admission: Adults £5.00, Child £3.00, Family £13.00.
Getting there: Car - 20 minutes (8 miles) on A10. **Bus** - Stagecoach 9 towards Chatteris, get off at Landbeach, Research Park Entrance, bus takes 30 minutes, walk 15 minutes.

Grafham Water

Marlow Park, Grafham, Huntingdon, Cambridgeshire, PE28 0BH
Tel: 01480 812154
www.grafham-water-centre.co.uk
On the Northern Shore is an exhibition centre showing how the reservoir was built and a cafe. You can walk around the reservoir and you can also hire bikes from the centre.

Hinxton Watermill

Mill Lane, Hinxton CB10 1RD
www.cambridgeppf.org/hinxton-watermill.shtml
On the River Cam with inner mill workings intact. In the pretty village of Hinxton, constructed in 17th century.The exterior of the mill can be enjoyed at any time of the year from the riverside footpath. The mill is especially worth visiting on one of the summer open days.

Houghton Water Mill see page 63

Mill Street, Houghton, Huntingdon, Cambridgeshire, PE28 2AZ
Tel: 01480 301494
www.nationaltrust.org.uk/houghton-mill
A large 5 storey timber-built watermill on an island in the Great Ouse.

Ickworth House Park and Gardens

The Rotunda, Bury St Edmunds, IP29 5QE
Telephone: 01284 735270
ickworth@nationaltrust.org.uk
www.nationaltrust.org.uk/ickworth
A lovely 1800 acre landscape with a Georgian Italianate palace. The Ickworth family and subsequent Lord Hervey's gave the house an interesting and eccentric history, full of intrigue. Acres of woodland that can be explored by foot or by bike. Has a cafe and restaurant, gift shop, plant and garden centre. There are living history days, and events such as archery and out door theatre.
Open: Varies. Gardens 10:00-17:30. Park dawn to dusk.
Admission: Park Adult £3.10, Family £6.30. House upgrade Adult £5.00, Child £2.20, Family £12.00.
Getting there: Train - Bury St Edmunds (3 miles from the Station). **Car** - A14.

Oliver Cromwell's House

29 St Mary's Street, Ely, Cambs, CB7 4HF
Tel: 01353 662062
tic@eastcambs.gov.uk

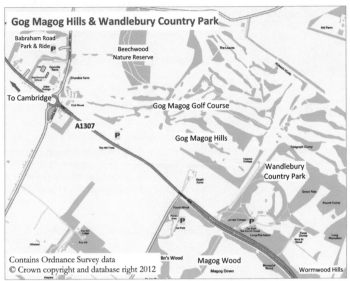

Gog Magog Hills & Wandlebury Country Park

Contains Ordnance Survey data
© Crown copyright and database right 2012

Domestic life in the 17th Century in a variety of re-created period rooms as well an exhibition detailing the Civil War. Mrs Cromwell's kitchen, try dressing-up or playing with the toys of the time or venture into the Haunted Bedroom.

Paxton Pits Nature Reserve
See page 70

St. Mary's Church - Buckdon
Buckden, Cambridgeshire
enquiries@stmarysbuckden.org.uk
www.ely.anglican.org/parishes/buckden
Buckden Towers is famous as a residence of the Bishops of Lincoln from the middle of the 13th century to the 19th century. The first Vicar of the Church was William de Bugden in 1217. It has carvings of animals around the porch. Open every day.

The Manor
Hemingford Grey, Huntingdon, Cambridgeshire, PE28 9BN
Tel: 01480 463134
diana_boston@hotmail.com
www.greenknowe.co.uk
Built in the 1130s the Manor is one of the oldest continuously inhabited houses in Britain and much of the original house remains virtually intact over 900 years. It was used during World War II by Lucy Boston to give gramophone record recitals twice a week to the RAF.

city centre. 110 acres of woods and chalk grassland in the gentle Gog Magog Hills. A great place to wander with children. The grasslands are grazed by Texel sheep and Highland Cattle. Site of Iron Age hill fort. In the 17th century a racing stable was built inside the old hillfort for King James II.

There are many myths about the gods Gog and Magog. Some say they were buried nearby, and that on Fleam Dyke lies a golden chariot. Gervase of Tilbusy wrote a ghostly tale in 1219 that Wandlebury was ruled by a dark night-rider that no mortal could defeat. One day a brave Normal knight called Osbert took up the challenge and won.

There is a picnic site, marked walks and nature trail through wooded parkland. There is a Banyard bird hide on the northern edge of Varley's Field, for watching wildlife. Some hardened paths are buggy and wheelchair friendly.
Open: from dawn until dusk every day.
Admission: Free.
Getting there: Bus - Citiplus X13 towards Haverhill. **Car** - off the A1307 (£2.50 parking charge) 3 miles from Cambridge.

Wimpole Hall Estate
Wimpole Hall, Arrington, Royston, Cambridgeshire SG8 0BW
Tel: 01223 206000
wimpolehall@nationaltrust.org.uk
www.wimpole.org

Wandlebury Country Park
Wandlebury Ring, Gog Magog Hills, Babraham, Cambs CB22 3AE
Tel: 01223 243830
www.cambridge ppf.org/wandleb ury-country-park
Attractive parkland with woodland walks & a nature trail located within 5 miles of the

Built by Sir John Soane in 1794 for the 3rd Earl of Hardwicke, who was passionately interested in farming and agricultural improvement. The Home Farm and gardens have been producing vegetables, meat and eggs throughout the estates history and still do today. Best seen in summer. The gardens are Victorian, but much has now been modified.

The park, landscaped by Bridgeman, Brown and Repton, has lovely views, a Gothic folly and serpentine lakes. The garden has thousands of daffodils in April and colourful parterres in July and August. There are hip-carrying infant seats for loan, a children's guide and quiz/trail. It has a picnic area, cafe and children's play area.
Open: Feb – Nov - Daily 10:30-17:00. Hall: Park: Everyday dawn to dusk. Nov– mid Feb11:00-16:00.Park: Everyday dawn to dusk
Admission: Hall: Adult: £10.30, Child £5.80. Farm: Adult: £8.40, Child £5.80, NT Adult: £3.95, NT Child: £2.60. Estate ticket for Hall & Farm: Adult: £15.50, Child: £8.40, Family: £40.70.
Getting there: Cycle - National Trust-permitted cycle path to entrance from Orwell (A603). **Car** - 8 miles SW of Cambridge off A603, Junc 12 of M11. By Foot - Wimpole Way from Cambridge. **Bus** - Citi 2 towards Addenbrooks Hospital, get off on Cherry Hinton Road, 15 minutes from Cambridge Centre. Or alight Arrington (1 mile) or Orwell (2 miles) Shepreth 5 miles. Taxi service from Royston 8 miles

East Anglia
The Lodge
Sandy, BedfordshireSG19 2DL
Tel: 01767 680541
thelodgereserve@rspb.org.uk
www.rspb.org.uk/reserves/guide/t/thelodge
The Lodge is an RSPB reserve with minor exhibitions and seasonal, child oriented events in The Lodge itself, as well as outdoor trails and bird or wildlife spotting. The woodland, heath and acid grassland along the Greensand Ridge cover 180 hectares, and are being restored to form the largest stretch of heathland in Bedfordshire. 5 miles of trails, gardens, Iron Age banks and picnic area.
Open 7am to 9pm.
Admission:£4 per car.
Getting there: By Car 45 minutes (21 miles) on A603, B1042. **By Bus and Train** is more

difficult, involving changing in London and taking 2 hours.

Kimbolton Castle

Kimbolton PE28 0EA
www.kimbolton.cambs.sch.uk/page/?title=Kimbolton+Castle&pid=2
Only open to the public a few times a year. Kimbolton Castle, Katherine of Aragon's last residence, was largely rebuilt as the 18th century country house of the Earls and Dukes of Manchester, owners for nearly 350 years. The Castle is set in extensive, wooded grounds, with pleasant walks.
Open: Only specific Public dates see website.
Admission:: Adults: £5, Children £2.50
Getting there: By Car 55 minutes (33 miles) on A14. **By Bus** X5 towards Milton Keynes, change St Neots, take Bus 150 towards Tilbrook, get off at Kimbolton. Takes 1 hour 15 minutes.

Longthorpe Tower

Thorpe Road, Longthorpe, Peterborough, Cambridgeshire, PE1 1HA
Tel: 01733 268482
customers@english-heritage.org.uk
www.english-heritage.org.uk
Opens on a Saturday between 1 Jul - 31 Aug, from 12pm - 5pm.

Lyveden New Bield

Harley Way, Oundle, Peterborough, Cambridgeshire, PE8 5AT
Tel: 01832 205358
www.nationaltrust.org.uk/lyveden-new-bield
Elizabethan lodge and moated garden. Begun in 1595 by Sir Thomas Tresham to symbolise his Catholic faith, Lyveden remains unaltered since work stopped on his death in 1605. It has a water garden, with terraces and spiral mounds. There are miles of footpaths in the open countryside and nearby Rockingham Forest.

Mountfitchet Castle

Stansted, Essex CM24 8SP
Tel: 01279 813237
www.mountfitchetcastle.com
The only motte and bailey castle in the world that has been faithfully reconstructed on its original site. An insight into Norman England, you can meet the tame deer, smell log fires and wander in and out of the castle and Norman Village. Also a Hill Toy Museum and Dinosaur Encounter. It has a tea room

Open Daily 10:00-17:00
Admission: Adults £9.95, Children over 3 yrs £7.50
Getting there: Car - 40 minutes (30 miles) on M11, A120. **Train** - 35 minutes, get off at Stansted Mountfitchet Station and it's a 10 minute walk.

Peckover House & Garden

North Brink, Wisbech, Cambs PE13 1JR
Tel: 01945 583463
www.nationaltrust.org.uk/peckover-house
Georgian brick town house with walled garden. Includes displays on the Quaker banking family who owned it and the Peckover Bank. It has a 2 acre Victorian garden which includes an orangery, summer houses, roses, herbaceous borders, fernery, croquet lawn and 17th-century thatched barn.

Walpole Water Gardens

Chalk Road, Walpole St. Peter, Wisbech, Cambs, PE14 7PH
Tel: 07718 745935
www.walpolewatergardens.co.uk
This is an unusual place with over 20 kinds of eucalyptus, as well as palms, banana trees, bamboos, cannas, grasses and much more. It also has a tea room, and shop selling exotic plants and Koi carp.
Open: Closed Monday and Tuesday except Bank Holidays.
Admission: Free.

Country Parks

Coton Countryside Reserve

Coton, Cambridgeshire
www.cambridgeppf.org/coton-countryside-reserve
The Cambridge Past, Present and Future Preservation Group (a local charity) have turned 27 acres of arable fields into accessible meadows with 4 miles of routes. Part of it is concrete and suitable for pushchairs, cycles and wheelchair users. There is a visitor guide on the website, with marked paths, which are worth sticking to unless you want to end up on the rifle range! You can see Beetle banks, grassy mounds in the middle of fields to provide winter houses for insects and spiders, and Black Poplars, now one of the rarest native timber species in Britain.
Getting there: Bus - 15 minutes, Citi 4 towards Lower Cambourne. **Car** - 15 minutes (5 miles) on A1134 and A1303.

Clare Castle Country Park

Maltings Lane, Clare, Suffolk CO10 8NJ
www.clare-uk.com/pages/clare-castle-country-park-602
Extensive grounds and parkland around the ruins of 13th century Clare Castle. Several walks around the park, the river Stour, a nature trail, old station house and a visitor centre. It is in the picturesque, historic town of Clare, just two minutes walk from the town centre.
Admission: Free.
Getting there: Car - 50 minutes (26 miles). **Bus** - 1 hour 10 minutes, X13 to Haverhill, then 236 to Clare.

Hinchingbrooke Country Park

Brampton Road, Huntingdon, Cambridgeshire, PE29 6DB
Tel: 01480 451568
www.huntingdonshire.gov.uk/Parks%20and%20Countryside/Hinchingbrooke%20Country%20Park/Pages/default
170 acre Country Park near Huntingdon. Free access to woods, lakes and meadows. Disabled access to visitor centre, toilets, hardened paths. Fishing platforms and wildlife garden. Electric wheelchairs available for use. Watersports available to people of all abilities The house was originally a medieval nunnery converted by Cromwell family in the 16th century, later extended by the Earls of Sandwich.
Open: All year.
Admission: Free for park. Pay for house.
Getting there: Bus - 1 hour 27 minutes, Busway A to Histon, then Busway B to Hinchingbrooke Park. **Train** - 1 hour 19 minutes, to Hitchin then Huntingdon then walk 15 mins. **Car** - 45 minutes (20 miles), A14 and A1.

Milton Country Park

Milton, CB4 6AZ
www.miltoncountrypark.org
A large park created from old gravel pits. The paths are suitable for bicycles and wheelchairs, as well as those on foot. There is a Visitor Centre with café, two play-areas, multiple viewing platforms, a sensory garden and sunclock. There are also regular events such as the Halloween Twilight Walk and Easter Egg Hunt.
Open: All year.
Admission: Free.
Getting there: Car - Junction of the A10 and A14 to Milton Village.

There are some wonderful, quirky and inspiring events around Cambridgeshire. The summer gets busy with Cambridge Strawberry Fair, the International Cambridge Folk Festival, Duxford Air Show, as well as village fetes and outdoor shows. The Cambridge Science Festival and Wordfest have plenty to inspire children. For sheer English eccentricity, there are the World Pea Shooting Championships, Stilton Cheese Rolling and Ely Eel Day.

Wordfest - Cambridge
www.cambridgewordfest.co.uk
In Spring, Summer and Winter. Plenty of activities for kids, it is a literary festival that is friendly and fresh.

January

Robbie Burns Night - 25th
Various, Cambridgeshire
Eat Haggis on Burns night, various restaurants and pubs around Cambridgeshire.

February

Anglesey Abbey Snowdrops - Cambridge
Anglesey Abbey, Cambridge
www.nationaltrust.org.uk/anglesey-abbey
240 varieties of snowdrops to see, some originating at the gardens. This garden is fantastic all winter.

Lent Bumps - late Feb/early March
www.cucbc.org/lents
College bumps rowing race in lower river.

March

Cambridge Science Festival
www.cam.ac.uk/science-festival
A fantastic event for the kids, there are hundreds of different science projects to see and interact with. The departments really make an effort to make science interesting and it is free.

The Shire Horse Society Spring Show - Alwalton
Grand Arena, Alwalton, Peterborough
www.shire-horse.org.uk/spring-show-18
For anyone with horse mad children.

Bible Dicing- Whitsun
All Saint's Church, St Ives, Whitsun
In St Ives since 1678, a strange dicing event originating from Dr Robert Wilde, poet and Puritan clergyman.

April

Duxford Spring Air Show
Imperial War Museum, Duxford www.iwm.org.uk/visits/iwm-duxford Magnificent air shows and family events featuring World War aircraft.

Ely Eel Day
Centre of Ely
www.visitely.org.uk
Procession with an Eel through Ely town, wth fun family activities.

May

Stilton Cheese Rolling
May Day Bank Holiday
www.stilton.org/cheese_rolling
Cheese Rolling has become an annual event in Stilton and every May Day in the main street teams battle for the honour of being called the 'Stilton Cheese Rolling Champions'.

June

Arbury Carnival
Arbury Town Park, Campkin Rd, Cambridge

CALENDAR OF EVENTS

www.arburycarnival.org
A carnival and family fun day out.

Dragon Boat Festival - Peterborough
River Nene, Peterborough
www.dragonboatfestivals.co.uk/dragon-boat-festivals/peterborough

Hemingford Abbots Flower Festival
www.hemingfordabbots.org.uk
This vivid flower show is held every other year. The last one was in 2013.

Peterborough Heritage Festival
www.vivacity-peterborough.com/festivals/heritage-festival
Costumed re-enactment from living history groups, with a children's zone, market and music.

Strawberry Fair - Cambridge
www.strawberry-fair.org.uk
A popular event on Midsummer Common, with stalls, activities and local bands.

July

Cambridge Shakespeare Festival
www.cambridgeshakespeare.com
A seven week long event held in Cambridge Universities private gardens. A nice way to enjoy a picnic. In July and August.

Flying Legends
Imperial War Museum, Duxford
www.iwm.org.uk/visits/iwm-duxford
One of the world's most celebrated air shows, full of thrills and nostalgia.

CALENDAR OF EVENTS

Godmanchester Gala - Godmanchester
www.godmanchestercommunityassociation.org
This is an event held annually since the Queens Silver Jubilee. On Sunday there is an open air concert picnic.

World Pea Shooting Championships & Village Fair -
WitchamVillage Green, Witcham
www.witcham.org.uk/_sgg/m1m6_1
This annual competition and village fair sees contestants from far and wide try their hand at pea shooting. Other attractions include face-painting, stalls, games, a bouncy castle, barbecue and cream teas.

St Ives Carnival & Music Festival
www.stives-town.info/st_ives_carnival
The St Ives Carnival and Music Festival is a two day event normally held over the weekend prior to the local schools breaking up for the summer holidays.

Cambridge Folk Festival
Cherry Hinton Hall, Cambridge
www.cambridgefolkfestival.co.uk
One of the most famous folk festivals in the world. It is held in Cherry Hinton Hall site. Ry Cooder and Joan Armatrading have sung here.

Kimbolton Country Fayre
Kimbolton Castle
www.kimboltoncountryfayre.com
Events, stall, classic cars, entertainment.

August

Fenland Country Fair
Stow cum Quy Park
www.fenlandfairs.com
A traditional country fair. Usually vintage vehicles, sheepdog demos, falconry displays and more.

Equifest - Peterborough
East of Engalnd Showground, Peterobourgh
www.equifest.org.uk
Horse show, classes and competitions.

Milton Maize Maze
The Milton Maize Maze, Rectory Farm Shop, A10 Milton By-pass, Milton, Cambridge
Tel: 01223 860 374
www.themiltonmaizemaze.co.uk

July to September. In autumn the maize fields are burned into a huge maze which is great to get lost in.

September

Bridge the Gap Walk - Cambridge
www.cam.ac.uk/open-cambridge
The chance to visit Colleges while raising money for charity in September.

Cherry Hinton Festival
Cherry Hinton, Cambridge
www.cherryhintonfestival.moonfruit.co.uk
A family fun day, samba music and more.

East of England Autumn Show - Peterborough
East of England Showground, Peterborough
www.eastofengland.org.uk
Country life show with crafts, shire horses, donkeys, dogs and birds.

Cambridge Film Festival
www.cambridgefilmfestival.org.uk
Hosted by the Arts Picturehouse, this is a good mix of films, shorts, documentaries and also a children's film festival. There is an open air cinema at Grantchester too.

Open Cambridge Weekend
www.cam.ac.uk/open-cambridge
Local residents get a chance to visit properties normally closed to the public.

Cambridge Dragon Boat Festival
River Cam, Fen Ditton, Cambridge
www.dragonboatfestivals.co.uk/dragon-boat-festivals/cambridge

Stourbridge Fair
Stourbridge Common, Cambridge
www.theleperchapel.org.uk
Annual Recreation of the ancient fair. Stalls selling cheese, honey, medeieval dancing and history talks. See page 53.

October

Cambridge Festival of Ideas
www.cam.ac.uk/festival-of-ideas
Arts and humanities event from the University of Cambridge.

World Conker Championships - Oundle, Northamptonshire
www.worldconkerchampionships.com
Thousands flock to this market town to watch the winner take the Conker Throne.

November

5th November - Bonfire Night
The annual bonfire and fireworks event to celebrate the capture of Guy Fakes. This may be subject to change, but in the past has generally been held in the following local areas. Most are free to attend.
Cambridge - Midsummer Common
Peterborough - Ferry Meadows (Sat nearest)
Huntingdon - Coneygreat Park
Hemingford Grey
Kimbolton Castle - large display, pay for admission. www.kimboltonfireworks.co.uk
Graham Village
Godmanchester - Judiths Field
Sawtry - Greenfields
Ely - Cherry Hill Park
Saffron Walden - The Common
St Neots - Enesbury Rovers Football Club
St Ives - London Road
Arrington - Wimpole Hall, pay for admission.
Exning - Exning Cricket Ground.

December

Mill Road Winter Fair - Cambridge
www.millroadwinterfair.org
The road is taken over with stalls, a carnival parade, food and entertainment.

King's College Carols - Cambridge
24th December
www.kings.cam.ac.uk/events/chapel-services
Popular carol service, people queue for hours to get in. Be at the queue before 9am to hopefully get a place.

Peterborough Christmas Market
www.peterborough-christmas-market.co.uk

Library	Address	Storytime (pre school)	Rhymetime (0-3yrs)
Arbury Court Library	Arbury Court, Cambridge CB4 2JQ	Thurs 10:30-11am (please bring a cushion to sit on)	
Bar Hill Library	Gladeside, Bar Hill, Cambridge CB23 8DY	Sat 10:30-11am	
Buckden Library	Buckden Millennium Centre, Burberry Rd, Buckden, St Neots PE19 5UY	Tues 2:30pm	
Burwell Library	The Causeway, Burwell CB25 0DU	Tues 10:30-11:30am	Once a month, check for dates.
Cambridge Central Library	1st Floor, Grand Arcade, Cambridge CB2 3QD	(0-18 months) Thur 2:30-3pm, Sat 10:30-11am (18 months to 5yrs)Mon 10:30-11am & Sun 3-3:30pm	
Cambourne Library	Sackville Way, Great Cambourne, Cambridge CB23 6HL	Fri 9:30-10am (Alternates Rhymetime / Storytime)	
Chatteris Library	2, Furrowfields Road, Chatteris PE16 6DY	Tues 2:15-2:45pm	Thurs 10-11am
Cherry Hinton Library	High Street, Cherry Hinton, Cambridge CB1 9HZ		Weds 2-2:30pm
Ely Library	6, The Cloisters, Ely CB7 4ZH	Weds 10:30-11am.(18 months to 3yrs) 2-3pm Weds, Fri 2-3pm.(Birth to 18 months)	
Fulbourn Library	The Swifts, Haggis Gap, Fulbourn, Cambridge CB21 5HD	Third Sat of month 10:30-11am	
Great Shelford Library	10-12 Woollards Lane, Great Shelford CB22 5LZ	Alternate Tues (0-18months) 10-10:30am	
Huntingdon Library	Princes Street, Huntingdon PE29 3PA	Weds 10:30-11am	Friday 10:30-11am (birth to 18 months).
March Library	City Road, March PE15 9LT	Monday 9:45-10:30am (18 months up to 3). 10:45-11:30am(birth to 18 months).	
Milton Road Library	Ascham Road, Cambridge CB4 2BD	Check for details.	
Linton Library	High Street, Linton, Cambridge CB21 4JT	Tues 2-2:30pm	
Peterborough Central Library	Broadway Peterborough PE1 1RX Tel: 01733 864280 libraryenquiries@vivacity-peterborough.com	· Stories and Rhymes. Tues & Sat, 10:30-11am and Fri & Sat, 2:15-2:45pm. Thur 1.30- 2pm. · Chatterbooks reading group for 10-12 yrs. First Thur of the month, 4-5pm. · Chatterbooks for 4-6 yrs. Third Sat of the month, 2:30-3:30pm. · Fast and Furious reading group for 7-9 yrs. Fourth Sat of the month, 2:30-3:30pm. · Lexicon book Group for teenagers. Second Thur of the month, 4-5pm. · Homework Club (years 3 to 8), every Sat from 10am to 12pm.	
Ramsey Library	25, Great Whyte, Ramsey Huntingdon PE26 1HG		Fri 10:30-11am
Rock Road Library	Rock Road, Cambridge CB1 7UG		Once a month.
Sawston Library	Village College, New Road Sawston CB22 3BP	Second week of month, Weds 10-10:30am	
Sawtry Library	Fen Lane, Sawtry, Huntingdon PE28 5TQ		Weds 10-10:30am
St Ives Library	4 Library Row, Station Rd, St Ives PE27 5BW	Thurs 10:30-11am & Sat 11-11:30am	Weds 10:10:30 or 11:15-11:45am
St Neots Library	Priory Lane, St Neots PE19 2BH		Mon 2pm. (Babies up to 18 months) Friday 10-11:15am
Warboys Library	High Street, Warboys PE28 2TA	Thurs 10:30-11am	Tues 11-11:30am
Whittlesey Library	31-35, Market Street, Whittlesey PE7 1BA	Fri 10:30-11am	
Willingham Library	Church Street, Willingham CB24 5HS	Check website for details	
Wisbech Library	Ely Place, Wisbech PE13 1EU	Weds 10:30-11am	Monday 10:30-11am
Yaxley Library	Lansdowne Road, Yaxley PE7 3JL	Third Tues of month 10:30-11am	Fri 10:30-11am

> **For all Libraries Please Note:** Usually Sessions Term Time Only

Information from www.cambridgeshire.net

Ely (ee-lee) is a charming and historic place. It has a Georgian and medieval centre and pretty riverside walks running out into the fens around it. It is also one of the fastest-growing cities in Europe.

It's only 15 minutes by train from Cambridge. On a sunny day you can walk by the river, and see the ponies, ducks and geese. The Cathedral is the main attraction, and is quite spectacular. You could also take a walk on the 'spy' trail, visit the old Gaol at the Museum, or join in the local festivities on Eel or Apple Day.

The odd name harks back to the days when Ely was an island marooned in the 'sea' of fens, which was full of eels that you can eat locally to this day.

Getting there from Cambridge:
Train - 15 minutes. **Bus** - 50 minutes (Stagecoach Bus 9 towards Chatteris). **Car -** 40 min's (19 miles) on the A10.

Getting Around
The railway station is about 10 minutes walk from the city centre, and

there are frequent and reliable buses. There are long stay car parks outside the centre in Barton Rd, Fishermans, Newnham St and Ship Lane.

Attractions
Ely Cathedral
Chapter House, The College, Ely CB7 4DL
www.elycathedral.org
This is a majestic sight, dominating the flat fens all around. Built in 1082, it is famous for its unique Octagon Tower and Lantern Tower which is floodlit at night.
Open: Summer: 09:00 – 17:00. Winter: 10:00 – 16:00. Access may be restricted during services and events.
Admission: Adults £7.00, Concessions £6.00, Children under 12 free. Admission on Sundays is free.

Eel Heritage Walk
A self-guided tour following brass way markers set into the pavement, through Jubilee Gardens and across into the Cathedral grounds.

Stained Class Museum
The South Triforium,
Ely Cathedral, Ely CB7 4DL
Tel: 01353 660347
info@stainedglassmuseum.com
This houses the national collection of British Stained Glass.
Open: Summer Mon to Fri 10:30-17:00, Sat 10:30-17:30, Sun 12:00-18:00. Winter as above but Sunday 12:00-16:30.
Admission: Adults £4.00, Concessions £3.00.

Ely Museum
The Old Gaol Market St, Ely CB7 4LS
Tel: 01353 666655
A small museum located in the Bishops Gaol, with local history, Roman artefacts and a condemned cell.
Open: Summer 10:30-17:00, Winter 10:30-16:00 (closed Tues), Mon - Sat. Sundays 13:00-16:00 or 17:00.
Admission: Adults £3.50, Children £1 (<5's free).

Jubilee Gardens
A lovely park by the riverside. It has a child's play area, sculptures, a bandstand and geese.

Jubilee Gardens Super Spy Trail
www.elysociety.org.uk/index.php/walks

www.elysociety.org.uk/wp-content/uploads/2011/10/jubilee_gardens-web.pdf
An interesting leaflet (see web site link) with a list of items for children to discover around the gardens. From the Ely Society.

Ted Coney's Family Portraits
49 Waterside, Ely CB7 4AU
tedconey@btinternet.com
Tel : 01353 650038
www.tedconeysfamilyportraits.co.uk
A collection of paintings on family life. A pop-up gallery opens on Sunday afternoons. Ted will give a tour if arranged.

Eating Out
Peacocks Tearoom
65 Waterside, Ely CB7 4AU
Tel: 01353 661100
Not open Monday or Tuesday.

Wildwood Restaurant - Italian
15 High Street, Ely CB7 4LQ
Tel: 01353 659587
ely@wildwoodrestaurants.co.uk
Good childrens play area at the back, candy floss machine, wood fired pizzas.

Ely Events

April/May - Ely Eel Day
An annual celebration with a parade outside Ely Cathedral to Jubilee Gardens, including an eel throwing competition (not real eels). Traditionally on the last Saturday of April but varies.

June - Ely Cathedral Flower Festival

October - Ely's Apple Festival
Palace Green, Ely
In celebration of the great Biritish apple.

Soham Pumpkin Fair
Soham, Nr Ely

Ely Library
6 The Cloisters, Ely CB7 4ZH
Tel: 0845 0455225
www.cambridgeshire.gov.uk
Rhymetime for all under-fives, their parents and carers is Sundays, 2pm. Baby rhymetime for children from birth to 18 months is Wednesdays, 2pm (Term time only)

Ely Children's Centre
High Barns, Ely CB7 4RB
Tel: 01353 611594
elychildrenscentre@cambridgeshire.gov.uk
www.cambridgeshirechildrenscentres.org.uk/ely
Located within Spring Meadow Infant & Nursery School. For families of children under 5 yrs.

Indoor Activities

Ely Cinema
Waterside, Ely CB7 4BB
info@adec.org.uk
www.adec.org.uk/cinemaShopping
Independent local cinema showing the best recent films, from family films, Hollywood blockbusters and arts picture house films.

Planet Zoom
Strikes Bowl Multiplex,
Angel Drove, Ely CB7 4DT
Tel: 01353 668 666
www.elystrikesbowl.co.uk
Soft play snake slides, fun activity towers and more.
Admission: 90 mins; 2's & over - £4.50/4.95

Prickwillow Engine Museum
Main Street, Prickwillow, Ely CB7 4UN
Tel: 01353 688360
www.prickwillow-engine-museum.co.uk
Engine and pump collection.

Treetops Soft Play
12 Lancaster Way, Ely CB6 3NW
Tel: 01353 665111
www.treetopsely.co.uk
Multi level jungle themed adventure play frame and a dedicated zone for toddlers and crawlers.
Admission: Under 1yr and

adults free. 1yrs and over £4/4.50

Outdoor Activities

Ely Sailing Club
www.elysailingclub.org.uk/Ely_Sailing_Club

Mepal Outdoor Centre
Chatteris Road, Nr Ely Cambs CB6 2AZ
Tel: 01354 692251
info@mepal.co.uk
www.mepal.co.uk
Outdoor activity centre for all ages.

Shopping

Ely Market Place
General Market held on Thursdays on 1st, 3rd and 5th Saturday of every month. The Craft and Collectables Market happens every Saturday. The Ely Farmers Market is on the 2nd and 4th Saturday of the month. The Flower, Food and Craft Market takes place on the last Sunday of the month.

Public Toilets
Barton Rd
NewnhamSt
Sacrist Gate

Cloisters
Palace Green
Ship Lane

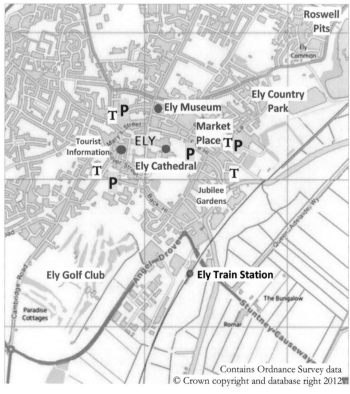

Contains Ordnance Survey data
© Crown copyright and database right 2012

Huntingdon grew up around a river crossing on the Great Ouse and was a staging post for Danish raids. Today, the Riverside Park is good place to watch boats pass by. In Norman times, the town had sixteen churches but it declined after the Black Death. It was once the site of Huntingdon Castle built in 1068. This is now a public open space and is the site of the Castle Hills Beacon.

Getting there

Bus - every half hour on Fens/the busway B towards Hinchingbrooke Park (1 hour) or Whipped Coaches/1B. **Car** - 35 minutes (18 miles) on A14.

Attractions

The Cromwell Museum
Grammar School Walk, Huntingdon PE29 3LF
Tel: 01480 375 830
His life and legacy through portraits, documents and objects associated with Cromwell.
Admission: Free
Open: Summer (April to October) 10:30-16:00 (closed for lunch 12:30-13:30) Tues - Sun. Winter Tues - Sun 13:30-16:00

Houghton Mill see page 54
Houghton, Huntingdon PE17 2AZ
Tel: 01480 301494
www.nationaltrust.org.uk/houghton-mill
A five storey working 18th century watermill on the Great Ouse river. Follow the family Cat and Rat trail around the mill.
Admission: Adult £4.00, Child £2.00, Family £10.00
Getting there: Train - Huntingdon Station is 3.5 miles. **Car** - signposted off

A1123. **Bus** - as for Huntingdon, 3.5 miles from station.

Johnsons Old Hurst Farm Shop
Church St, Old Hurst, Huntingdon PE28 3AF
Tel: 01487 824658
The farm shop is a nice stopover. It has tea rooms, play area with toy tractors and fort. You can't go in but you can see the farm.

Eating Out

The Crown Inn
Bridge Rd,, Huntingdon PE28 3AY
Tel: 01487824428
Fantastic Sunday lunch treat.

The Brampton Pie Company
16 Chequers Court, Huntingdon
Great pies in the middle of Huntingdon.

Frankie & Benny's
Towerfields, Kings Ripon Road, Huntingdon PE29 7EG
Tel: 01480 437 240
www.frankieandbennys.com
This chain restaurant has plenty for kids, even fussy ones.

Playgrounds

Managed by the Town and District Council
www.huntingdontown.gov.uk
Beacon Close
Nursery Road (near the fire station)
Great Northern Street
King George V, St Peter's Road
King George V, Hartford
Snowdonia Way and Dartmoor Drive
Whinfell Close
Stukeley Meadows
Aerial & Embankment Slides at Hinchingbrooke Country Park
Riverside Park   Moorhouse Drive
Maryland Drive Mayfield Crescent
Devoke Close

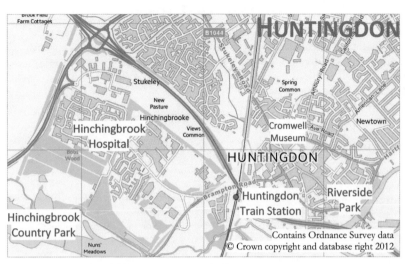

Contains Ordnance Survey data
© Crown copyright and database right 2012

Bevan Close
Beech Close
Bloomfield Park
Devoke Close
Gamer Court

Indoor Activities

Norris Museum
The Broadway, St Ives Cambs PE27 5BX
Tel: 01480 497314
bob@norrismuseum.org.uk
www.norrismuseum.org.uk
The story of Huntingdonshire from earliest times to the present day, includes a life-size model of an Ichthyosaur.

Cineworld - Huntingdon
Abbots Ripton Road, Tower Field Leisure Park, Huntingdon PE29 7EG
Tel: 0871 200 2000
www.cineworld.co.uk/cinemas/36

Crystal Country Play Barn
Crystal Lakes, Low Road, Fenstanton, Huntingdon PE28 9HU
Tel: 01480 493394.
www.crystallakesleisure.com
Soft play area, slides, toddler area, cafe.

Leos Funzone
One Leisure Huntingdon, St Peters Road, Huntingdon PE29 7DA
Tel: 01480 388600
www.leosfunzone.co.uk
Climbing walls, slides, swings, spinning panels, wobble floors, ball pools, interactive games.

Admission: £4.40 under 9s £3 under 1s

Huntingdon Toy Library
Huntingdon Nursery School, Ambury Road, Huntingdon PE29 1AD
Costs: Membership of Toy Library is £1.00 per year.Toys all cost 25p each per week to hire.
Over 500 toys, games, books, tapes and CD's all of which are for hire, Every Thursday during term time: 9.00-11.00 am and 12.45-2.30 pm

Huntingdon Town Children's Centre
Ambury Road, Huntingdon PE29 1AD
Tel: 01480 375216
office@huntingdon-nur.cambs.sch.uk
www.cambridgeshirechildrenscentres.org.uk/huntingdon-town
Services Offered include:
Baby clinics, Toy Libraries, Toddler Sessions e.g. Moorplay, Breakfast Clubs, Support Groups – Post Natal Support, Emotional Support

Daffodil Children's Centre & Toy Library
Next to Godmanchester Community Primary School, Park Lane, Godmanchester, Huntingdon PE29 2AG
Tel: 01480 375116
godmanchesterchildrenscentre@cambridgeshire.gov.uk

A large selection of toys, books and games available to borrow free of charge for families with children up to 5 years old.
Open: Monday to Friday 9am to 3pm.

Huntingdon Library
Dryden House, St. Johns St, Huntingdon PE29 3NU
Tel: 0845 045 5225
www.cambridgeshire.gov.uk
Storytime on Wednesdays 10.30-11am

Public Toilets
The Bus Station Princes St
Princes St Car Park

Sports Centres
Huntingdon Leisure Centre
St Peters Road, Huntingdon PE29 7DA
Tel: 01480 388600
www.huntingdonshire.gov.uk
25 metre pool and leisure centre. Swimming is free for Advantage and Classic members. Swimming classes for children.

One Leisure Ramsey
Abbey Road, Ramsey PE26 1DP
Tel: 01487 710275
oneleisureramsey@huntsdc.gov.uk
www.huntingdonshire.gov.uk
20 metre pool. Swimming is free for Advantage and Classic members.

One Leisure Sawtry
Green End Road, Sawtry, Cambs PE28 5UY
Tel: 01487 832161
www.huntingdonshire.gov.uk
20 metre pool.

Sports Clubs
Blue Vision Twirling Team
21 Owl Way, Hartford Huntingdon PE29 1YZ
Tel: 01480 436516

The Splash Academy - Huntingdon
Hinchingbrooke School, Brampton Road, Huntingdon PE29 3BN
Tel/Fax: 01480 375697
Kids swimming lessons.

Grafham Water Sailing Club
Perry, Huntingdon PE28 0BU
Tel. 01480 810478
admin@grafham.org

Huntingdon & District Cricket Club
12 St Peter's Road, Huntingdon PE29 7AA

Huntingdon Rowdies Youth Football Club
1 Gimber Court, Huntingdon PE29 1GQ
Tel. 01480 823077

Huntingdon Town Football Club
Wykeham House, Market Hill, Huntingdon PE29 3NR
Tel: 07787 577688,
sallyreif@aol.com

Huntingdon Olympic Gymnastics Club Limited
Claytons Way, Huntingdon PE29 1UT
Tel. 01480 52343
huntgymnast@tiscali.co.uk

Huntingdon Tennis Centre,
King George V Field, St Peter's Road, Huntingdon PE29 7DA
Tel. 01480 411412
www.huntingdontennis.org.uk

ST IVES
St Ives is 12 miles from Cambridge on the banks of the river Great Ouse. You can take the Guided Bus way there from Cambridge. It has a 15th Century Bridge and chapel over the river and is one of only three such surviving bridges in England. On the first and third Saturdays of each month an excellent Farmer's Market takes place.

Getting there
Bus - the Fens/the busway A towards Wyton Airfield (20 minutes) or busway B towards Hichingbrooke Park. **Car** - 30minutes (16 miles) on A14 and A1096.

Indoor Activities
St Ivo Leisure Centre
Westwood Road, St Ives PE27 6WU
Tel: 01480 388500
oneleisurestives@huntsdc.gov.uk
www.huntingdonshire.gov.uk
25 metre pool and leisure faciilities.

Swavesey Screen (Cinema)
Swavesey Village College, Gibraltar Lane, Swavesey CB24 4RS
Tel: 01954 234476
karen@start-arts.org.uk
www.ticketsource.co.uk/swavesey vc
A monthly community screening programme using the facilities of Swavesey Village College.

Eating Out
White Hart
Sheep Market, St. Ives PE27 5AH
Tel: 01480 463275
Nice lunch pub food.

PR Massala
Market Lane, St. Ives
Good indian food, for kids the milder options go down a treat.

St Ives Children's Centre
Wheatfields Primary School, Nene Way, St Ives PE27 3WF
Tel: 07776 494100
stiveschildrenscentre@cambridgeshire.gov.uk
www.cambridgeshirechildrenscentres.org.uk
It covers St Ives, Hemingford Grey, Hemingford Abbotts, Wyton, Hougton, Holywell and Needingworth. They run a variety of activities for children.

St Ives Toy Library
Broad Leas Centre, Pig Lane, St Ives PE27 5QB
Tel: 01480 462069
Borrow toys & children's videos at a small cost. Free playtime and refreshments for children. Tue 9.15am-11.00am. Term time.

St Ives Library
4 Library Row, Station Road, St Ives PE27 5BW
Tel: 0845 045 5225
www.cambridgeshire.gov.uk
Storytime and Rhymetime.

Public Toilets
The Bus Station, Station Rd
Globe Place Car Park

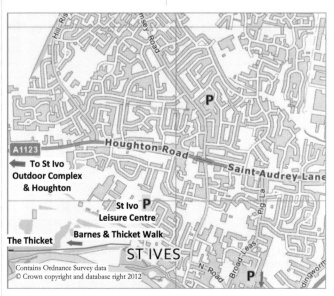

Contains Ordnance Survey data
© Crown copyright and database right 2012

The headquarters of thorough bred breeding and training. If you get up very early you can see them train through the morning mist. It is a market town in Suffolk and has over 50 horse training stables and two large racetracks. It is also home to the Newmarket Sausage, a pork sausage from a traditional recipe.

Getting there from Cambridge
Train - 20 minutes. **Bus -** 40 minutes (Stagecoach Bus 11 towards Bury St Edmund's or 12 towards Ely). **Car -** 30 min's (14 miles) on A1304.

Attractions

Brandon Country Park
Bury Road, Brandon, Suffolk
Tel: 01842 810185
www.brandonsuffolk.com/high-lodge.asp

Hill Lodge Forest Centre
Santon Downham, Brandon
01842 815434
Lovely park with adventure play area and cafe.

Mildenhall Museum
King Street, Mildenhall, Suffolk
IP28 7EX
Tel: 01638 716970
www.mildenhallmuseum.co.uk
The history of Mildenhall, has holiday activities for kids, and exhibits.

National Horseracing Museum
99 High Street, Newmarket, Suffolk., CB8 8JH
Tel: 01638 667333
admin@nhrm.co.uk
www.nhrm.co.uk
The stories and history of horse racing. You can try a horse simulator and dress up as a jockey.

Newmarket Racecourse
Westfield House, The Links, Newmarket, Suffolk. CB8 0TG
Tel: 01638 675500

www.newmarketracecourses.co.uk
From the oldest race in history to the 21st Century, Newmarket hosts some of the world's top thoroughbred racing: Events include the Guineas Festival in May, the July Festival in high summer and the Future Champions Day in October.

The National Stud
Wavertree House, The National Stud, Newmarket, Suffolk, CB8 0XE
Tel: 01638 663464
tours@nationalstud.co.uk
www.nationalstud.co.uk
British Thoroughbred breeding. Set in 500-acres close to Newmarket, it opened its gates to the public for the first time in the mid-1970's. It remains the only working stud farm in the UK.

A tour will take you to the Foaling Unit and nursery paddocks where in the early spring, you may see a newborn foal.

Wild Tracks
Chippenham Road, Kennett, Newmarket CB8 7QJ
Tel: 01638 751918
www.wildtracksltd.co.uk
Activity park with go karting, quad treks, archery and shooting.

Eating Out

Charlottes Tea Room and Bistro
3 High St, Newmarket CB8 8LX
Tel: 01638 668432
Nice tea room with a view of the Clock Tower.

Central Fish Bar and Restaurant
20-22 Market Street, Newmarket
Good fish and chips, just across from the National Horseracing Museum.

Pizza Express
75 High St., Newmarket CB8 8NA, England

NEWMARKET

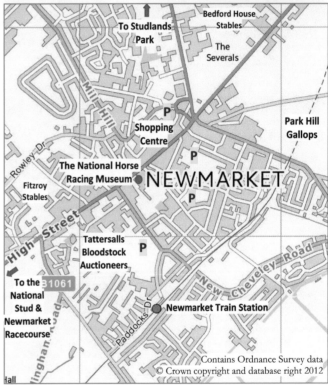

Contains Ordnance Survey data
© Crown copyright and database right 2012

Tel: 01638 664 646
Bright and modern pizza place, with family friendly options including make your own pizza.

Indoor Activities

Newmarket Leisure Centre
Exning Road, Newmarket CB8 0EA
Tel: 01638 782500
www.angcomleisure.com

The Cinema at Newmarket
The Stable, 65 High St, Newmarket Upstairs next to Goldings
Tel: 01638 667200
www.cinemaatnewmarket.org.uk
Non profit volunteer run group showing DVD films. Check in advance for listings.

Kings Theatre
Fitzroy Street, Newmarket
Tel: 01638 663337
www.nomadskingstheatre.com

Peterborough is a Cathedral City 40 miles north of Cambridge. It is a large town but compact in the centre and has good public transport. You can take a trip on the steam engines at Nene Valley Railway, visit the Museum or go swimming in the Art Deco outdoor lido. The Cathedral is the burial place of Katharine of Aragon, the first wife of Henry VIII. Five miles out of town is the interesting Flag Fen Archaeological Park.

Getting there:
Train - 50 minutes. **Bus** - National Express/350 1 hour 5 minutes. **Car** - 55 minutes (40 miles) on A14, A1 (M), A1139

Getting Around
Most of the city centre is pretty manageable on foot or with a buggy. It has a good range of car parks and public transport system. The cycle routes, or 'green wheel' are available in their Visitor Information Centre for £1.50. However you can also check out information on their website: www.travelchoice.org.uk

The buses are run by stagecoach. A family day ticket can be the cheapest option if travelling with children. It has citi 1 to 6 buses. Take the citi 3 to get to Planet Ice, and the citi 1 to get to the East of England Showground and Ferry Meadows. The lovely steam train Nene Valley Railway runs through Ferry Meadows from the river by the city centre.

Attractions
Burghley House
Burghley Park Stamford, Lincolnshire PE9 3JY
Tel: 01780 752451
www.burghley.co.uk
An Elizabethan mansion with 18 state rooms and parklands designed by Capability Brown. It now has a 'Garden of Surprises' with mirrors, water and sculptures. **Open:** during the summer, check website for details.

East of England Showground
East Of England Agricultural Society, Peterborough PE2 6XE
www.peterborougharena.com
This has some of the biggest events in the region, including the East of England Show; Just Dogs Live; Equifest; Truckfest.

Ferry Meadows Country Park
Ferry Meadows, Ham Lane, Peterborough PE2 5UU
Tel: 01733 234193
www.neneparktrust.org.uk/ferry-meadows
A large 500 acre open area along the River Nene, through woodlands and meadow. There is a visitor centre, and also horse riding, fishing, sailing and boat trips.

Flag Fen Archaeological Park
The Droveway, Northey Rd, Peterborough PE6 7QJ
Tel: 01733 313414
Parkinfo@flagfen.org
www.flagfen.org
This is a Bronze Age site with the oldest wheel in England and an ancient wooden track through the Fens. It is set in 37 acres of wild fenland and historic reconstructions. There are regular events such as the bronze sword casting.
Admission: Adult £5.00, Senior or Disabled Citizen: £4.50, Child £3.75, Children under 5 yrs free
Getting there: Car - 1 hour 10 minutes (40 miles) on A10 then A1101. From Jct 5 of the A1139 turning at the Dog in the Doublet Pub. Train - 45 minutes towards Kings Lynn. 5 miles from Peterborough station

Green Wheel
www.pect.org.uk
A network of cycle routes that circle the city with spokes leading to the centre.

Nene Valley Railway
Eastern terminus of the Nene Valley Railway.
Tel: 01780 784444
nfo@nvr.org.uk
www.nvr.org.uk

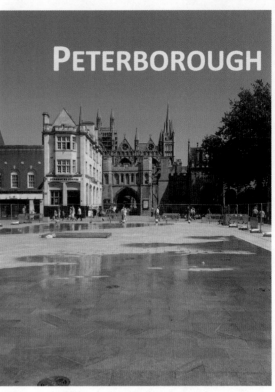

PETERBOROUGH

This is a heritage railway, with a Thomas the Tank Engine as well as other activities. It uses part of the original London and North Western line from Northamptonshire into the Cathedral city of Peterborough and the stations of Yarwell, Wansford, Ferry Meadows (Nene Park) and Orton Mere. Check website for open days. It is also worth checking the website to book Thomas Big Adventure and Santa specials.

There is a Museum, shop, cafe, Exhibition Engine Shed and Loco Yard. A 'Rover Ticket' allows unlimited travel on the day of purchase. Stations at Ferry Meadows in the heart of the 500 acre Nene Park, Orton Mere and Peterborough

Peterborough Museum
Priestgate, Peterborough PE1 1LF
Tel: 01733 864663
Gallerymuseum@vivacity-peterborough.com
www.vivacity-peterborough.com/museums-and-heritage
Recently improved with a £3.2 million grant, thousands of items in one of the city's most historic Georgian buildings.
Open: Daily. Closed Mondays (open Bank holiday Mondays).

Admission: Free.

Peterborough Cathedral

Minster Precincts, Peterborough PE1 1XS
Tel: 01733 355315
www.peterborough-cathedral.org.uk
The Cathedral is one of the finest Norman buildings, and is a stunning place with a fine ceiling. It's especially atmospheric at Christmas time.
Open: Mon-Fri 09:00-17:00, Sat 09:00-15:00, Sun 12:00-15:00
Admission: Free but donations are politely requested.

Planet Ice

1 Mallard Road, Peterborough PE3 8YN
Tel: 01733 260 222
pet.boxoffice@planet-ice.co.uk
www.planet-ice.co.uk/arena/Peterborough
A skating arena open daily with cafe. It has parent and toddler sessions on Sundays from 10:00-11:00.
Admission: £9.50 with skate hire. Family of 4 £32.00

Sacrewell Farm and Country Centre

Thornhaugh, Peterborough PE8 6HJ
Tel: 01780 782254
info@sacrewell.org.uk
www.sacrewell.org.uk
Hidden away in a quiet valley setting near the A1, it has a restored Mill. The farm animal collection, restaurant and a play areas, walks and trails. You can tour the farm by tractor, feed the animals and meet Shire horses.

Teamworks Karting Peterborough

4 Venture Park, Stirling Way, Peterborough PE3 8YD
Tel: 08451803020
info@teamworkskarting.com
www.teamworkskarting.com/peterborough
Indoor high speed electric karting, open 7 days a week. One for the older kids who like speed and excitement!

Eating Out

Frankie & Benny's Restaurant

Boongate Retail Park, Peterborough PE1 5AH
Tel: 01733 890225
www.frankieandbennys.com
Reasonably priced food, plenty of choice for kids.

Giuliano's

10 East St, Crowland, Peterborough, PE6 0EN
Tel: 01733 211055

Warm and welcoming Italian restaurant, reasonably priced and you won't feel out of place with kids. Reservations recommended.

Jimmy's World Grill and Bar

35 New Road, Peterborough PE1 1FJ
Tel: 01733 564930
www.jimmysworldgrill.co.uk
For more adventurous kids, this offers a buffet with food from around the world, and a popular ice cream Teppan-yaki station.

Sub Xpress

8c Serpentine Green Shopping Centre, Hampton, Peterborough PE7 8BE
Tel: 01733 893344
Healthy toasted sandwiches and pizzas. GM free. It does a kids Meal with a toy, cookie, fruit juice and sub sandwich.

Playgrounds

www.peterborough.gov.uk/leisure_and_culture/parks,_trees_and_open_spaces/playgrounds.aspx
There are over 200 playgrounds in Peterborough for children. The local council has details.

New Ark Adventure Playground

Hill Close, Reeves Way, Peterborough PE1 5LZ
Tel: 01733 340605
www.newarkadventureplayground.co.uk
There is sand play, swings, slides, rocking logs, tyre swing, cable ride.

Parks

Bretton Park

One of the largest green open spaces, in the centre of North Bretton.

Central Park

Park Crescent Peterborough PE1 4DY
www.neneparktrust.org.uk
A park in the north of the city centre, it has a sunken garden, sensory garden, two play areas and a paddling pool, aviary and tennis courts. There are also tea rooms open all year round.

Itter Park

On Fulbridge Rd in Paston.

The Embankment

Along the river Nene and within easy walking distance of the city centre.

Peterborough Events

Peterborough Heritage Festival - June
Battle displays and re-enactments.

Peterborough Arts Festival - July
Grand finale in Central Park.

Truckfest - May
Haulage and trucking event, with monster trucks and motorcycle display teams.

Peterborough Dragon Boat Festival - June
River Nene

East of England Show - July
British farming and rural life.

Festival of the Forties - July
Three days of 1940's big bands.

Equifest - August
Horse show and extravaganza.

Peterborough Italian Festival - September
Includes flag dancing, singing and food.

Burghley House Flower Festival - October

The Autumn Show - October
Animals of all shapes and sizes and Giant Vegetable Competition.

Whittlesey Straw Bear Festival
Tradition of dressing a ploughman in straw, calling him a straw bear and parading him through town.

Nature Reserves and Wildlife Areas

Cuckoos Hollow
Originally an area of pastureland surrounded by dykes, now redesigned to create a lake, with ducks, swans and grebes.

Holywell ponds, Longthorpe
A medieval fish pond, and wildflower meadow. Car parking is limited.

Eye Green
A 25 acre site with a lake, woodland and reed beds.

Stanground Wash
Good for bird watching.

Stanground newt ponds
A collection of small ponds and a meadow.

The Boardwalks
This lies alongside the river Nene at Thorpe Meadows, with willow, marshland and ponds.

Thorpe Wood
An ancient woodland full of wild flowers.

Woodfield park, Dogsthorpe
19 acres of parkland, with wetlands, meadow, a skate park and playground.

Woodston ponds
Previously managed by British Sugar to take washings from the sugar beet, and now leased to the Wildlife Trust. Good place to see water birds.

Peterborough Central Library
Broadway, Peterborough, PE1 1RX
Tel: 01733 864280
libraryenquiries@vivacity-peterborough.com
www.vivacity-peterborough.com/venues/peterborough-central-library

Indoor Activities

Activity World
Padholme Road East, Peterborough PE1 5XH
Tel: 01733 314446
www.activityworld.co.uk
For children up to a height limit of 1.5m, houses a variety of exciting play equipment such as "The Drop Slide", The Giant Hamster Wheel" and the "Spiders Web Tangle Tower".
Admission: Under 4s £5.10 Over 4s £6.30 Adults £1.30Activity World Ltd

Big Sky Adventure Play
24 Wainman Road Shrewsbury Ave, Orton, Longueville, Peterborough PE2 7BU
Tel: 01733 390810
www.bigsky.co.uk
This has a huge King Kong climbing wall (for adults too), Skyrider, Kart Track Riders and Trampolines plus the New Bouncy Castle.

The Broadway Theatre
46 Broadway, Peterborough, PE1 1RT
Tel: 0844 850 0 850
www.thebroadwaytheatre.co.uk
All kinds of live entertainment including music, theatre, comedy and even films.

City Gallery
Priestgate, Peterborough PE1 1LF

Tel 01733 864663
arts@vivacity-peterborough.com

Dave the Clowns Fun House
Cresset, Bretton, Peterborough, PE3 8DX
Tel: 01733 265705
www.davetheclown.co.uk
Bright, colourful softplay for children up to six years old hosted by Dave the Clown.
Admission: 30 mins - £1.80 to 2hrs - £3.20

Key Theatre
Embankment Road, Peterborough, PE1 1EF
Tel: 01733 207237
www.vivacity-peterborough.com/venues/key-theatre

Laserforce
23 Brook St, Town Centre, Peterborough PE1 1TU
Tel: 01733 894549
www.laserforceuk.co.uk
Laser indoor activity centre.

Peterborough Museum
Priestgate, Peterborough PE1 1LF
Tel: 01733 864 663

Showcase Cinema Peterborough
Mallory Road, Boon Gate, Peterborough
Tel: 0871 220 1000
www.showcasecinemas.co.uk

Sports

The Vivacity Card
This card offers discounts on the Vivacity managed centres and activities. For example the £22 Vivacity Sports Pass with additional savings off swimming and a range of sports or the Sports PLUS Pass from just £6 per week, offering you full access to the gyms and pools, with discounts off a range of sports and services.

Vivacity have a range of indoor and outdoor sporting facilities at four leisure centres across the city – with over 46 sporting activities. Based in the city, Orton, Werrington and Netherton.

Football
There are various football clubs across the city, see the Peterborough Telegraph Sports Section and local leisure centres.

Peterborough United Football
mfox86@hotmail.co.uk
www.theposh.com
Peterborough United Development programme coaches footballing talent in young people. Members could play in the Peterborough & District Junior Alliance League.

Football Fundamentals
Werrington Leisure Centre
For children aged 2-4 and 5-7 years old.

Sports Centres

Art-Deco Lido - Outdoor Pool
Bishops Road, Peterborough, PE1 1YY
Tel: 01733 864761
www.vivacity-peterborough.com
It first opened in 1936 and is one of the few survivors of its type. There are three heated pools and a sunbathing terrace, open from May to September. The main pool is 0.9m to 2.7m deep.
Open: Daily 09:00-18:00
Admission: Adult £4.70, Child £3.00

Deepings Leisure Centre
Park Road, Deeping St James, Peterborough PE6 8NF
Tel: 01778 344072
www.harpersfitness.co.uk
When the school day is over the facilities are available for the community. They have an Olympic size pool and a learner pool. Also roller skating on a Friday evening.

Lakeside Leisure
Ferry Meadows Watersports Centre, Nene Park, Ham Ln, Peterborough
Tel: 01733 234418
www.lakesideleisure.com

Manor Leisure Centre
Station Rd, Peterborough
Tel: 01733 202298

Peterborough Town Sports Club
Bretton Gate, Peterborough
Tel: 01733 262202
www.ptsc.org.uk

Regional Fitness and Swimming Centre
Bishops Road, Peterborough PE1 5BW
Tel: 01733 864760

Werrington Sports & Recreation Centre
Staniland Way, Werrington, Peterborough PE4 6JT
Tel: 01733 576606

PETERBOROUGH

www.vivacity-peterborough.com/venues/werrington-leisure-centre
Football, martial arts, squahs, trampolining, roller skating and more.

Shopping

Cathedral Square Peterborough
City Centre, Peterborough PE1
This is lovely on a sunny day, with cafes and farmer's market.

Peterborough Garden Park
Peterborough PE1 4YZ
www.peterboroughgardenpark.co.uk
For garden lovers, this has a huge glass atrium.

Peterborough City Market
Northminster, Peterborough PE11AY
Tel: 01733 343358
A covered market with fruit, vegetables, clothing, meat and fish.

Queensgate Shopping Centre
Peterborough PE1 1NT
Tel: 01733 311666
www.queensgate-shopping.co.uk
Large shopping centre with over 90 stores.

Rivergate Shopping Centre
Viersen Platz, Peterborough PE11EL
Tel: 01733 313743
Family shopping and independent traders too.

Serpentine Green Shopping Centre
The Serpentine, Hampton, Peterborough PE7
In Hampton to the south of Peterborough, includes Britains largest Tesco Extra store.

Public Toilets
Peterborough Railway Station
Rivergate Shopping Centre
Car Haven, St Peter's Road
St Peters Arcade
Queensgate Bus Station (Shopping Centre)

Healthcare
A pharmacist can give advice or you can telephone NHS Direct 0845 46 47
www.nhsdirect.nhs.uk

Dental Helpline 01223 415126
Dental Emergency Service 01733 295854 office hours or 01223 471798 out of hours.

NHS Walk-in Centre (minor illnesses and injurires) Tel: 01733 293800 Bourges Boulevard near ASDA

GP Surgery. To register with a GP call 01733 477725. Out of hours call 01733 293838
Emergencies: 999

Accident and Emergency department is at Peterborough District Hospital, off Thorpe Rd, Peterborough.

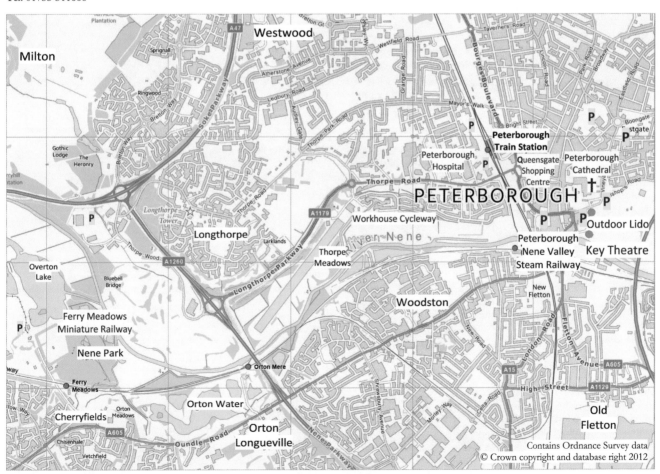

Contains Ordnance Survey data
© Crown copyright and database right 2012

SURROUNDING AREA

Chatteris

Known for its Christmas lights which are funded by community donations. It also has a small museum and a good fish and chip shop (Petrou Brothers in West Park St).

Chatteris Community Cinema
King Edward Road,The King Edward Centre, Chatteris
Tel: 07759 049619
www.chatteriscommunitycinema.co.uk

Imperial War Museum Duxford

Cambridgeshire CB22 4QR
Tel: 01223 835000 duxford@iwm.org.uk.
www.iwm.org.uk/visits/iwm-duxford
Regular air shows and famous aircraft, from the wars, reconditioned. Collections of tanks, military vehicles and artillery in the UK It has three cafés on site - The Mess Restaurant, Wing Co Joes Café and Station 357. It is a good day out with kids interested in history and vehicles. There are also benches for a picnic.

Open: Daily, Winter 10:00-16:00 (last admission 15:00), Summer 10:00-18:00 (last admission 17:00).
Admission: Adult £17.50; Child (under 16) free.
Getting there: Car - Just south of Cambridge at Junction 10 of the M11 motorway. On Sundays there is a direct Myalls 132 bus service from Cambridge to air shows. **Train**: nearest stations are Whittlesford, Royston and Cambridge. There are taxi ranks at both Royston and Cambridge stations but not Whittlesford.

Linton

Attractions

Linton Zoo   See page 84

Spotted Giraffe
The Grip Industrial Estate, Linton, Cambs CB21 4XN
Tele: 01223 892 226
spotgiraffe@gmail.com
www.spottedgiraffe.co.uk
Indoor cafe and play area for children.

Conkers Children's Centre
Cathodeon Centre, Linton CB21 4JT
Tel: 01223 893594
www.cambridgeshirechildrenscentres.org.uk/linton
Activities and support for parents and young children,
Open: Wednesday to Friday 9:30 - 12:00 noon

Linton Library
Cathodeon Centre, Linton, Cambridge CB1 6JT
Tel: 0845 0455225
www.cambridgeshire.gov.uk
Storytime for all under-fives on alternate Wednesdays 2.15-2.45pm (term-time only)

Paxton Pits Nature Reserve

Little Paxton, Huntingdon, Cambridgeshire PE19 4ET.
Tel: 01480 406795
paxtonpits@huntingdonshire.gov.uk
www.paxton-pits.org.uk
75 hectares of gravel pits, meadows, scrub and woodland next to the River Great Ouse. There is a wealth of wildlife to enjoy all year round, and a network of marked paths. During May there are large numbers of Nightingales and many species of orchid in the meadows .The Visitor Centre has a childrens corner, with activities for our younger visitors and a nature table, including some of the mammoth finds from the quarry.
Open: Daily. A Visitor Centre is open most weekends, with Volunteer Wardens, leaflets, maps and refreshments.
Getting there: Car - 35 minutes (19 miles) on A428. Train - St Neots it is 2 miles from the station along the Ouse Valley Way. Bus - see St Neots info.

Fishing - Cloudy, Rudd and Hayling Lakes Little Paxton Fisheries. Permits from Ouse Valley Specialist Angling, 25-31 Huntingdon Street, St Neots.
Tel: 01480 386088
Sailing - Paxton Lakes Sailing Club
Tel: 01707 322141
Waterskiing - South Lake Ski School
Tel: 01480 216966

Royston

Royston is very close by train from Cambridge, and is a reasonably sized market town, with a museum, caves and nearby Wimpole Hall stately home (see page 91).

Getting there from Cambridge:
Train - 20 minutes. **Car -** 30 minutes (13 miles) o the A10.

Indoor Activities

Melbourn Sports Centre
The Moor, Melbourn, Nr Royston

Hertfordshire SG8 6EF
Tel: 01763 263313
graham@mc-sport.co.uk
www.melbournsports.com
A 20 metre swimming pool and lessons offered.

Royston Museum

5 Lower King Street, Royston SG8 5AL
Tel: 01763 242587
www.roystonmuseum.org.uk
Has the Royston Tapestry project, local history and a collection of ceramics and glass. Royston Museum A significant and varied collection of exhibits, especially glass and ceramic work.
Open: Wed, Thur & Sat 10:00-16:45
Admission: Free.

Royston Cave

Royston Cave Melbourn Street, Royston
Tel: 01763 245484
www.roystoncave.co.uk
This curious circular cave is hidden beneath the pavement. It is cut into the 60m (197ft) layer of chalk which underlies the town. Legend suggests that in the 13th century it was used as a secret meeting place by the Knights Templar. It has an extensive range of wall carvings.
Open: Check website. Open weekends Easter to September. Additional open Wed in August.
Admission: Check website.

Eating Out

Lazy Days Cafe

113 Cambridge Rd, Wimpole, Royston SG85QB
Great place for a fry up.

Saffron Walden

A picturesque, medieval town, with St Mary's Church, the largest parish church in Essex. Nearby, Saffron Walden Museum is one of the oldest purpose built museum buildings in the country, completed in 1835. It has everything from mammoth tusks to mummies, and the ruins of a Castle keep.

On the eastern side of Saffron Walden Common is the largest turf labyrinth still surviving in Europe. Children can follow 'path' through the turf, which winds for about one mile within a circle 100 feet (30.5 meters) in diameter.

For kids interested in skating and bikes, you can visit the One Minet Skate Park at the rear of Lord Butler Leisure Centre, Peaslands Road.

Getting there from Cambridge

Train - 20 minutes towards London Liverpool Street, get off at Audley End and take the Bus 59 towards Haverhill (8 minutes). **Bus** - Citi 7 to Saffron Walden (10 hour 10 minutes). **Car** - 35 minutes (16 miles) on A11 then B184.

St Neots

18 miles west of Cambridge, St Neots still retains its rich heritage. It dates back over 1000 years to the Medieval Priory of St. Neot. The name of the town comes from the Cornish saint. It has a museum housed in the former magistrates court. It has a Lost Priory and you can walk in the footsteps of the famous 19th Century Eynesbury Giant. The Riverside Mill and lock in Eaton Socon are also worth a look.

It has some green open areas, the Common, Priory Park and Riverside Park. There are lakes for boating and fishing, picnic areas, children's play areas.

Getting there from Cambridge

Bus - 35 minutes, Bedford/X5 towards Oxford. **Car** - 35 minutes (19 miles) on A428 then B1428. **Train** - 1 hour, change at Hitchin.

Indoor Activities

Crafty Monkey

12 Moores Walk, St Neots PE19 1AG
Tel: 01480 219222 07522750174
Crafty Monkey pottery painting and build a bear studio.

Little Snappers, St Neots

St Neots Leisure centre, Barford Road, Eynesbury, St Neots Cambridgeshire PE19 2SA
Tel: 01480 388700
stneotsleisure@huntsdc.gov.uk
www.huntingdonshire.gov.uk/leisurecentres

Under 5s. Bouncy castle, ball pool, tricycles and soft play building.

St Neots Museum

The Old Court, 8 New St, St Neots PE19 1AE
Tel: 01480 388921
curators@stneotsmuseum.org.uk
www.stneotsmuseum.org.uk
St Neots and River Ouse history.

Eating Out

The Horseshoe Restaurant

90 High St, Offord D'Arcy, St. Neots PE19 5RH
Tel: 01480810293
www.theoffordshoe.co.uk
Try the shoeburger, beef burger, salad and battered onion rings in a bun. Lunch and early bird menu best for kids.

The Eatons Children's Centre

Bushmead Primary School, Bushmead Road, Eaton Socon, St Neots PE19 8BT
Tel: 01480 358340
eatonsoconchildrenscentre@cambridgeshire.gov.uk
www.cambridgeshirechildrenscentres.org.uk
Provides services such as stay and play groups, for both Eaton Socon and Eaton Ford. The centre is based at Bushmead Primary School, Bushmead Road, Eaton Socon, St. Neots, PE19 8BT.

Butterfly Children's Centre

Winhills School, St Neots PE19 2DX
Tel: 01480 358350
stneotschildrenscentre@cambridgeshire.gov.uk
www.cambridgeshirechildrenscentres.org.uk
A wide variety of groups and learning opportunities are currently available, both in centre and within local community venues, including a toy library, stay and play groups, speech and language therapy and more.
Open: Monday - Thursday: 8.45am - 4.30pm, Friday: 8.45am - 1pm

St Neots Toy Library Session

Winhills School, St Neots PE19 2DX
Tel: 01480 375222
office@winhills.cambs.sch.uk
www.winhills.cambs.sch.uk/content.php?page=childrenscentre
Books, toys, puzzles & videos to borrow
Children's play area and tea and coffee available. Fridays during term time 9am - 11am

Villages in Cambridgeshire

Buckden and Kimbolton
Home of Catherine of Aragon (captive by orders of her estranged husband King Henry VIII). Kimbolton dates from the Romans, and has a castle built by the de Bohun family.

Elsworth
This is 9 miles from Cambridge, and listed in the Domesday Book. It has a pretty church with poppyhead bench ends.

Elton
This is a pretty village, with a historic Hall.

Grantchester
The nearest, and walkable from Cambridge. See page

Hemingford Abbots
On the banks of the Great Ouse, with half-timbered and thatch cottages. Nearby Hemingford Grey Manor is one of the oldest inhabited buildings in Britain.

St Andrews Church, Chesterton, once a village outside Cambridge

---

St Neots Library
Priory Lane, St Neots PE19 2BH
Tel: 0845 045 5225
www.cambridgeshire.gov.uk
Mondays 2pm - 2.30pm Rhymetime for babies held 11-11.30am alternate Tuesdays (term-time only)

St Neots Events
St Neots Folk Festival - June
Rowing Regatta - July
Medieval Heritage Festival - end July
Food & Drink Festival - early August
Charity Dragon Boat Race Festival - end August
Music in the Park - September

Public Toilets
Tebbutts Rd Car Park
Riverside, The Paddocks, Eaton Ford

South St

The Henry Moore Foundation

Perry Green, Much Hadham, Hertfordshire, SG10 6EE
Tel: 01279 844104
Lovely landscape and gardens, in Moore's family home Hoglands. Studios and gardens created by his wife Irina. It has a visitor centre, shop and covered picnic area.
Open: April to October, Wed - Sun and Bank Holidays 111:00-17:00.
Admission: Adults £12.50, Under 18s £6.00, Under 5's free. Family ticket (2 adults and 2 children) £27.
Getting there: Car - 50 minutes (33 miles)- take M11 leave at junction 8A, then A120, A1184. Satnav postcode SG10 6EE. **Train** - 50 minutes to Bishop's Stortford. Shuttle service to Perry Green (Centrebus South 5) 35 minutes.

Wisbech

This used to be a busy trade centre. Stroll along the Brinks or round the Crescent to see some fine Georgian houses. Peckover House on North Brink, a Quaker banking family, or Elgood's Brewery. Wisbech has two museums; the Wisbech and Fenland.

The town is also a gateway to the Cambridgeshire Fens. Fenland is a unique landscape formed by nature and shaped by people over more than 6000 years.

The Luxe Cinema
Alexandra Road, Wisbech
Tel: 01945 588808
www.theluxecinema.com
A nice local cinema, which has leather chairs and sofas and is very comfortable.

Kings Cross Train Station

Getting There (from Cambridge)

Car - 1 hour 23 minutes (central London).

Train - 50 minutes (Kings Cross), also Liverpool Street. Watch the times that you can travel, often commuter times can be much more expensive and crowded. A family rail ticket or network card can cut the costs.

For fans of Harry Potter, check out the Platform 9¾ at Kings Cross Train Station.

Bus - 2 hours 25 minutes to London Victoria

Getting Around

It does get crowded in London, so it is wise to keep an extra eye on children, particularly in getting on and off buses and tubes, and try to avoid rush hour. However, it now much easier with buggies and baby changing with better facilities on public transport and better accessibility. All London taxis are also wheelchair accessible. The main website with details of buses and tubes is Transport for London. www.tfl.gov.uk

Bus
All of the 700 London buses are able to take buggies, and have low floors, but can get crowded at tourist areas and at commuter times. A person with a buggy can use the wheelchair space if someone is not using is, but if a wheelchair gets on they have priority.

Barclays Cycle Hire
www.tfl.gov.uk/road users/cycling

They have a distinct blue mud guard. You can pick up a bike from several docking terminals, paying with your credit or debit card. And then when you've finished, you just dock it back. The website has cycling safety tips for around London.

By Boat
The Thames has many river cruises, for example from Tate Britain to Tate Mod-

ern which only takes 20 minutes, or a longer trip to Greenwich.

London Taxis
The Black London Hackney Cabs can be hailed by the road or at taxi ranks. Fares are displayed.

London Underground
Free for accompanied children under 11. Some tube stations now have lifts and disability access, so if you have a buggy, a disability and/or several kids this can be handy. A full list of these stations are available on the website 'step free' or phone to order the guide on 0343 222 1234. There is also a tube toilet map. Use the wider gates at the ticket barriers.
www.tfl.gov.uk/gettingaround

Oyster Cards
You can purchase these at most London Underground stations, and they can be very handy otherwise you will have to rely on ticket machines for each journey. Or you could get a London day travel card with travel in London included.

Kid Friendly Attractions

Some of the best things to do with children in London are free; the Science Museum, Tate Galleries; walking down the Southbank and seeing the different buskers, performers and skateboarders.

In the summer the beautiful parks in London come alive with people. Hyde Park, Regents Park and St James Park are well maintained and great for picnics, to play games or wander around. Hampstead Heath and Richmond Park are huge and also great to explore. There are playparks dotted around the city, and Corams Fields are central. Further afield, there are Theme Parks. There is a lot of choice for eating out, and although it can be expensive, there are many budget and

interesting family friendly places to have lunch or dinner too.

Museums

British Museum
Great Russell St, London WC1B 3DG
Nearest tube station: Tottenham Court Rd/Holborn
The Egyptian mummies and huge ancient Roman and Greek sculptures are favourites with kids. The huge, airy main hall is wonderful.

Horniman Museum
100 London Rd, London SE23 3PQ
www.horniman.ac.uk
Nearest train station: Forest Hill Train Station
16 acres of landscaped gardens, a family friendly anthropological museum with many hands on activities. It's a bit out of the centre though.

London Transport Museum
Covent Garden Piazza, London WC2E 7BB
www.ltmuseum.co.uk
Nearest tube station: Covent Garden
Great for any child that likes buses and trains. You can guide a tube through tunnels on a simulator.

Natural History Museum - Free
Cromwell Rd, London SW7 5BD
www.nhm.ac.uk
Nearest tube station: South Kensington
The huge dinosaur skeleton is a great way to introduce children to the wonders of the ancient natural world. But there is much more, such as the earthquake simulator and life size blue whale.

V&A Museum of Childhood - Free
Cambridge Heath Rd, London E2 9PA
www.museumofchildhood.org.uk
Nearest tube station: Bethnal Green (no lift)
Many toys behind glass but also ones that you can touch and play with in 'activity stations', with lego, sandpit etc.

Tate Modern & Tate Britain - Free
Tate Modern, Bankside, London SE1 9TG
Nearest tube station: Southwark
Tate Britain, Millbank, London SW1P 4RG
Nearest tube station: Pimlico
www.tate.org.uk
Both of these can be fantastic places to bring kids, with huge rooms filled with modern and historic art.

National Army Museum - Free
Royal Hospital Rd, London SW3 4HT
www.nam.ac.uk
Nearest tube station: Sloane Square
This has a great kid's zone for under 10's, they can dress up in soldier's uniforms, rock climb, crawl through tunnels. The Kids Zone has a small charge.

Science Museum - Free
Exhibition Rd, London SW7 2DD
www.sciencemuseum.org.uk
Nearest tube station: South Kensington
An amazing place to stimulate your child's curiosity. It has new exhibitions on the Hadron Collider, exploring the Universe, and loads of interactive exhibits, This has a garden for 3-6 year olds with a multi-sensory area and giant building blocks.

HMS Belfast
The Queen's Walk, Tooley Street SE1 2JH
www.iwm.org.uk/visits/hms-belfast
Nearest tube station: London Bridge
Europe's largest preserved World War II warship, great for exploring and imagining what life aboard would be like. Admission: Adults £15.50, Child free (2014 prices)

Other Attractions

Battersea Park Children's Zoo
Battersea Park, Chelsea, Embankment SW11 4NJ
www.batterseaparkzoo.co.uk
Nearest train station: Queenstown Rd Battersea
Battersea Park is a good area for kids, with a paddling pool and large open spaces and playgrounds. It also has a zoo.

Hamleys Toy Shop
188-196 Regent St, Soho, London W1B 5BT
www.hamleys.com
Nearest tube station: Regent St
It was established in 1760 and has 7 floors packed full of the latest games. Although it's very hard to leave empty handed!

London Zoo
Outer Circle, Regent's Park, NW1 4RY
www.zsl.org/zsl-london-zoo
Nearest tube station: Regents Park
This has a wide variety of animals and activities for the kids to do. It is also

next to Regents Park which is central and good to roam around with smaller children.

Sea Life London Aquarium
Riverside Building, Westminster Bridge Rd, SE1 7PB
www.visitsealife.com/london
Nearest tube station: Waterloo/Westminster
This can take a few hours, it's quite big. It has sharks, jellyfish, penguins and many interactive activities and is located just next to Westminster.

Skateboard Park - Southbank
www.londonskateparks.co.uk/skateparks/southbank
Nearest tube station: Waterloo
Teenagers can watch the daring cyclists and skateboarders from the river. Although this area is under threat now from development of the Southbank.

Walk from Big Ben to the Tate Modern and beyond
Start at Big Ben, cross the river, turn left, past the London Eye, the Barbican Centre and South Bank, stop off at the Tate Modern with its fantastic Turbine Hall entrance, then onto to London Bridge and over the river again to the Tower of London.

West End Theatres
Nearest tube station: Leicester Square/Covent Garden/Picadilly Circus
The West End has several shows that are for kids and adults alike. Although tickets are often expensive, if you like musicals these can be spectacular and make a special day out.

London Parks

Coram's Fields
93 Guildford Street, WC1N 1DN
Nearest tube station: Russell Square
A 7 acre playground in central London, adults are only permitted with a child and no dogs, glass or bicycles allowed.

Hampstead Heath
Nearest rail station: Hampstead Heath
A huge park, 320 hectares, not central but with plenty or space to fly a kit or run around. Good views from Parliament Hill.

Sea Life London Aquarium

Hyde Park
London W2 2UH
Nearest tube station: Hyde Park Corner/Knightsbridge/Lancaster Gate
www.royalparks.org.uk/parks/hyde-park
This is a huge park, right in the centre, with a lake, meadow and paths all around for cycling or skating.

Regent's Park
Chester Rd, London NW1 4NR
Nearest tube station: Regent's Park
Designed by John Nash in 1811. It has lovely rose gardens in the summer, and a large outdoor sports area for football, softball, rugby and cricket.

Richmond Park
Richmond, Greater London TW10 5HS
Nearest tube station: Richmond Station and then 371 or 65 bus.
2000 acres of grassland, trees and home to free roaming deer. Good cycle paths and power kiting. Great views from the top of the hill.

St James's Park
Horse Guards Road, London SW1A 2BJ
Nearest tube station: St Jame's Park
Near the Royal Palaces, a smaller park, with a lake with pelicans (watch them being fed at 2.30pm). This is the area to find Horse Guards Parade and the Mall, with the famous guards that keep very still. It is also near Downing Street and well known landmarks.

Theme Parks

Chessington World of Adventure
Leatherhead Rd, Chessington, Surrey KT9 2NE
Tel: 0871 663 4477
www.chessington.com
Nearest train station: Chessington South (10 minutes walk)
12 miles from London on the A243. It is closed during winter. Theme park with rides for kids of all ages.

Jurassic Encounter Adventure Golf
World of Golf, Beverley Way, New Malden, Surrey KT3 4PH
Tel: 020 8949 9200
www.jurassicencounter.com
Prehistoric themed course.

Legoland Windsor
Winkfield Rd, Windsor SL4 4AY
Tel: 0871 222 2001
www.legoland.co.uk
Nearest train station: Windsor
It has three rollercoasters and six water rides, including Spinning Spider, Laser Raiders, Vikings River Splash and more.

Thorpe Park
Staines Rd, Chertsey, Surrey KT16 8PN
Tel: 0871 663 1673
www.thorpepark.com
Nearest train station: Staines (take 950 shuttle link Bus)
Aimed at older children and adults, but plenty for all with five water rides and five rollercoasters.

Eating Out

Carluccios

Garrick Street, Covent Garden, London, WC2E 9BH
Tel: 020 7836 0990
www.carluccios.com
Nearest tube station: Covent Garden
The kids menu is a miniature version of the adult menu and comes with crayons, puzzles and games. Several restaurants in the UK.

Julie's

135 Portland Road, Holland Park, London W11 4LW
Tel: 020 7229 8331
www.juliesrestaurant.com
Nearest tube station: Holland Park
This is a swish, funky restaurant that actually has a crèche for kids aged 2 – 12 years old from 1-4pm on Sundays. It has Sunday roast lunches for £20.

Giraffe

Several London locations, including 7 Kensington High St, London W8 5NP
Behind the Royal Festival Hall, Riverside Level 1, Southbank Centre, Belvedere Rd, London SE1 8XX
Tel: 020 7042 6900N
www.giraffe.net
This has friendly service and a big kids menu and activity kit.

Leon

73-76 Strand, London WC2R 0DE
3 Spital Square, London E1 5DW
12 Ludgate Circus, London EC4M 7LQ
www.leonrestaurants.co.uk

Skate boarding at the Southbank Centre

Nutritious food, a good range of children's meals, like meatballs and rice box, humus and cucumber pot, and sweet potato falafel. The kids menu comes with an activity pack.

Pizza Express

Several London locations, includiing Canary Wharf (2nd floor, Cabot Place East), 5 Fenchurch St, Bankside (Benbow House, 24 New Globe Walk) and 1 Byward St, EC3R 7QN
www.pizzaexpress.com
For luscious pizzas and salads, you are never far away from a Pizza Express and their set price Piccolo menu includes dough balls, side salad, pizza or pasta, sundae or fudge cake and Bambinoccino.

Rainforest Café

20-24 Shaftesbury Ave, London W1D 7EU
Tel: 020 7434 3111
www.therainforestcafe.co.uk
Nearest tube station: Piccadilly Circus
Fun jungle-themed decorations and moving guerillas and animals. The menu is average, and it can have loud birthday parties.

Sticky Fingers

1a Phillimore Gardens, Kensington, W8 7QG
Tel: 020 79385338
www.stickyfingers.co.uk
Nearest tube station: High St Kensington
Bill Wyman's (from the Rolling Stones) American-themed restaurant. Kids menu has fruit kebabs, burgers and fish fingers.

Tips for Travelling Around London with Kids

- Stay in one area for most of the day, or around central London if you want the biggest tourist spots.

- If you have a buggy, check ahead on the Transport for London website on which stations have lifts. If there is not a lift, it may be better to use the bus.

- Avoid rush hour.

- If you do take the tube, be careful with young ones and hold their hands getting on and off. They are very regular so if there is too much of a rush there will always be a next one.

- London Taxi Cabs will fit in the whole family, and although more expensive can save your sanity at the end of the day if buses are late/it's raining.

- Be realistic about how much travelling or walking a child, or teenager, or even you can handle.

- Some of the shops and streets of London are interesting days out in themselves. A walk along Oxford Street in the Christmas Lights seeing the window displays can be real festive sight, even if it is incredibly busy. The shops are a teenagers delight. Fortnum and Mason, Hamleys and Harrods have great displays and exotic foods and magical games. Fun if your kids are prepared to leave without hassling you to buy half the shop! Portobello and other markets can be fun too.

Discover the winding rivers, marshes and beautiful sprawling beaches of Norfolk and Suffolk. You could take a boat on the broads, or a cycle ride along the Bure Valley Cycle Path. Or have a traditional bucket and spade holiday by the sea in the pretty villages of Wells or Southwold. There are adventures to be had in the imaginative outdoor Bewilderwood or see squirrels and rabbits scamper past your lodge at Centre Parcs.

Norfolk Broads

www.visitnorfolk.co.uk/explore-norfolk/norfolk-broads.aspx

Huge expanses of marsh land and canals for a gettting away from it all holiday. There are many nature reserves with birds, butterflies and protected species. The county has shingly coastline and is dotted with pretty villages and seafront flint houses and fishing boats. The county's town, Norwich has a castle, cathedral and parks for the kids.

Getting around

You can hire a variety of boats from large cabin cruisers for a few weeks to smaller boats for a few hours.

Boating holidays are operated by Blakes (0870 2202 498; www.blakes.co.uk) and Hoseasons (01502-502588; www.hoseasons.co.uk) among others. Typically, a boat for two to four people costs around £500 to £850 for a week.

Meanwhile boat yards around Wroxham and Potter Heigham hire out boats for shorter cruises. In mid summer, prices start from £30 for two hours.

You could also try canoeing. Alternatively, you could walk or cycle on riverside paths and stop off at a pretty village for lunch.

Attractions

Bewilderwood
Hornig Rd Hoveton
www.bewilderwood.co.uk
An activity forest playground with jungle bridges, tree houses and magical places to swing, climb and jump. There are also marsh walks, boat trips, mazes and other activities.

Getting there: Bus No 12a from Norwich drops you right at the door.
Admission: adult/child £13.50/10.50
Open: 10am-5.30pm Mar-Oct

Bure Valley Steam Railway
www.bvrw.co.uk
This steam railway runs between Aylsham and Wroxham. Some book up well in advance. You could take the train and then canoe back.
Admission: Adult/child £8.50/6

Fairhaven Woodland and Water Garden
School Road. South Walsham, Norfolk NR13 6DZ
www.fairhavengarden.co.uk
50 hectares of woodland and a private broad.

Toad Hole Cottage
How Hill
This tiny cottage was home to a marshman and his family. Nearby is a beautiful thatched Edwardian mansion and a picturesque nature trail.

Waveney River Centre
www.waveneyriver centre.co.uk

Wroxham
This is a lively town and you can hire boats here. It has a Junior Farm at Wroxham Barn.

Villages
Potter Heigham - Small medieval bridge and fishing.
Ranworth - View from the church top.
Woodbastwick - Lovely thatched medieval flint church.
Stalham, Horning, Coltishall, Acle and **Reedham.**

Norwich Tourist Office
The Forum, Kenneth McKee Plain, Norwich, Norfolk NR2 1TF
Tel: 01603-213999
www.visitnorwich.co.uk

Walking
Wherryman's Way follows the route of the River Yare from Norwich.
Angles Way along the Norfolk/Suffolk border.

Cycling
Thebroadsbybike.org.uk
Tag-a-longs and baby seats, and child cycles can be hired from most major cycle hire services in the area. Trips include:
Hoveton to Coltishall
Weaver's Way
Bure Valley Cycle Path

Fishing
Barton Broad by boat.
Wroxham Broad by boat.
River Thurne at Martham and Potter Heigham.

Seaside Holidays in Norfolk and Suffollk

Cromer
Famous for its crabs. It has a pier, seaside shows and tea shops.

Great Yarmouth
A bright seaside town, with piers, donkey rides and golden mile amusement arcades. It also has a Sea Life Centre. The Pleasure Beach has a rollercoaster and a log flume.

Hunstanton
Pretty town green and walk along it's pink striped cliffs. It also has a Sea Life Sanctuary.

Sheringham
Take a steam train on the North Norfolk Poppy Line. Hilltop Outdoor Centre has active outdoor activities such as archery.

Southwold
A very pretty town with an old pier next to the sea. You can walk along the seafront to nearby villages. It has a sandy beach, pebble walled cottages, cliff tops and a quaint pier which has unusual hand made slot machines.

Wells-next-to-Sea

Winding streets, whelk and shrimp boats, long sweeping beach.

Wildlife

There are many national reserves which are reknowned by bird, water and insect life. Hickling Broad has the swallowtail butterfly. There is also Berney Marches and Ranworth Broad.

Banham Zoo (see page 83)

Kenninghall Rd, Banham, Norfolk NR16 2HE
Tel: 01953 887771
www.banhamzoo.co.uk

Thrigby Hall Wildlife Gardens

Filby Rd, Thrigby, Great Yarmouth NR29 3DR
Tel: 01493 369477
www.thrigbyhall.co.uk

Pensthorpe Nature Reserve

Pensthorpe Road, Fakenham, Norfolk NR21 0LN
Tel: 01328 851465
www.pensthorpe.com

Snettisham Park

Bircham Rd, King's Lynn PE31 7NG
Tel: 01485 542425
www.snettishampark.co.uk

Theme Parks

Pleasurewood Hills Theme Park

Leisure Way, Lowestoft, Suffolk NR32 5DZ
Tel: 01502 586000
pleasurewoodhills.com

Dinosaur Adventure

Weston Park, Lenwade, Norwich NR9 5JW
Tel: 01603 876310
www.dinosauradventure.co.uk

Suffolk

{Suffolk}The Stour Valley{Stour Valley} has some beautifully preserved villages that are from the Middle Ages, and on the coast, long beaches spotted with seaside towns. Bury St Edmunds has a historic centre, and nearby Centre Parcs is a favourite

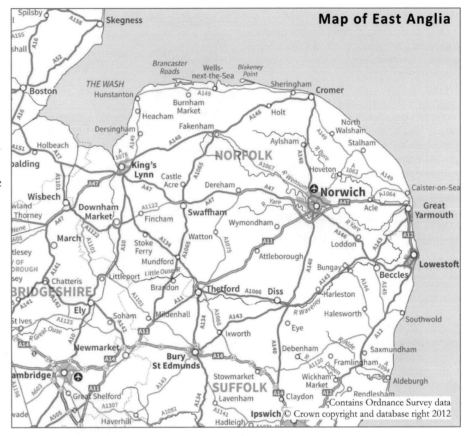

Map of East Anglia

Contains Ordnance Survey data
© Crown copyright and database right 2012

for a car free break where you can cycle around the forest and fly down the water flumes.

Walking and Cycling Routes

www.discoversuffolk.org.uk
From Suffolk County Council, 18 Easy Going Trails guide, each walk can be accessed by buggies or a wheelchair user. Range from third of a mile to 8 miles long.

Attractions

Bury St Edmunds

See the historic old town and Abbey Gardens, or explore the countryside at Knettishall Heath

Centre Parcs Elveden Forest

Elveden Forest, Brandon, Suffolk IP27 0YZ
SAT NAV use postcode IP24 3TR.
Tel: 08448 267723
www.centerparcs.co.uk/villages/elveden
This is a popular resort for families. You stay in chalets in the forest, and walk or cycle around the park as cars

are only allowed for drop off. The subtropical swimming paradise is free, and has fun pools and chutes, but all other activities are extra.

Lavenham

A lovely medieval town, with hundreds of preserved wooden framed 15th century buildings, thatched cottages, local curiosity shops and tearooms.

Sutton Hoo

Tranmer House, Woodbridge, IP12 3DJ
Tel: 01394 389700
suttonhoo@nationaltrust.org.uk
www.nationaltrust.org.uk/suttonhoo
A well known archaeological site, 255 acres with views over the River Deben. A buried ship was found here, the final resting place of Raedwald, King of East Anglia until AD 625, and was stuffed with a fabulous wealth of Saxon riches.
Getting there: Sutton Hoo is 2 miles east of Woodbridge and 6 miles northeast of

Ipswich off the B1083. Buses 71 and 73 go to Sutton Hoo, 10 times per day Monday to Saturday, passing through Woodbridge (10 minutes) en route to Ipswich (40 minutes).
Open: 10.30am-5pm
Admission: Adult/child £7.50/3.90

West Stow Anglo-Saxon Village
Icklingham Rd
Open: 10am-5pm
Admission: Adult/child £6/4

Woolpit
Unspoilt villages and the tall Victorian spire of Woolpit St Mary's.

Suffolk Tourist Information Centre
152 High Street Aldeburgh
Suffolk IP15 5AQ
Tel: 01728 453637
atic@suffolkcoastal.gov.uk
www.suffolkcoastal.gov.uk

Bury St Edmunds Tourist Information Centre
6 Angel Hill, Bury St Edmunds,
Suffolk IP33 1UZ
Tel: 01284 764667
tic@stedsbc.gov.uk
www.stedmundsbury.gov.uk

Lincolnshire

This is quite sparsely populated and has some stunning stately homes. Lincoln has a grand Gothic Cathedral and the town itself is perched high on a hill. Here you can also find the tasty Lincolnshire sausage, regional pork pies and Lincolnshire Poacher cheese.

It includes the historic houses of Gainsborough Old Hall, Harlaxton Manor, Tattershall Castle, Thornton Abbey, Belton House and Burghley House. The seaside resorts of Skegness and Cleethorpes are the most well known, but Sutton-on-Sea, and Chapel St Leonard are all also on the sea with long sandy beaches in many of these places. Skegness has a famous Jolly Fisherman mascot, and is a favourite for a traditional seaside holiday.

Places to Stay

Check the Tourist Information Centres for local cottages and hotels. There are a few family favourites listed here that should meet different accommodation needs.

Cley Windmill
Cley-next-the-Sea, Holt, Norfolk NR25 7RP
Tel: 01263 740209
www.cleywindmill.co.uk
Not all of the rooms are suitable for young children, but for an unusual self catering/bed and breakfast option it's hard to beat, and beautifully restored.

Kelling Heath
Weybourne, North Norfolk
Tel: 01263 588181
www.kellingheath.co.uk
Set amongst 250 acres of woodland and heathland, and very close to the coastline at Weybourne. Woodland lodges, caravan and camping.

Potters Leisure Resort
Coast Road, Hopton on Sea NR31 9BX
www.pottersholidays.com
5* Holiday Village which does family breaks in the school holidays.

Premier Inn Norwich Nelson City Centre
Prince of Wales Road, Norwich NR1 1DX
www.premierinn.com
Central location, comfortable, reasonably priced.

Fish, Crab and Chips

Fresh seafood, farm shops and markets are all great places to try local delicious food. Cromer is famous for its crabs, and there are some brilliant fish and chip shops.

Cookies Crab Shop
Salthouse, Holt, North Nofolk NR25 7AJ

www.salthouse.org.uk
A shellfish and sandwich shop, there is a garden overlooking the salt marshes. Phone to check that they are open (sometimes closed if it is wet).

Grosvenor Fish Bar
28 Lower Goat Lane, Norwich NR2 1EL
Tel: 01603 625855
www.fishshop.com

HMS Hinchinbrook
6 Marine Parade, Great Yarmouth NR30 3AH
Tel: 01493 843588

My Plaice Fish and Chips
45 Baker Street, Gorleston,
Norfolk NR31 6QT

The Boundary
64 High Street, Market Deeping,
Lincolnshire PE6 8EB
www.boundaryfishandchips.co.uk

Campervans

Yet another option is to hire a motorhome or campervan. It's more expensive than hiring a car but it does help you save on accommodation costs, and gives almost unlimited freedom.

Sites to check include these:
Cool Campervans
www.coolcampervans.com
Just Go
www.justgo.uk.com
Wild Horizon
www.wildhorizon.co.uk

SPORTS, ARTS & ACTIVITIES FOR CHILDREN

This section contains information on local activities; sports, swimming, arts, drama, music and more in the Cambridge area. It is packed with clubs that your child could join to develop their athletic talents, fitness and creativity.

There are also general groups like the Girl Guides or the Scouts. Most indoor pools offer swimming lessons, and the area is well serviced with sports centres.

Girl Guides

Join Girlguiding: Register your interest or call on 0800 1 69 59 01.
General enquiries: 020 7834 6242
www.girlguiding-anglia.org.uk
www.girlguiding.org.uk
The girl guide association is a charity where girls can meet up locally, and under the supervision of vol-

unteer leaders, can build friendships, learn life skills and have fun. Rainbows are for girls aged 5 to 7, Browies from 7 to 10 who become a member of a six and follow a programme called 'Brownie Adventure'. Guides are from 10 to 14 and try out activities from adventure sports to performing arts or community action projects. There is also a senior section from 14 to 26 years.

Scouts - not just for boys

scouts.org.uk
Over 400,000 young people in the UK are in the scouts. It was started over a 100 years ago and is still going strong today. You can join your local group for a fee of between £50 to £100 a year to cover facilities and costs. The emphasis is on

fun and adventure, building confidence and friendships.

There are badges and awards in hiking, healthy eating, camping, IT, mechanics and more. Children can join from aged 6, with the Beaver Scouts. They usually meet weekly to take part in games, crafts, singing, good turns. Cub scouts are from 8-10, then Scouts. As well as weekly meetings, there are chances to have holidays and camps with adventure activities.

NOTE:
Please check the details, websites or by phone to check activities. Whilst the author has tried to ensure that these are as accurate as possible, they are subject to change.

Swimming Pool/ Leisure Centre	Address	Contact	Swim Prices* *Subject to change	Opening Times	Pool Size	Facilities
Bottisham Swimming Pool and Sports Centre (Indoor pool)	Lode Road, Bottisham, CB25 9DL	Tel. 01223 811121 www.bottishamvc.org/sportscentre	Membership or from £2.30	See website for lesson timetable	25m long	Four lane pool and good disabled facilities. Swimming lessons and fitness. Sports hall, gym, tennis/netball courts, astroturf, football pitch, dance studio.
Cherry Hinton Water Play Area (Outdoor pool)	Cherry Hinton Hall, Cherry Hinton Road, Cambridge CB1 8DW	Tel: 01223 213352 www.cambridge.gov.uk/cherry-hinton-water-play-area	Free	May to September	Max depth 0.4m	Two small paddling pools. The water shelves gently to a max depth of 0.4 metres, and the pools are fenced in for safety.
Coleridge Paddling Pool (Outdoor pool)	Coleridge recreation ground, Davy Road, Cambridge	Tel: 01223 213352 www.cambridge.gov.uk/coleridge-paddling-pool	Free	May to September	Depth 0.2 to 0.45m	The pool is fenced off, with seating and toilets available nearby.
Jesus Green Outdoor Lido (Outdoor pool)	Jesus Green, Off Chesterton Road, CB4 3AX	Tel: 01223 302579 www.cambridge.gov.uk/jesus-green-outdoor-pool	Adult £4.10 Junior £2.15	Can vary. Generally Mon-Sun: 10:30-19:30	91m long	14m wide, but very long . 1.2m to 2.5m depth. Shower and toilet facilities, basket store room. Opened in 1923.
King's Hedges Learner Swimming Pool (Indoor pool)	Jedburgh Court, Buchan Street, Cambridge CB4 2XH	Tel: 01223 353248 www.better.org.uk/areas/cambridge	Adult swim £3.30	Mon-Fri: 09:00-18:00 Sat: & Sun: 09:00-16:00	15m long	Indoor pool and also outdoor pool and children's playground.
Lammas Land/Sheeps Green Learner Pool (Outdoor pool)	Lammas Land via Barton Road, Cambridge	Tel: 01223 302580 www.cambridge.gov.uk/sheeps-green-learner-pool	Free	Mon- Sun: 10:00-17:30 May to September	Depth 0.9m	A lifeguard is present during opening hours. 0.9 metres deep.
Parkside Swimming Pool (Indoor pool)	Gonville Place, Cambridge CB1 1LY	Tel: 01223 446100 www.better.org.uk/areas/cambridge	Adult swim £4.10	Mon to Weds: 07:00-21:30 Thurs: 07:00 - 17:00 Fri: 07:00 - 21:30 Sat - Sun: 08:00 - 17:30	25m long	Eight lane competition-standard pool. Teaching and Diving pool. Children's Leisure pool. Two flume rides. Health suite with jacuzzi, sauna and steam room. Exercise studio. Cafe. Used for competitions so sometimes it may be closed to the public. The building itself won a major Architecture Award.
Cambourne Fitness & Sports Centre	Back Lane, Great Cambourne CB23 6FY	Tel: 01954 714070	N/A	Mon-Fri: 06:30 - 22:00 Sat & Sun: 08:00 - 20:00	No Pool	Four court sports hall, exercise studio, fitness suite.
Chesterton Sports Centre (Indoor pool)	Gilbert Road, Cambridge CB4 3NY	Tel: 01223 576110 www.chestertonsportscentre.org.uk	Adult swim £3.50 Junior swim £2.25	Mon, Wed, Fri: 07:00 - 22:00 Sat & Sun: 08:00 -18:00	17m long	17 metre swimming pool for training or fun. Sports hall, tennis courts, astroturf, gym and cafe.
Kelsey Kerridge Sports Centre	Queen Anne Terrace, Cambridge CB1 1NA	Tel: 01223 462226 info@kelseykerridge.co.uk www.kelseykerridge.co.uk	N/A	Daily 09:00 - 23:00 Bank Holidays: 09:00 - 19:00	No Pool	Largest sports hall in the Cambridge area, can be used for a range including badminton, football, basketball, volleyball. Long mirrored room with sports floor for archery, tablet tennis, martial arts, cricket, and fitness studio. Outlooks gym and free weights gym.
Netherhall Sports Centre	Queen Edith's Way, Cambridge CB1 8NN	Tel: 01223 712142 www.netherhallsports.com	N/A	Mon - Fri: 17:00 - 22:00 Sat & Sun: 09:00 - 17:00	No Pool	Sports hall, gym, dance studio, atrium hall, football pitch, 5 floodlit netball/tennis courts, grass pitches.
The Park - Cambridge Regional College Sports	Kings Hedges Road, Cambridge CB4 2QT	Tel: 01223 418280 www.thepark-cambridge.co.uk	N/A	Mon -Thur: 07.15 - 22:00 Fri: 07.15 - 21:00 Sat & Sun: 09:00-16:00	No Pool	Two squash courts, two sports halls, climbing wall, Gym, exercise studio, floodlit outdoor 5-a-side all weather pitch. Varied activities.

SPORTS & SWIMMING

Parkside, Abbey, King's Hedges and Chesterton are all excellent local indoor pools. Cambridge is fortunate to also have a number of outdoor pools most of which are free. There will be some improvements in local pools, with Parkside getting a new gym facility and Abbey Pool upgraded.

There are many good Leisure and Sports Centres, such as the Kelsey Kerridge and Chesterton. There is a handy sports table for quick reference.

From fishing to football there should be something for your child. It is recommended that you check ahead first, as prices, times and facilities can change.

Indoor Swimming Pools

Abbey Swimming Pool
Whitehill Road, Cambridge CB5 8NT
Tel: 01223 213352
www.better.org.uk/leisure/abbeyleisurecomplex
Swimming lessons, aqua aerobics. It also has an exercise studio, Astroturf pitch, grass pitch, fitness suite.

Chesterton Sports Centre
Gilbert Road, Cambridge CB4 3NY
Tel: 01223 576 110
www.chestertonsportscentre.org.uk
This has a swimming pool, as well as sports facilities. Children's swimming lessons including Rookie Lifeguard and Synchronised Swimming

King's Hedges Learner Swimming Pool
Jedburgh Court, Buchan St, Cambridge CB4 2XH
Tel: 01223 353248
www.better.org.uk/areas/cambridge
This is a 15m pool. It runs swimming lessons for children from 5 months upwards.

Parkside Swimming Pool
Gonville Place, Cambridge CB1 1LY
Tel: 01223 446100
www.better.org.uk/leisure/parksidepools
Parkside Pool is the biggest in Cambridge with eight lanes, 25 m long competition standard. It has a children's pool and two flume rides. It is sometimes closed to the public for competitions.

Outdoor Swimming Pools

All the listed outdoor paddling pools are free to use, except Jesus Green.

Cherry Hinton Water Play Area
Cherry Hinton Hall, Cherry Hinton Rd, Cambridge CB1 8DW
Tel: 01223 213352
These two small paddling pools can be found in the grounds of Cherry Hinton Hall. The water shelves gently to a maximum depth of 0.4 metres, and the pools are fenced in for safety. Open May to September.

Coleridge Paddling Pool
Coleridge recreation ground, Davy Rd, Cambridge
Tel: 01223 213352
The pool is fenced off, with seating and toilets available nearby. The pool varies from 0.2 to 0.45 metres in depth. Open from May to September.

Jesus Green Outdoor Lido
Jesus Green, Off Chesterton Rd, Cambridge CB4 3AX
Tel: 01223 302579
Open from May to September during the summer, usually Monday to Sunday 10:30 to 7:30pm, earlier on Tuesday and

Friday. Great outdoor pool on Jesus Green, perfect for a sunny day. There is an admission charge.

Lammas Land Pool

Lammas Land via Barton Road, Cambridge
Tel: 01223 302580

It is closed for the winter months, open May to September. The site also has a large playground, toilets and a refreshment kiosk.

Sheeps Green Learner Pool

Sheep's Green via Barton Road, Cambridge
Tel: 01223 302580

The pool is 0.9 metres deep and is free to use. Male and female changing rooms are available. A lifeguard is present during opening hours, which are 10am-5.30pm, Monday to Sunday. The pool is open from May to September. It is close to Lammas Land Pool.

Swimming Lessons

These are available at all of the indoor pools listed. In addition, there are some independent providers that also use the local pools to teach swimming to children.

Dolphin Baby Swim

Cambridge, Bury St Edmunds, Bishops Stortford and a beautiful pool near Newmarket.and Bishops Stortford
Tel: 01223 564064
www.dolphinbabyswim.com

Birthlight gentle approach for parent and baby. Baby swim classes (from 6 weeks to 6 years old).

Baby swimming classes are offered in 'Cutie the Clam' (0-3 months), through to 'Smiley the Turtle' (3-4 years).

At Kings Hedges Pool; Granta School Pool; Grove Pool; Parkside Pool; Windmill Pool.

Benefits of Learning to Swim

Your child will learn a valuable safety skill for life.
It builds confidence.
It develops physical coordination.
Swimming is a healthy form of exercise.
It can be great fun to splash around and learn the different swimming techniques.

Sports Centres in Cambridge

See the Sports Table for contact and main details. Below are a taste of what each has to offer specifically for children.

Abbey Pool & Leisure Centre

Junior fitness and swimming lessons.

Bottisham Swimming Pool and Sports Centre

It has holiday and term-time kids activities, as well as Tots Ballet, Kidz Dance, Tennis Academy and Football Coaching.

The Park - Cambridge Regional College Sports -

It has holiday activities, and a Sports Academy to encourage young players.

Chesterton Sports Centre

Children's term time after school and Saturdays (10-12 week courses) and holiday activities for 4-16 yrs. Including Zumbatomic, Rookie Lifeguard, Trampolining, Football, Syncronised Swimming and Tennis.

Kelsey Kerridge Sports Centre

This has extensive holiday activities for kids. Little Kickers is football training for kids from 18 months to 7 years. Cambridge Karate Club, Kickboxing, Aikido and Shotokan Karate are run from here.

Netherhall Sports Centre

A range of sporting activities during the school term and school holidays for children from the age of 4 to 12 years plus.

FREE Swimming
www.better.org.uk

Under 3s

Free during public-swimming sessions. Must be accompanied at all times by a person over 17 years of age. Please notify receptionist.

Surrounding Area

- See individual towns for details.

Art-Deco Lido - Outdoor Pool

Bishops Road, Peterborough, PE1 1YY
www.vivacity-peterborough.com

Deepings Leisure Centre

Park Road, Deeping St James, Peterborough PE6 8NF
www.harpersfitness.co.uk

Mepal Outdoor Centre

Chatteris Road, Nr Ely Cambs CB6 2AZ
www.mepal.co.uk

Lakeside Leisure

Ferry Meadows Watersports Centre, Nene Park, Ham Ln, Peterborough
www.lakesideleisure.com

Manor Leisure Centre

Station Rd, Peterborough PE7 1UA
www.fenland.gov.uk/leisure

Melbourn Sports Centre

The Moor, Melbourn, Nr Royston G8 6EF
www.melbournsports.com

Newmarket Leisure Centre

Exning Road, Newmarket, Suffolk CB8 OEA
www.angcomleisure.com

St Ivo Leisure Centre

Westwood Road, St Ives Cambs PE27 6WU
www.huntingdonshire.gov.uk

Peterborough Town Sports Club

Bretton Gate, Peterborough
www.ptsc.org.uk

Regional Fitness and Swimming Centre

Bishops Road, Peterborough PE1 5BW
www.vivacity-peterborough.com

Werrington Sports Centre

Staniland Way, Werrington, Peterborough PE4 6JT

BETTER Card holders aged 17 or under

Parkside Pool - Monday, Wednesdays and Fridays, 4-6pm. **Abbey Pool** - Tuesdays and Thursdays, 4-6pm BETTER leisure upgrade subscription required (available from Abbey Pools, Parkside Pools).

Cricket

Cambridge Granta Cricket Club
Clare Sports Ground, Bentley Road,
Cambridge CB2 8AW
Cambridgegrant.play-cricket.com
Six senior week-end teams, two mid-week teams, ten junior (age 6-15) teams.

Babraham Cricket Club
Babraham Cricket Ground, Babraham Park,
Babraham CB22 3AG
Babraham.play-cricket.com
Three Saturday and one Sunday cricket teams run during summer. Midweek Twenty/20 side. Juniorsections for U11, U12,U13, & U15. Winter coaching.

Sawston Cricket Club
Spicers Sports Ground, New Road, Sawston
CB2
Sawston.play-cricket.com
Cricket for local community at both junior and senior levels and coaching for junior members.

Bar Hill Cricket Club
Village Green, The Spinney, Bar Hill,
Cambridge CB23 8SU
Tel: 01954 201212
Info@barhillcricket.org.uk
www.barhillcricket.org.uk
Two Saturday League sides and one Sunday friendly side. Small friendly club where everyone is welcome.

Coton Cricket Club
Coton Recreation Ground, Coton
Rob.kaye@btinternet.com
Coton.play-cricket.com
All standards of rowers, coxes and coaches are welcome.

Cambridge Schools Cricket Association
Clare College Sports Ground, Bentley Rd,
Cambridge CB2 8AW
Under 11 team manager & organiser of cricket coaching for children aged 9-15 yrs.

Hardwick & Shepreth Cricket Club
Hardwick Recreation Ground, Ashmead Drive, Cambridge CB3 7XT
C.fuller@bioc.cam.ac.uk
Hardwick.play-cricket.com

Fishing

Earith Lakes Fishery
The Lakes, Holme Fen,
Drove Colne,
Huntingdon,
Cambridgeshire PE28 3RE
Tel: 01487 740301
orenb36@hotmail.com
www.earithlakes.com
Open all year. Two gravel pit lakes of 16 and 18 acres set in Farmland. Clear water. Big fish lake (4lb-27lbs) can only be fished on sporting ticket. Rainbow, Brown, Golden, Blue, Triploid and Pike.

Headfen Lakes
Little Downham, near Ely
Tel: Marcus Bailey 07971 574375
www.headfenlakesfishery.co.uk
3 coarse fishing lakes containing carp, tench, barbel, chub, bream, roach, perch and gudgeon. Day tickets are available on site.

New Lake
Barway, near Ely, Cambridgeshire
5 acre lake with two islands, and landscaped surround. Members log hut, 2 toilets secure parking. Catfish , carp, specimen fish in nearly all species. Suitable for disabled anglers.

Lawn Farm Fishery
Elsworth, Cambridge CB3 8JX
Tel: 01954 719260
ros@lawnfarmfisheries.fsnet.co.uk
The Fishery was opened in 1999 and is well stocked with coarse fish. Situated on the access road to Elsworth by the A428.

Waterbeach Angling Club
Waterbeach Road, Landbeach, Cambridge
CB25 9FA
info@waterbeachac.co.uk
www.waterbeachac.co.uk
Angling with still waters and rivers. Strong junior section. Wheelchair access to Atkins Water and Magpie Lake.

Welney Angling Club
"Shanedeh" Bedford Bank, West Welney,
Wisbech, Cambridgeshire PE14 9RJ
Tel: 01354 63863

w@edenfab.co.uk
www.welneyanglingclub.co.uk
These rivers are mostly dead straight with hardly any flow, they contain pike, some zander, lots of roach, perch, rudd & the odd carp. Normal water rules apply. Day tickets on bank. Night fishing is allowed.

Sea Fishing

Breakaways Sea Angling Club
43 Squires Court, Eaton Socon, St Neots,
Cambridgeshire PE19 8PB
Tel: 01480 476656
nastyhero@cufc.fsworld.co.uk

Cambridge & District Sea Angling Society
Social Club, Fulbourn Hospital,
Fulbourn, Cambridge
Tel: 01223 860881
Dedicated to promoting sea fishing in the Cambridge region.

Football

Football Clubs

Cambridge City Football Club
The Pro-Edge Stadium, Milton Road,
Cambridge CB4 1UY
Tel: 01223 357973
info@cambridgecityfc.com
www.cambridgecityfc.com
It has girls and boys teams from under 10s upwards. The Development Centre is run in close association with 1stStep Sports.

Cambridge Regional College - Football Academy
The Park, Kings Hedges Rd,
Cambridge CB4 2QT
Tel: 01223 418249/226315.

www.thepark-
cambridge.co.uk/index.php?page=SC-sports-
academy
In partnership with Southend United
Football Club, to launch careers of
young players in a 3 year course.

Football Mash Up Session
Abbey Pools, Cambridge CB5 8NT
Small Sided 'game - based' Football
coaching sessions lasting 10 weeks.
Targeting new players (boys & girls aged
14 – 17) Cost £2.00 per session

Cambridge United Football Club
The R Costings Abbey Stadium, Newmarket
Rd, Cambridge CB5 8LN
www.cambridge-united.co.uk
Tel:01223 566500
info@cambridge-united.co.uk
Youth Trust:
Tel: 01223 729204
info@cambridgeunitedtrust.co.uk
Various activities in it's Youth Trust
programme which includes Academy
and Development Centre. Can book
online for football sports camps and
courses. Half day courses in
Cambridgeshire for 4-16 years and 1
and 2 day holiday camps for 4-12 years.
Also professional sports camps of 1 to 5
days.

Kelsey Kerridge
Queen Anne Terrace, Cambridge CB1 1NA
www.kelseykerridge.co.uk
Indoor football. The Main Hall consists
of 2 indoor football pitches that are
available for hire. Half Main Hall e.g. 1
x 5-a-side indoor football pitch (room
hire per hour) £26.05 off peak £34.55
peak.

Little Kickers
Tel: 01954 719872 lsteven@littlekickers.co.uk
www.littlekickers.co.uk
Little Kickers is football training for
kids from 18 months to 7th birthday.

Book through website. Three venues in
Cambridge:
Cambourne church, Jeavons Lane, Great
Cambourne, CB23 6AF - Thursday
mornings
Impington Sports Centre, New Rd,
Impington, CB24 9LX - Saturday
mornings
Kelsey Kerridge, Queen Anne Terrace,
CB1 1NA - Saturday and Sunday
mornings

Young Dribblers
Hills Road Sports & Tennis Centre, Cambridge
Tel: 07900 263700
youngdribblers@live.co.uk
www.youngdribblers.co.uk
Football Fun for 2-5 Years olds. Also in
Gamlingay and Arbury Community
Centre.

Cambridgeshire Football Association
www.cambridgeshirefa.com
Skills Sessions - Children aged 5-11 can
access high quality coaching through the
FA Tesco Skills Programme.
Mini-Soccer and Youth Clubs - Clubs
provide structured opportunities for
children to be part of a team, train and
play in matches against other teams.

Local Football Clubs
You can search for local clubs, with age
range and postcode on the Football
Association website. A search for 10
mile radius of Cambridge for under 7's
produced 16 clubs:

Bar Hill Colts
The Spinney, Bar Hill, CB23 8SU
Tel: 01954 204801
www.barhillcolts.co.uk

Bottisham
Bottisham Village College, Lode Road,
Bottisham, CB25 9DL
Tel: 01223 812591
www.bottishamfc.co.uk

Burwell Swallows
Buntings Path, Burwell, CB25 0EG
Tel: 01638 611513
www.clubwebsite.co.uk/burwellswallowsfc01

Cambourne
Back Lane, Great Cambourne, CB23 6FY
Tel: 01954715959
www.cambournefc.org.uk

Cambridge Comets
Cambridge Regional College
The Park, Kings Hedges Road, Cambridge
CB4 2QT
ihart@camre.ac.uk
www.thepark-
cambridge.co.uk/index.php?page=SC-clubs-
teams

Cottenham Colts
www.cottenhamcolts.com
www.facebook.com/CottenhamUnitedColts

Fulbourn Falcons Colts
Fulbourn Capital Park Sports, Cambridge
Road, Fulbourn, CB21 5EF
www.fulbournfalcons.co.uk
stanjones47@yahoo.com
Tel: 01223 573186 (Evening)

Haslingfield Colts
High St, Haslingfield, CB23 1JW
Tel: 01223 870484
www.haslingfieldcolts.co.uk

Hardwick Harriers
Egremont Rd, Hardwick, CB23 7XR
Tel: 07810 372393
www.hardwickharriers.co.uk

Histon Hornets
New Rd, Impington, CB24 9LU
www.clubwebsite.co.uk/histonhornets
Tel: 01223 575151

Longstanton Colts
Over Rd, Longstanton, CB24 5DW
Tel: 01954 789858

Melbourn Dynamos
The Moor, Melbourn, Royston,
Cambridgeshire, SG8 6EF
www.melbourndynamos.co.uk

Milton Colts
Milton Community Centre, Coles Rd, Milton,
CB24 6BL
www.clubwebsite.co.uk/miltoncoltsfootballcl
ub
Tel: 01223 561255

Shelford & Stapleford Strikers
Haverhill Rd, Stapleford, CB22 5BX
Tel: 01223 561753
www.sass-fc.com

Swavesey Spartans
High St, Swavesey, CB24 4QU
Tel: 01480 382015
www.swaveseyspartansfc.co.uk

Teversham Colts
Fulbourn Rd, Teversham, CB1 9AJ

Tel: 01223 813595
www.tevershamcoltsfc.co.uk

Waterbeach Colts
Cambridge Rd, Waterbeach, CB25 9NJ
Tel: 01223 566687
www.waterbeachcolts.org.uk

Football for Girls
Most clubs cater for girls' football and Cambridgeshire has a healthy number of girls in Charter Standard Club, Development and Community clubs.

S-Tech Cambs Girls' League
The league offers mini soccer football up to Under 12 and 9 v 9 competition and/or 11 v 11 at under 13 age groups and above.

FA Girls' Talent Development
Cambridge also has a Centre of Excellence. Contact:
danielle.quelch@hotmail.co.uk

Primary & Secondary School League
The Girls' Primary & Seconday School competition organised by the FA. Girls' football contact 01223 209036
Beverley.Clarkson@CambridgeshireFA.com
ESFA Tesco Cup Primary School Competition (Years 7&8)
Cambridgeshire FA organises the girls' competition.

Golf

Bourn Golf Club
Toft Rd, Bourn, Cambridge CB23 2TT
Tel: 01954 718057
info@bourngolfandleisure.co.uk
This privately owned course was first opened in 1991, and is 6498 yards (off the white tees) in length. It is in quiet, rolling countryside. A river runs throughout, which in combination with 3 lakes results in 11 holes having water hazards. For all levels.

Cambridge Golf Club
Longstanton, Cambridge CB4 5DR
Tel: 01954 789388
cambridgegolf@tiscali.co.uk
www.cambridgegolfclub.net
The course is a maturing parkland course designed as two loops of nine, both finishing at the clubhouse, with ponds, ditches and lakes (where you could catch roach, or carp up to 14 lb). There is also a floodlit driving range and a practice putting green.

Cambridge Lakes Golf Course
Trumpington Rd, Cambridge CB2 2AJ
Tel: 01223 324242
bob@cambridgelakes.co.uk
Beginners/Inexperienced players. You can hire all the equipment you need including bag, clubs and balls. Casual dress allowed. No restrictive rules & regulations (except that you play safely and respect the course and other players).

Cambridge National Golf
Comberton Rd, Toft, Cambridge CB3 7RY
Tel: 01223 264700
meridian@golfsocieties.com
Cambridge Meridian has short game and long game practice areas and first class tuition.

Ely City Golf Club
107 Cambridge Road, Ely CB7 4HX
Tel: 01353 662751
info@elygolf.co.uk
www.elygolf.co.uk
19 hole course located on the site of an old 2nd World War Prisoner of War Camp. Using borrowed tractors and machinery and the goodwill of the members this 'self help, home made' course quickly gained in popularity.

Girton Golf Club
Dodford Lane, Girton, Cambridge CB3 0QE
Tel: 01223 276169
secretary@girtongolfclub.sagehost.co.uk
Opened in 1936. Girton is an easy walking, tight parkland course with mature bushes and trees. Visitors are welcome to play at the course on Monday to Friday; no handicap certificate is required but telephone in advance to confirm.

Gog Magog Golf Club
On A1307, Shelford Bottom, Cambridge CB22 3AB
Tel:01223 247626
www.gogmagog.co.uk
Two 18 hole golf courses open to members and visitors.

Hemingford Abbots Golf Course
New Farm Lodge, Cambridge Road, Hemingford Abbots, Cambridgeshire, PE28 9HQ
Tel: 01480 495000
hagcenquiries@tiscali.co.uk
www.hemingfordabbotsgolfclub.co.uk
18 self catering units, with 9 holes, but with its varied tee positions offers 18 holes over 5414 yards.

Gymnastics and Trampoline

Cambridge Aspire Trampoline Academy
Comberton, The Leys School, Chatteris and Ely
www.cambridge-aspire.co.uk
For children from age 2¾ upwards.

Cambridge Cangaroos Trampolining
cangaroos.org
Cambridge Cangaroos was formed in June 2004, is now thriving. Based at Sawston Sports Centre and operate satellite centres at Cambridge Regional College and Saffron Walden.

Cambridge Gymnastics & Trampoline Club
Venues: Morley Memorial School, Cambridge Fitness & Sports Centre, Parkside Federation Coleridge Campus, The Leys Sports Complex
Cambridge.gymandtrampclub@ntlworld.com
Tel: 01223 510144
www.cambridge-gymnastics.co.uk
Gymnastics activities for ages 3-16 years including: Floor, Vault, Beam, Rhythmic Gymnastics, Co-ordination.

Dynamics Gymnastics
Parkside Community College, Cambridge CB1 1EH
info@dynamicsgymnastics.co.uk
www.dynamicsgymnastics.co.uk
National gymnastics for young people aged 4 - 16.

Horse Riding

Bridge Farm Riding School
Smithy Fen, Cottenham CB24 8PT
Tel: 01954 252284
info@bridgefarmschool.co.uk
www.bfrs.co.uk

Explore the galleries with their Junior Fun Tour.

Folgate
Folgate La, Walpole St. Andrew, Wisbech, Cambridgeshire PE14 7HY
Tel: 01945 780456

Rectory Farm
7 Offord Rd, Graveley, St. Neots, Cambridgeshire, PE19 6PP
Tel: 01480 830336

Sawston Riding School
Common Lane, Sawston CB2 4HW
Tel: 01223 835198
enquiries@sawstonridingschool.co.uk
www.sawstonridingschool.co.uk

The Ridings
The Ridings, Apethorpe Rd, Nassington, Peterborough, Cambridgeshire, PE8 6QZ
Tel: 07731 862343

Tick Fen Riding Stables
Gleewalk Farm, New Road, Tick Fen, Warboys, Cambridgeshire, PE28 2UF
Tel: 01354 695459 or 07910 030441
www.tickfenriding.co.uk

The Coach House Stables
Old Coach House, High Street, Chippenham, near Newmarket, Ely, Cambridgeshire, CB7 5PP
Tel: 01638 720415
linda@coachhouseriding.co.uk
www.coachhouseriding.co.uk

The Old Tiger Stables
22 Northfield Road, Soham, Ely, Cambridgeshire CB7 5UF
Tel: 01353 720125
l.websterward@btinternet.com

Witcham Equestrian Centre
Mepal Rd, Witcham, Ely, Cambridgeshire CB6 2LD
Tel: 01353 777588

Woodwalton Stud & Training Centre
Raveley Road, Woodwalton, Nr Huntingdon, Cambridgeshire PE28 5YX
Tel: 07725 478586
bev.wing@btinternet.com
www.woodwaltonstud.org.uk

Yaxley Riding Centre
99 Main St, Yaxley, Peterborough, Cambridgeshire PE7 3LP
Tel: 01733 245783

Broadway Farm Stables
High St, Lolworth, Cambridge, Cambridgeshire CB23 8HG
Tel: 01954 780159

Chestunut Farm Equestiran Centre
109 St Pauls Road, Walton Highway, Wisbech, Cambridgeshire PE14 7DD
Tel: 07815 765147
wendy.whatley@btinternet.com
www.chestnutequestrian.vpweb.co.uk

Hall Farm Stables
Hall Farm Stables, Waterbeach, just off the A10

Hill Top Equestrian Centre
180 High Street, Yelling, Cambridgeshire PE19 6SD
Tel: 01480 880232
hilltop.equestrian@ntlworld.com
www.hilltopec.co.uk

Grange Farm Equestrian Centre
Wittering Grange Cottage, Leicester Rd, Wansford, Peterborough PE8 6NR
Tel: 01780 782459

Hockley Green Riding Stables
Hockley Cl, Shudy Camps, Cambridge CB1 6RB
Tel: 01799 584289

Loves Enterprises Equestrian Centre & Riding School
Loves Land, Crowland Rd, Eye, Peterborough, Cambridgeshire PE6 7TT
Tel: 01733 222132

Lynch Farm Equestrian Club
Lynch Farm, Orton Wistow, Peterborough, Cambridgeshire PE2 6XA
Tel: 01733 234445

Manor Farm
Sawtry Way, Wyton, Huntingdon, Cambridgeshire PE28 2DY
Tel: 01480 498000

Monarch Farm Riding Stables
St. Francis Toft, The Green Hilton, Huntingdon, Cambridgeshire PE28 9NB
Tel: 01480 830426
emy2@dialstart.net

Moorfield Riding Centre
Moor Rd, Milking Nook, Peterborough, Cambridgeshire PE6 7PQ
Tel: 07710 660799

Ms Louise Gripton
Sponge Drove, Willingham, Cambridge, Cambridgeshire, CB24 5JN
Tel: 07787 561070

Northbrook Equestrian Centre
New Road, Offord Cluny, St. Neots, Cambridgeshire PE19 5RP
Tel: 01480 812654
northbrookec@gmail.com
www.northbrookequestriancentre.com

National Horse Racing Museum
Newmarket. See page 108. The story of the people and horses involved in racing from its Royal origins to Lester Piggott.

Martial Arts

Cambridge Academy of Martial Arts

The Sports Hall, St Bede's School, Coleridge Community College Gym, Netherhall School
Tel: 01223 565020
info @ cama.org.uk
www.cama.org.uk
7-13yrs Savate Tiger Cubs. Kickboxing and fighting arts from 14 years.

Cambridge Aiki Dojo

Wednesdays at Chesterton Sports Centre, Gilbert Rd, Cambridge CB4 3NY
cambridgeaikidojo@yahoo.co.uk
Tel: 07800 784 777 / 07845903451
hwww.cambridgeaikidojo.co.uk
From 7yrs upwards. Training in Aikido.

Cambridge & Impington Tang Soo Do Club

Mondays: Manor School, Arbury Road, Cambridge CB4 2TF
Thursdays: Mayfield School, Warwick Rd, Cambridge CB4 3HN
Tel: 01223 273983
Gymnasium, Sports Centre, Impington Village Collge, New Rd, Impington, CB24 9LX
ITel: 01354 692378.
www.cambstsd.co.uk
Juniors from 7years upwards

Cambridge Ki-Aikido Club

Chesterton Community College, Gilbert Rd, Cambridge CB4 3NY
kifed@hoardinghopes.com
Tel: 07790 613026
Mondays, over 5 yrs.

Cambridge Kung Fu Ltd

Various Cambridge venues including: Hills Road Sports Centre, Berwick Bridge Community Primary School, Netherhall Sports Centre, St. Matthews Primary School.
Tel: 01223 368229
www.cambridgekungfu.com
From 2yrs upwards, Mini Monkyes up to Junior Warriors (11yrs), Snow Leopards (young people with disabilities).

Cambridge Schools Of Tae Kwon Do

Tuesdays: Queen Emma Primary School, Gunhild Way, Cambridge CB1 8QY
Thursdays: Newnham Croft Primary School, Chedworth St, Cambridge CB3 9JF
Tel: 07963 473595
contact@cambs-tkd.co.uk
www.cambs-tkd.co.uk
7yrs upwards.

Carisma

Kelsey Kerridge, Queen Anne Terrace, Cambridge CB1 1NA
Manor Community College, Arbury Rd, Cambridge CB4 2JF
Tel: 01223 501493
www.carisma.org.uk
Kickboxing, Multicombat & Self defence Recommend upwards of 13 yrs and children taller than 4'6".

Comberton Judo Club

Comberton Leisure, West St, Comberton CB23 7DU
www.combertonjudo.org
For ages 7 yrs upwards.

Just Karate

Meadows Community Centre, 1 St Catharine's Rd, Cambridge CB4 3XJ
Tel: 07981 395258
info@justkarate.co.uk
www.justkarate.co.uk
Age 5 upwards at the Meadows Centre in Cambridge.

Pa Kua Martial Arts

Kelsey Kerridge, Queen Anne Terrace, Cambridge CB1 1NA
Tel: 0781 3486599
info@pakuauk.com
www.pakuauk.blogspot.ie
Over 7s. The classes are running in Cambridge & Ely, from Tuesday to Saturday.

Play Capoeira

Multi Arts Community Space, 47-51 Norfolk St, CB1 2LD
info@cambridge-capoeira.co.uk
www.capoeira-cambridge.co.uk
Kids class on Thursdays.

Pro Martial Arts Schools

Chesterton Sports Centre, Gilbert Road, Cambridge CB4 3NY
Tel: 07951 018002
www.promartialartsschools.com/.../Cambridge.
Aged 5-12yrs, kickboxing.

Seni Ki Ryu Martial Arts

Cambridge - Cottenham - St Ives - Bar Hill - Caldecote - Huntingdon
Tel: 01480 457398
www.skrmartialarts.com
Seni Ki Ryu Martial Arts is a hybrid style which means a 'composite or mixture of traditional martial arts styles' for kids, teens, and adults

Rugby

Cambridge Rugby Union Football Club

Volac Park, Grantchester Rd, Cambridge CB3 9ED
Clubhouse: 01223 312437.
www.crufc.co.uk
Sunday mornings, boys and girls 6-17yrs. Large club with split age groups and contacts for each, best to check website.

Little Scrummers Rugby Ltd

Netherhall Sports Centre, The Netherhall School Queen Edith Way, Cambridge CB1 8NN
Tel: 07738591232
mail@littlescrummers.com
www.littlescrummers.com
For boys and girls aged 2 years to 6 years.

Shelford Rugby Union Football Club

The Davey Field, Cambridge Rd, Great Shelford CB22 5JJ
Tel: 01223 843357
shelfordphysio@aol.com
www.shelfordrugby.co.uk
Has a youth section.

Tennis

Bar Hill Tennis Club
Tennis courts, Hanover Close off Viking Way, Bar Hill
www.barhilltennisclub.co.uk
Provides tennis facilities for the local community. Work and Rebound Techniques, and Trampolining (for ages 7-16 years).

Cambridge Lawn Tennis Club
Wilberforce Rd, Cambridge CB3 0EQ
Tel: 01223 312550
info@cambridgeltc.com
www.cambridgeltc.com
Competitive and social tennis. 7 artificial grasses, 3 hard, 6 grass courts, plus short tennis court practice wall, clubhouse, social area and shop. There is an extensive mini tennis programme. It is a community-based not-for-profit club

Fulbourn Tennis Club
Recreation Ground, Home End, Fulbourn, Cambridge CB21 5ER
info@fulbourntennis.co.uk
www.fulbourntennis.co.uk
4 all weather courts (2 floodlit). Small clubhouse shared with bowls club. Some coaching. Mon & Weds 6.00pm-8.00pm; Sats 2.00-6.00pm club sessions for full members.

Hills Road Sports and Tennis Centre
Purbeck Road, Cambridge CB2 8PF
Tel: 01223 500009
nmoss@hillsroad.ac.uk
www.hrsfc.ac.uk
For aged 4-18 yrs in its performance programme.

Mike's Tennis Academy
Cambridge, Ely, Barton and Cambridgeshire
20 Selwyn Road, Cambridge CB3 9EB
Text: 07702 291099
marketing@mik
www.mikestennis.com
Runs Tennis Camps from 4-17 yrs, coaching and club activities all year round.

Netherhall Tennis Club
Netherall Sports Centre, Queen Edith's Way, Cambridge
www.netherhallsports.com/clubs/netherhall-tennis-club
Training for kids from aged 6 yrs.

Free Outdoor Tennis Courts
Most managed by Cambridge City Council
Barnwell Tennis Court, CB5 8RQ
Cherry Hinton Hall Recreation Ground, CB1 3TH
Christ's Pieces Park, CB1 1LN
Coleridge Recreation Ground, CB1 3PN
Jesus Green, CB5 8AL
King George V Playing Fields, Trumpington, CB2 9JJ
Lammas Land Recreation Ground, CB2 7AD
Nightingale Avenue Recreation Ground, CB1 8SG
sessions for girls only (fees apply). Email to apply.

Water Sports

Cambridgeshire Canoeing Association
Tel: 01223 832128 (Evening Only)
An organisation set up to promote canoeing.

Cambridge Canoe Club
Tel: 01223 365425
committee@cambridgecanoeclub.org.uk
www.cambridgecanoeclub.org.uk
The Club caters for both the recreational and competitive paddler who wishes to take part in canoeing and kayaking in and around Cambridge.

Cam Sailing Club
Clayhythe Waterbeach, Cambridgeshire
Tel: 01223 440 462
lynne.easy@btinternet.com
www.cam.net.uk/home/sail
The Cam Sailing Club is a friendly, family club, but with a large racing programme.

Grafham Water Centre
Perry, Huntingdon, Cambridgeshire PE28 0BX
Tel: 0845 6346022
info@grafham-water-centre.co.uk
www.grafham-water-centre.co.uk
Activity centre, with courses in sailing, canoeing and windsurfing and more.

St Neots Canoe Club
The Priory, Priory Lane, St Neots PE19 2BH
Tel: 01480 472302
phil@gcmiles.freeserve.co.uk

Purvis Marine
Boatyard, Hartford Road, Huntingdon, Cambridgeshire, PE29 3RP
Tel: 01480 453628
purvismarine@yahoo.co.uk
Small motor boats can be hired by the hour or day from Purvis Marine.

Miscellaneous

Cambridge Community Circus
www.chaos.org.uk/ccc
Offers workshops for children aged 7 and over, such as beginners juggling.

Cambridge Floorball Club
Chesterton Sports & Leisure, Cambridge
info@cambridge-floorball.org.uk
www.cambridge-floorball.org.uk
Floorball, also know as unihockey, innebandy, salibandy, is a fast paced indoor game played with plastic sticks a light airflow ball. For children (5-13) on Sunday afternoons.

Comberton Village College Squash Club
West Street, Comberton, CB23 7DU
Tel: 01223 264149
join@combertonsquash.com
www.combertonsquash.com
Free Saturday morning junior sessions, for mini-squash (primary school children) and graded sessions for secondary school children. Also sessions for girls only (fees apply). Email to apply.

Comberton Netball Club
Comberton Specialist Sports College (part of Comberton Village College) West Street, Comberton, CB3 7DU
www.comberton-netball.co.uk
info@comberton-netball.co.uk
Netball for girls and ladies from the age of 11. No upper age limit.

Cottenham Roller Skating Club
Cottenham Sports Centre, High Street, Cottenham, Cambridgeshire CB24 8UA
sportscentre@cvcweb.net
www.sports.cvcweb.net
Tel: 01954 288760
Roller skating session for beginners and improvers skates available for hire.

SWIMMING & SPORT

Kartsport
The Depot, Royston Road, Cambridgeshire CB23 3PN Tel: 01954 719 192 (near Caxton)
www.gokartingcambridge.co.uk
Has a Cadet School for ages 8-16 yrs to learn go-kart racing, racing lines, overtaking etc.

Netherhall Archers
Netherhall School, Queen Edith's Way, Cambridge CB1 8NN
www.netherhall-archers.org
beginners@netherhall-archers.org
Beginners course run approx 3 times a

year in Autumn, Spring & Summer. To go on the waiting list for the next course please use email above.You must confirm your place with the club prior to the course starting – numbers are strictly limited.

Planet Ice (Ice Skating) - Peterborough
1 Mallard Road, Peterborough PE3 8YN
pet.boxoffice@planet-ice.co.uk
www.planet-ice.co.uk/arena/peterborough
pet.boxoffice@planet-ice.co.uk
Tel: 01733 260 222
Popular ice skating rink. It has parent and toddler sessions (18months to 5 years) on Sunday 10-11am. Also Planet Ice Shows, Learn to Skate Programme (6 weeks, £60) including toddlers.

Mission Impossible 7
The Netherhall School Sports Centre, Queen Edith Way, Cambridge CB1 8NN
Toni.Race@cdnl.org
11-15yrs train 5-6pm Mondays. Email to book. People of all netballing abilities are welcome.

Team Cambridge Cycling Club
www.cambridgecc.org.uk
The club has a juvenile/junior section. The club has a fully qualified BCCS coach who advises on all aspects of training for racing & assists

newcomers to the sport in getting started. To join complete online form.

Yoga for babies and children

Baby Yoga
Tel: 01223 479658
Sally@joyfulbabies.co.uk
www.joyfulbabies.co.uk
Yoga and relaxation for baby and mother.

Camyoga
Camyoga South Studios, Chaston House, 1 Mill Court, Great Shelford, Cambridge CB22 5LD
Central Studios, Thomas House, 14 George IV St, Cambridge CB2 1HH
Tel: 01223 847930
info@camyoga.co.uk
www.camyoga.co.uk
Adult Yoga but also recently started Yoga for kids aged 8-15yrs, Pregnancy Yoga and Baby Yoga for parents and babies.

YogaBugs
Ross Street Community Centre, 75 Ross Street, Cambridge CB1 3UZ
www.thehealing-house.com
christine@healing-house.com
Yoga classes: for pregnancy birth preparation workshops baby yoga postnatal yoga yoga bears for mums and toddlers yoga for children aged 3 - 7yrs.

Babies & Toddlers

Family fitness
Parkside Swimming Pool, Gonville Pl, Cambridge CB1 1LY
www.cleversteps.co.uk
Tel: 07728832961
Hello@cleversteps.co.uk
Creative education classes for parents to exercise with their children. Thursday mornings: separate age groups classes for kids, toddlers and babies (crawling upwards). £6 -8 per session.

Little Gym
Units 1-3 Chesterton Mill, French's Rd, Cambridge CB4 3NP
Tel: 01223 324 554
cambridge@thelittlegym.co.uk
www.thelittlegym.co.uk/cambridge
Non-competitive, progressive approach to motor skill development for 4 months to 12 yrs.

TigerTots Baby & Preschool Gymnastics
The Fulbourn Centre, Home End, Fulbourn, Cambridge CB21 5BS
Tel: 07775 853123
tigertots@ntlworld.com
www.tigertots.co.uk

Suitable for babies as young as 8 weeks, preschool gymnastics is a foundation for children's natural physical development.

Youth Disability Sports

Football

Downs Syndrome and CP (Cerebral Palsy) Football - Cambridge
Impington Sports Centre, New Road, Impington, Cambridgeshire CB24 9LX
www.cpfootball.co.uk/cambridge
Set up to provide opportunities to play football, in inclusive mainstream settings, or pan-disability or those specific to children with ambulant cerebral palsy. Saturday morning sessions, 11am-12noon, £2 for ages 6-11yrs.

Histon Hornets
ollie.waterson@gmail.com

Netherton United
kered56@aol.com

St Ives Rangers

roger.bates50@ntlworld.com
Clubs have the opportunity to play in the Cambridgeshire Ability Counts League.

General Sports

Ability Plus Group - Cambridge & Peterborough

rebecca.gilbertson@livingsport.co.uk
www.abilityplusgroup.co.uk
Living Sport, the Cambridgeshire and Peterborough Sports Partnership works with the 'Ability PLUS Group' promoting sport and physical activity for people with disabilities or additional needs.

Act 4 Kidz - Ely

S Club, Paradise Centre, Newnham street, Ely CB74P
Various locations around Ely.
www.act4kidz.com

This is an enthusiastic voluntary group that aims to offer children and young people with special needs, aged 3 – 19 years living in Cambridgeshire, access to exciting sport and social activities.

English Federation of Disability Sport - National

Tel: 01509 227750
federation@efds.co.uk
www.efds.co.uk
National body and charity dedicated to disabled people in sport throughout England.

Sports Zone - Cambridge

Cherry Hinton Village Centre, Colville Road, Cherry Hinton, Cambridge
www.cambridge.gov.uk
These multi sports sessions are run on the fourth Sunday of every month from 1pm - 3pm (some months the date may vary). They are for 5 - 18 year olds with a disability.

Specific Sports

Barton Group Riding for the Disabled

South Cambs Equestrian Centre, Foxton Road, Barrington CB22 7RN
jTel: Mrs Jo Cowland 01223 871061 (Evening)
ocowland@hotmail.com
A riding school which offers support for children and young people with spe-

cial needs, disabled people and people with a learning disability.

Blind & Visually Impaired Tennis

Hills Road Sports & Tennis Centre
Steve Morley, Sports Development Team at Cambridge City
Steve.morley@cambridge.gov.uk
www.cambridge.gov.uk
The game is played with a larger than normal sponge ball that contains small bells and the rackets have shorter handles and larger hitting areas. Tuesday from 12 – 2pm

Goalball

Steve Morley, SportsDevelopment Officer on 01223 457000
Steve.Morley@cambridge.gov.uk
www.goalballuk.com
Goalball is a sport that was devised as a rehabilitation programme for visually impaired World War II veterans. It is the only team sport played at the Paralympics by the visually impaired but is a totally inclusive sport since all participants wear blindfolds. Friday at the Frank Lee Centre at Addenbrookes.

Hereward Heat Wheelchair Basketball Club

Cambridge Regional College and Comberton Village College
Tel: 01354 695560
sspilkawba@aol.com
Hereward Heat WBC runs a wheelchair basketball junior section the "Hotshot Wheelies". For ages 10 to 16.

Snow Leopards - Cambridge

Tel: 01223 368229.
www.cambridgekungfu.com/kids/snowleopards
A Kung Fu class for children and young people with physical and/or learning disabilities. Saturdays at Netherhall Sports Centre, Cambridge 2.30pm – 3.30pm.

Swimming, Fishing and Water Sports

Cambridge Disabled Kids Swimming Club

Sally Abbott on 01223 315024
syabbott@bigfoot.com
www.cdksc.co.uk
The swimming club is aimed at children of any age from birth to 19 with any

disability. As far as possible, sessions are run by a qualified instructor with several volunteers.
Family Fun Session
Venue: Abbey Leisure Centre
Day: Saturdays. **Time:** 4.30pm – 6pm
Age range: Approx 0 – 8 years
Swimming instruction for improvers / older children
Venue: Chesterton Sports Centre, Gilbert Road, Cambridge
Day: Sundays (term time only). **Time:** 4.30pm – 5.30pm
Age Range: 6 – 19 years
Family fun and water confidence in the hydrotherapy pool
Venue: Windmill Pool, Hinton Way, Fulbourn
Day: Saturday **Time:** 9.30am – 11am
Aimed at: Young children (under fives) plus those that need warmer water or a smaller, secure environment to swim.

Grafham Water Sailability

Grafham Water Centre, off Chichester Way, Perry PE28 0GW.
info@grafhamwatersailability.org.uk
www.grafhamwatersailability.org.uk
Grafham Water Sailability is a registered charity based at Grafham Water. It is run by disabled sailors and able-bodied helpers with the primary objective of enabling people with many types of disabilities to enjoy the fun of sailing – even if they've never been on the water before.

Paradise Pool Disability Swim Sessions - Ely

Paradise Pool, Newnham Street, Ely CB7 4PQ
Tel: 01353 665481
paradise.pool@harpersfitness.co.uk
The sessions are open to all people with disabilities and provide the opportunity for whole families to spend some recreational time together in a fun and relaxing environment

The Manderson Trust (Fishing)

themandersontrust@virginmedia.com
www.themandersontrust.co.uk
The Manderson Trust is a registered charity which provides a safe environment for disabled anglers. Parking close to where they choose to fish with toilet facilities (wheelchair access) and a centre providing light snacks, hot and cold drinks.

You may have a child who is keen on ballet or hip hop, a budding chef, guitar player or Picasso. Nurture their creative appetites with some of the local classes on offer. See also playgroups (page 173).

ART, MUSIC, DANCE & DRAMA

Art, Crafts and Cooking

Access Art
Grantchester Village Hall, Cambridge
Tel: 01223 262134
Drawings sessions for children aged 6-10.

Arty Crafts
10 Girton Rd Girton, Cambridge CB3 0LJ
Tel: 01223 277922
Tom@artycrafts.co.uk
artycrafts.co.uk
Art Holiday Workshops for children aged 5-12 in Cambridge. Typical cost £30/day.

Crafty Monkey - St. Neots
12 Moores Walk St Neots, PE19 1AG
Tel: 01480 219222
www.craftymonkeypotterypainting.com
Crafty Monkey Pottery painting and build a bear studio.

Fitzwilliam Museum Art Workshops
Trumpington St Cambridge CB2 1RB
Tel. 01223 332904
fitzmuseum-education@lists.cam.ac.uk
www.fitzmuseum.cam.ac.uk/dept/education
For families with children aged 2-12, art sessions at weekends and in school holidays Booking essential. Also 'Drop in and Draw'. On the first Saturday of each month visit the Fitz Family Welcome Point and collect drawing materials, activities and trails.

Kiddy Cook - Cambridge & Ely
Tel: 07867797831
Cambridge@kiddycook.co.uk
kiddycook.co.uk/cambridge
Cookie Tots and Kiddy Cook classes in Cambridge, Ely, Newmarket and the surrounding areas .Cookie Tot classes for 2-4 year olds, Kiddy Cook classes for 5-11 yrs.

Kids4Arts - Cottenham
Community Centre, Cottenham,CB24 8RZ
Tel: 01954 250466
sheeba3434@hotmail.com
kids4arts.yolasite.com
This runs groups for pre-school and primary school children which promote confidence and development

Sticky Kids
Ely Scout Hall, St John's Rd, Ely
Tel: 01353 650079
Messy play for 18 months to 4 years.

Scrapstore
Tel: 01223 457873
caroline.gill@cambridge.gov.uk
www.cambridge.gov.uk/ccm/content/community-and-living/children-and-young-people/scrapstore-events.en
Provides recycled materials for children and young people to use in art, craft and play activities. They also sell arts and crafts equipment at cost price.

Scribbles Ceramics - Newmarket
2 Park Lane, Newmarket, CB8 8AX
Tel: 01638 661 555
hello@studioscribbles.co.uk
Paint your own ceramic pottery. Parties and walk in painting.

Dance (& Ballet)

Colours of Dance Studio
Level 2, 182 Histon Road, Cambridge CB4 3JP
Tel: 01223 778268
www.coloursofdance.com
This has a studio in Cambridge, and offers dance from 2 years and upwards. For all ages and abilities, in ballet and modern dance. Also Mum & Toddler's classes. Additional casses in Great Wilbraham and Fulbourn.

Creative Movements
St Mary's Junior School,
6 Chaucer Rd, Cambridge CB2 7EB
Tel: 07837844759
Michelle@creativemovements.co.uk
www.creativemovements.co.uk
Toddler introduction to dance with storytelling.

Funky Footsteps
Level 2, 182 Histon Rd, Cambridge CB4 3JP
Tel: 01223 778268
Imogen@coloursofdance.com
www.coloursofdance.com

Toddlesr - half hour class of dancing and singing.

King Slocombe School of Dance
8 Emmanuel Road, Cambridge CB1 1JW
Tel: 01223 356023
Info@kingslocombe.com
www.kingslocombe.com

The oldest dance school in Cambridge. Classes at all levels from babies to professional in classical ballet. Also modern theatre, jazz, tap and contemporary.

Jandor School of Dancing
The Netherhall School & Sixth Form College, Queen Ediths Way, Cambridge CB1 8NN
www.jandor.co.uk

Monday and Tuesday evenings. Ballet, tap, modern and disco, jazz and gymnastics. Special tiny tots class for 2 years olds. Pupils prepared for grades & major examinations.

Pop Steps
Tel: 07933746995
Stardustdance@binternet.com
www.stardust-dance-and-fitness.co.uk

Suitable for boys and girls 5-9 yrs involve learning dance routines to favourite artists. Saturday 10.15-11am £3.50 per session. Held at Parkside Pool.

Pre School Dance Classes
St Marks Church Halls, 13 Barton Road, Newnham, Cambridge CB3 9JZ
Tel: 01223 564096
liz.anderson@ntlworld.com

Pre-school dancing classes for girls and boys. Ages 2 ¾ -4 ½ years. Wednesdays.

SIN Cru
Cambridge Combat & Fitness Centre, Harvest way, Cambridge CB1 2RA
sinstars@aol.com
Tel: 01223 403359
www.sincru.co.uk

SIN Cru is a collective of Bboys & Bgirls, DJs, MCs and Graffiti artists founded in 1995. Run several hip hop dance classes for different ages and levels during the week.

Stardust Dance and Fitness
Tel: 07933 746 995
stardustdance@btinternet.com
www.stardust-dance-and-fitness.co.uk

Offering both adult and children's classes in dance and fitness, including ballet, tap, modern, street dance, pop steps, ZumbAtomic (Zumba for kids).Venues: Parkside Pools; Arbury Community iCentre, Cambourne Sports Centre

Street Funk
Parkside Pools, Parkside, Cambridge
www.everyoneactive.com/Home/tabid/679
Tuesday 4-5pm for children aged 8-13 years. Based on street dance and hip hop. £3.15 per session.

Sylvia Armit School of Dance
Bourn, Haslingfield, Barton, Ely
Tel 01223 873 173
sylviaarmit@yahoo.co.uk
www.sylviaarmitschoolofdance.co.uk

A modern dance school located in East Anglia, UK. Classical Ballet and Russian, Tap Dance , Repertoire, Historical Dance and National Dance.

Splitz Theatre Arts
Fulbourn Centre and Bewick Bridge Primary School, Cherry Hinton, Cambridge
Tel: 01223 880389
www.splitz-ta.net/25

Classical ballet, funky jazz, hip-hop, English and American tap dance, and dance gymnastics. Also a theatre school.

The Jill Bridger School of Dance
Tel: 01480 469711
jillB999@aol.com
www.danceschool.biz

Classes in ballet, modern and tap in Cambridge and villages nearby. Fom aged 18 months to 18 years. Daytime 'Melody Movement' pre-school classes are held at St Ives, the Hub, Cambourne and Abbey Meadows Primary School, Cambridge. After school lessons at St Ives, Hardwick and Cambourne. Saturday classes at Abbey Meadows Primary School in Cambridge. New classes starting at the Histon and Impington Recreation Centre.

Ballet

Chesterton Ballet School
St George's Church Hall, Chesterfield Road, Cambridge
www.chestertonballetschool.co.uk
Tel: 01223 366588
chestertonballetschool@hotmail.com

Classes in Russian Classical Ballet, established in 1974. Various classes from Beginners 3 & 4 years old to Senior Pupils aged 16 years.

Dedikated
Queen Edith Primary School, Cambridge CB1 8QP
Tel: 01223 292562
www.dedikated.biz

A ballet school which runs Royal Academy of Dance ballet classes for children aged 3 years and upwards.

Eden Dance
Chesterton Sports Centre. Gilbert Road, Cambridge CB4 3NY
Tel: 01223 650861
info@edendance.co.uk
edendance.co.uk

Ballet and Tap dance for children, juniors and teens from 3 years plus.

The Russian Ballet School
YMCA Dance Studio, Gonville Place/The Salvation Army Community Centre 104 Mill Road, Cambridge and elsewhere
Tel: 01223 473402
www.therussianballetschool.co.uk

Ballet instruction (Russian style) for pupils from baby beginners age 5 upwards to advanced. National dance included. Performances and exams.

Stardust Children's Ballet
Parkside Pool, Cambridge
Tel: 07933746995
Stardustdance@binternet.com
www.stardust-dance-and-fitness.co.uk

Mini ballet (3-5yrs) and Primary ballet (5-7 yrs) on Saturday mornings, £3.50 per session at Parkside Pool.

Dance and Ballet in Other Areas
Octagon Studios - Ely
28D High St, Town Centre, Ely CB7 4JU
Tel: 01353 661919
info@octagonstudios.co.uk
www.octagonstudios.co.uk

A performing arts centre, a privately–owned business with a range of classes for all levels and ages. lasses in Ballet, Contemporary Dance, Jazz Dance and Tap.

Rosewood Dance Academy
Tel: 01353 720179
info@rosewooddanceacademy.co.uk

ARTS & MUSIC

www.rosewooddanceacademy.co.uk
Ballet, Modern Theatre and Jazz dance classes in Ely, Newmarket, Haddenham, Little Thetford, Waterbeach, Soham, Littleport.

The Studio - CT

Covering Cambridgeshire, Hertfordshire and Suffolk
www.thestudio-ct.co.uk
Offering street, freestyle, jazz, ballroom and latin amercian dancing. Competition level training. Children 3 - 17years. Classes in Foxton Primary School, CB2 6RN, see website.

The Jill Bridger School of Dance

St Ives, Hardwick and Cambourne. **See page 158**

The Lane Academy - Cambridge, Ely

Sutton, Sawton, Little Downham, Linton, Great Shelford, Ely.
Cambridge - St Faiths School, Milton Primary School.
Tel: Vanessa on 07590 109578, Sarah on 07903 210498
laneacademy@btconnect.com
www.laneacademy.co.uk
For ages 3 to 16. Pop and Jazz Street Dance Classes and Musiclal Theatre.

The Samara Ballet School - Burwell

35 High Street, Burwell CB25 0HD
Tel: 01638 744119
info@samaraballet.co.uk
www.samaraballet.co.uk
For the areas of East Cambridgeshire and West Norfolk. It provides ballet and tap classes, and also classes for preschool children.

Wendy Burke School of Dance - Huntingdon

Huntingdon Dancentre,
10 Orchard Lane, Huntingdon
Tel: 01480 434625
wendy.burke@hotmail.co.uk
www.dance4it.com
Based in the centre of Huntingdon, the School offers Ballet classes following the Royal Academy of Dance syllabus and Tap, Modern and Jazz, following the Imperial Society of Teachers of Dance Syllabus.

Drama

Bedazzle Theatre Arts

Meadows Community Centre, 1 St. Catharines Road, Cambridge CB4 3XJ
www.bedazzlearts.com
Singing, dancing, acting and arts and crafts courses for children, young people and adults with learning disabilities. Three hour weekly project driven courses. Stage shows.

Bodywork Company Dance Studio

25-29 Glisson Road, Cambridge CB1 2HA
Tel: 01223 314461
www.bodywork-dance.co.uk
For ages 3 to 18 to dance, drama, musical theatre and singing. This also houses Cambridge Performing Arts, a three-year performing arts course and a one year foundation course.

Stagecoach

Coleridge Community College, Radegund Road, Cambridge CB1 3RJ
Tel: 01223 359974
www.stagecoach.co.uk
This is a national performing arts network. Stagecoach Cambridge runs drama classes, dance classes and singing classes for 4-18 year olds.

Razzamataz Theatre Schools

CRC Sports Centre, Kings Hedges Road, Cambridge CB4 2QT
Tel: 01223 480025
cambridge@razzamataz.co.uk
www.razzamataz.co.uk
Courses from 4 years upwards. Dance, drama and singing together with opportunities to perform.

Theatretrain - Cambridge & Huntingdon

admin@theatretrain.co.uk
theatretrain.co.uk
In different venues around Cambridge, East and North, Bishops Stortford and Huntingdon, see website for details. Professional training in the performing arts for young people aged 6-18 years. Regular productions.

Helen O'Grady Theatre Company

Tel: 01462 713406
cambs-herts@helenogrady.co.uk
www.helenogrady.co.uk
Drama classes for 5 to 15 year olds. Multiple venues in the Cambridge area,

CAMBRIDGE & SURROUNDING AREAS

including Cambourne, Comberton, Milton, Linton and Queen Edith Primary School, Cambridge.

Splitz Theatre Arts

Fulbourn Centre and Bewick Bridge Primary School, Cherry Hinton, Cambridge
Tel: 01223 880389
www.splitz-ta.net/25
Classical ballet, funky jazz, hip-hop, English and American tap dance, and dance gymnastics. Also a theatre school.

Music

Cambridge
Arthur Bear's Music Time

Chesterton Methodist Church, Green End Road, Cambridge CB4 1RW
Tel: 01223514725
charshie21@hotmail.com
A fun and stimulating music session for babies and toddlers.

Baby Music & Cafe

St Thomas Hall, Ancaster Way, Cambridge CB1 3TT
Tel@ 07772286547
Kirstenpercival@gmail.com
Babymusiccambridge.co.uk
Music for babies, drop in sessions.

Baby Melody

The Friends Meeting House, Hartington Grove, Cambridge CB1 7UB
Tel: 01223 410896
Veronica.julian@ntlworld.com
0-1yr music sessions.

Cambridge Suzuki Young Musicians

info@suzukipianocambridge.org.uk
Offers a combination of Suzuki piano and Kodaly musicianship to children aged 3-18. Zero to four year olds, and 2.5 to 4 year programme.

Cambridge Youth Music

enquiries@cambridgeyouthmusic.org.uk
www.cambridgeyouthmusic.org.uk
This is a Charitable Trust launched in May 2005 by a group of local musicians and parents. It organises the Cambridge Young Musician of the Year and the Cambridge Young Composer of the Year competitions providing a platform for talented young musicians and composers in Cambridgeshire.

Music Shops

Millers Music Centre & Ken Stevens

12 Sussex Street, Cambridge CB1 1PW.
Tel: 01223 354452
webhelp@millersmusic.co.uk
www.millersmusic.co.uk

Miller's Music is one of the longest established companies in Britain and is believed to be the second oldest music shop in the country.

Cambridge Strings

72 King Street, Cambridge CB1 1LN
Tel: 01223 323388
sales@cambridgestrings.co.uk
www.cambridgestrings.co.uk

Cambridge Pianoforte

10-12 Kings Hedges Road, Cambridge CB4 2PA
Tel: 01223 424007
info@cambridgemusic.net
www.cambridgemusic.net

Wood, Wind and Reed

106 Russell Street, Cambridge CB2 1HU
Tel: 01223 500442
shop@wwr.co.uk
www.wwr.co.uk

Cambridgeshire Music

cm@cambridgeshire.gov.uk
www.cambridgeshiremusic.org

Schools throughout the county use Cambridgeshire Music to provide lessons in school. It's an initiative

from Cambridgeshire County Counciil. To request lessons, book an instrument or a taster session, register on the website or email (above). It is possible to have lessons out of school time at one of the area music academies across the county.

Cambridgeshire County Youth Orchestra

For children who have reached Grade 6/7 or above. Also **Cambridgeshire Youth Wind Orchestra** for children who have reached Grade 5 or above.

Take it Away Scheme

www.takeitaway.org.uk

Interest free loans for the purchase of musical instruments, supported by the Arts Council England. Applicants need to be either 18-25 or an adult applying for a child under 18. All applicants also need to be a UK resident and working at least 16 hours per week to be eligible. Visit one of the member music stores and mention scheme or on mail order (check website).

Cambridge Summer Music Festival

contact@cambridgesummermusic.com
www.cambridgesummermusic.com

An annual classical music festival that also has 'Music for Kids' - a programme for families.

Choosing Music Teachers

It can be difficult trying to choose a teacher, and many parents go through personal recommendations. Individual music teachers are not listed in this book, but can be found by searching websites, local adverts and directories. Cambridgeshire has a high number of qualified musicians offering individual lessons. But how do you choose with confidence?

There are a few websites that list teachers, with information on whether they belong to a musicians union, or are CRB checked and their training and memberships. You would have to verify these details yourself.

www.musicteachers.co.uk - useful section 'Guidelines for Choosing a Teacher in Safety and Confidence'. It advises to never leave your child with a relative stranger unless you are absolutely certain that this is an appropriate arrangement. If in any doubt, sit in on the lessons.

www.firsttutors.com/uk - this charges a small fee, and has a good search facility including area, instrument and level.

Kindermusik - Cambridge
Tel: 07895092505
Info: musicwithannari.co.uk
www.musicwithannari.co.uk
Newborn to 7 years dance and music.

Melody Makers
Bakehouse, next to Trumpington Church, Cambridge CB2 9LH
www.trumpingtonchurch.org.uk/melodymakers
This is a music group for babies and toddlers in the Trumpington/Newnham area.Wed mornings, costs £3 per family.

Music to Grow to - Cambridge & Ely
Cambridge Central Library & Ely
Tel: 01353 662022
www.musictogrowto.co.uk
Classes held in Ely and Cambridge. On Friday at Cambridge Library, and Monday and Thursday in Ely. Weekly music classes from birth up to school age.

Music for Little People
Buckden, Cambridge, Cambourne, Peterborough
Tel: 01480 812469
Karen@mflp.co.uk
www.musicforlittlepeople.co.uk
Classes for under 5s.

Rat-a-tat! Music Group for babies and toddlers
Old Vestry, St. Augustine's Church, Richmond Rd, Cambridge on Mondays & Baptist Church, Girton on Tuesdays.
info@ratatatmusic.co.uk
www.ratatatmusic.co.uk
A small, relaxed drop-in music group for 0-3 year-olds. Tea, coffee and snacks are provided at the end. Mondays 10am-11am £3.50 per family.

Rock College
Mullet Boy Studios, 20, Mercers Row, Cambridge CB5 8HY
Tel: 07835 610699
info@rockcollege.co.uk
www.rockcollege.co.uk
Rock College is for 8 year old upwards. Opportunity to learn how to put together a band to write, rehearse, record and rock out live shows.

Saturday Morning Community Music School
Perse Senior School, Union Road, Cambridge CB2 1HF

ew@perse.cambs.sch.uk
stephenperse.com/community/community-music-school
Individual lessons and music workshops for kids aged 7 - 18. Early Years Music Classes for children up to the age of 7.

Sing and Swing
St. Luke's Church, Cambridge
www.singandswing.co.uk
At Sing and Swing children learn through Dalcroze Eurythmics. Tuesdays, St Luke's Church, Cambridge Reception – Year 2 age. Cost £6.

Stringmoves
St John's College School, 63 Grange Road, Cambridge.
stringmoves@gmail.com
www.stringmoves.org
Dalcroze Eurhythmics and the opportunity to learn a stringed instrument within a whole musical experience, generally starting at age 5 or 6. Violin, viola and cello teaching, and general musicianship training, music theory and choir. Sat am.

Surrounding Area
Music For Little People! - St. Neots
Buckden, St Neots PE19 5TS
Tel: 01480 812469
www.musicforlittlepeople.co.uk
Music For Little People music classes for babies and children are for 0 to 5 years.

Sine Nomine
Histon Baptist Church, Histon.
www.sinenominechoir.co.uk
A choir for boys and girls aged 10 to 17. Monday evenings.

Swavesey Music School
Tel: 01954 230366.
acaldwell@swaveseyvc.co.uk
www.swaveseyms.co.uk
It is open to all children aged between 3 – 18 years and takes place every Saturday during term-time.

What age should my child start more formal music lessons?
There is no set age for lessons to start, and different teaching methods advise different ages. A good time is when a child is able to concentrate for longer periods, and shows an interest in playing an instrument. As a rough guide, 5-6 years earliest for piano and violin, 7 for guitar, 8/9 years for drums and wind instruments.

Music and a Child's Brain
Musicians have been shown to have significantly more developed left planum temporales, and have also shown to have a greater word memory. Musicians have larger brain volumes in brain areas which may cross over to speech areas.

Journal Nature Reviews Neuroscience 11, 599-605 (2010)

McMaster University have discovered that one-year-old babies who participate in interactive music classes with their parents smile more, communicate better and show earlier and more sophisticated brain responses to music.

Gerry et al (2012) Development Science; Vol 15, Issue 3; p398-407 May

Children with Special Needs

If you have a child with special needs, many of the activities and places listed in this book have provisions to enable your child to attend the centre or activity. It was worth checking out their websites or contacting them in advance.

There are also some local organisations that are specifically geared up to children or young people with special needs. Some of these are listed here. There is also a section in the chapter on Sports.

Activities

Disabled Children's Database (SCIP)
www.cambridgeshire.gov.uk/childrenandfamilies/specialneedsdisabilities/supportforsend/disabledchildrensdatabase/
Information on activities, support and events in Cambridgeshire, if you register on the SCIP database. It has useful publications on activities in the Cambridge, Fenland and Huntingdon area as well as Disability Sport.

Art and Music

ArtWorks - Cambridge
Head of Community Services, Cambridgeshire Mencap, Edmund House, 9 Church Lane, Fulbourn, Cambridge CB21 5EP
Tel: 01223 883130
info@cambridgeshiremencap.co.uk
www.cambridgeshiremencap.co.uk
ArtWorks is an arts based group and offers people with learning disability a chance to explore all aspects of creative work. Monday to Friday (10am to 3pm) and take place in Cambridge and March.

Lantern Dance Theatre Company - Ely
www.lanterndancetheatre.org.uk

Tel: 01353 662441
helenpettit@excite.comLantern
This is an award winning integrated contemporary dance company based in Ely. About half the members of the company have a disability.

The Junction - Total Arts - Cambridge
Venue: The Junction, Clifton Way, Cambridge CB1 7GX
www.junction.co.uk
This group runs term time on a fortnightly basis on Saturdays 11am – 3pm for 11-19 years.

The Music Box - Cambridge
The Music Box, 321, High Street, Cottenham, Cambridge CB24 8TX
Music and art for children with Autism, Learning Disabilities and other Special Needs, also one to one sessions.

Clubs and Support

Action for Children – Inclusion Project
Contact Centre on 0345 045 5203.
The Inclusion Project supports disabled children and young people aged 0-19 years to attend inclusive activities close to where they live. It is the child or young person who chooses which activity they would like to attend. However, Action for Children can provide guidance and suggestions if required.

Cambridge Down's Syndrome Baby and Toddler Group
Roz Brown on 07415 036099
dsbabytoddler@gmail.com
www.cambridgeshiremencap.co.uk/what-we-do/children.asp
The group meets on the first Saturday of every month (except January and August) from 10.30am -12.30pm at the Little Footsteps children's centre in Caldecote.

Cambridge Kids club @ Queen Ediths
Tel: 07960 412716
Info@cambridgekidsclub.com
www.cambridgekidsclub.com/queen-edith
Breakfast, after school and holiday care for children 4 to 14 years.

CHILDREN WITH SPECIAL NEEDS

CamPlay - Cambridgeshire
www.cambridgeshire.gov.uk/short-breaks
Contact Centre on 0345 045 5203
CamPlay provides two services: Holiday Clubs and Saturday Clubs. These are for disabled children and young people aged 6 - 19 years, with a moderate or severe physical or learning disability. The services are provided by Cambridgeshire County Council and are registered with Ofsted.

The **Holiday Clubs** run in Huntingdon, Ely, Wisbech, St. Neots and March in the summer holidays from 10am to 4pm. During Easter they run from venues in Wisbech, Ely, St Neots and Huntingdon. In the Christmas holidays they also run from a venue in East Cambs and Fenland and a venue in Huntingdonshire. If you have a Social Worker please speak to them requesting the CamPlay service. If you do not have a Social Worker then please call the Contact Centre on 0345 045 5203.

Cam Sight - Cambridge
North Cambridge Children's Centre, Campkin Road, Cambridge CB4 2DL
Tel: 01223 420033 info@camsight.org.uk
Runs a group for pre-school children with a visual impairment and their siblings. Every other Tuesday during term time from 10am – 12pm.

Crossroads Saturday/Sunshine Club – Cambridge
Venue: Castle School, Courtney Way, Cambridge CB4 2EE
Contact: Anna Bainbridge
Tel: 0845 241 0954 or 01480 499090
www.crossroadscarecambridgeshire.org.uk
This group runs fortnightly on Saturday mornings for groups 8 – 14 and 15 – 19 years. The Sunshine club for 5-11 years is for children with Autism.

Crossroads St Neots Community Group
Venue: The sessions are held at various locations across Huntingdonshire.
Contact: Anna Bainbridge

CHILDREN WITH SPECIAL NEEDS

Tel: 0845 241 0954 or 01480 499090
www.crossroadscarecambridgeshire.org.uk
This group runs fortnightly on Saturday.

Early Support - Helping every child succeed - Cambridgeshire

www.ncb.org.uk/earlysupport
www.cambridgeshire.gov.uk/childrenandfamilies/specialneedsdisabilities/earlyyears/earlysupport
Early Support is a way of working, that aims to improve the delivery of services for children 0-5 years who are disabled or have complex additional needs and their families.

Impington Opportunity Playgroup

Venue: The groups are meeting at a temporary venue – please contact: Sally Abbott. Tel: 01223 315024
syabbott@bigfoot.com
members.lycos.co.uk/iopg/
This is a pre-school playgroup for any children with special needs and their families. Monday and Friday afternoons 1 – 3pm during school term time.

Papworth Trust - Cambridgeshire

Tel: 07764 273326
www.papworth.org.uk/youthclub
Run youth groups in Huntingdon, Bury, March, Ely and Wisbech. These groups run term time only 7 – 9pm on different days throughout the week for 12-19 years.

Scope Saturday Club - Royston

Venue: Meldreth Manor, Fenny lane, Meldreth, Royston SG8 6LG
Contact: Grace Fordham
Tel: 01763 268111.
www.scope.org.uk
This group is run by Scope and takes place once a month 10.30am – 4pm for 8-19 yrs

Sense - Cambridge Resource Centre

Cambridge Resource Centre, The Coirnfield Suite, Glebe Farm, Knapwell CB3 8GG
Tel: 01954 267056
www.sense.org.uk
Sense provides support to children who have a dual sensory impairment or a single sensory impairment with additional needs.

Sensing Fun - Ely

Ely Children's Centre, High Barns, Ely CB7 4RB.

Pippa on 01353 611594
elychildrenscentre@cambridgeshire.gov.uk
A group for children under the age of five with special educational needs and their families, fortnightly 1pm - 2.30pm. 2nd and 4th Friday of the month.

Advocacy

Adders - National

www.adders.org
A national website with information on support on Attention Deficit Disorder.

ADDISS - National

Middlesex HA8 7BJ
Tel: 020 8952 2800 info@addiss.co.uk
www.addiss.co.uk
This is the national **A**ttention **D**eficit **D**isorder **I**nformation and **S**upport **S**ervice.

Cambridgeshire Deaf Association

8 Romsey Terrace, Cambridge CB1 3NH
Tel: 01223 246237(voice)
office@cambsdeaf.org www.cambsdeaf.org
This is a county-wide organisation, which acts as a focal point for the area's deaf community. It organises drop-ins in Fenland and Peterborough, a lunch-time club in Cambridge and deaf/hearing clubs in Cambridge and Huntingdon. CDA also run sign language classes to level 1 and 2.

Cambridge/Huntingdon Deaf Children's Society

Contact: Justin Lewis on 01223 300 361
cambridgeandhuntingdon@ndcsgroup.org.uk
Run by volunteer parents from all over Cambridgeshire with lots of experience in
bringing up children with different degrees of deafness. It meets on the 2nd Saturday of the month (except for August), usually in Hinchingbrooke Park, Huntingdon from 10am - 12.30pm.

Cambridge Dyslexia Association (CDA)

Tel: 0845 251 9002
news@cambsdyslexia.org.uk
www.cambsdyslexia.org.uk
The CDA is a registered charity set up to meet the needs of children and adults affected by dyslexia.

Speaking Up - Cambridge

Mount Pleasant House, Mount Pleasant, Cambridge CB3 0RN
Tel: 01223 555800
Advocacy Partners Speaking Up (APSU) provides advocacy, courses, participation projects and resources for people with learning disabilities, mental health issues and physical disabilities together with advocacy for carers.

The Dyspraxia Foundation - National

Office, 8 West Alley, Hitchin, Hertfordshire SG5 1EG
Tel: 01462 454986
dyspraxia@dyspraxiafoundation.org.uk
www.dyspraxiafoundation.org.uk
A countrywide charity for Dyspraxia, a developmental co-ordination disorder.

The National Autistic Society Cambridge Branch

National telephone helpline: 0845 070 4004 - 10am - 4pm
www.autism.org.uk
The National Autistic Society (NAS) champions the rights and interests of all people with autism.

Schools and Education

In most cases, children with special educational needs attend mainstream schools, however for those with more complex needs a special school may be offered. In Cambridgeshire there are six area and three county-wide special schools. There are also Independent special schools.

Admission to special school

www.cambridgeshire.gov.uk/childrenandfamilies/specialneedsdisabilities/schoolagespecial/applyforaschoolplace/admissiontospecialschool.htm

Spelling Success

Spelling Success, 3, Sudeley Grove, Hardwick, Cambs CB23 7XS
Tel: 01954 210762
www.spellingsuccess.co.uk
Tuition for Dyslexia and anyone who has difficulties spelling or reading, for all ages.

Ten Things to do Outside Before You're Ten

1. Play 'Pooh' sticks, like Pooh Bear, race sticks from a bridge.

2. Roll down a hill. If you can find one!

3. Find a minibeast with a magnifying glass and find out what it is.

4. Skim a stone across a lake.

5. Splash about in the rain, in a puddle, in wellington boots.

6. Fly a kite. There aren't many hills around Cambridgeshire but there are plenty of windy days. Try Coldhams Common or the Gog Magog hills. In Newmarket try the gallops or in Royston the Heath.

7. Go sledging and/or build a snowman in the snow.

8. Learn to ride a bike.

9. Kick around in autumn leaves.

10. Plant something, grow it, eat it! (Make sure it's edible!)

Growing potatoes

There are a wide range of childcare providers in Cambridge and the surrounding area. You may want to talk to other parents, check reports on Ofsted and visit a few before making your choice.

Nannies provide care in your own home, childminders in their own home. Childminders are registered with Ofsted, nannies do not, at present have to be registered. An au pair is a cultural exchange programme where young people abroad can live with you and learn about the UK in exchange for light household duties.

If you have a pre-school toddler, local playgroups are a good way to meet other parents and provide kids with a child friendly environment outside of home. There are also Children's Centres which provide support and advice for parents of 0-5yrs in certain areas.

Children from households receiving particular benefits may be entitled to some free childcare from two years old. All three and four year olds become eligible for free early learning places from the school term after their third birthday. This is 15 free hours per week over 38 weeks.

Cambridgeshire County Council has information on choosing childcare and a useful childcare directory.
www.cambridgeshire.gov.uk/childrenandfamilies/familyinformation

You may be eligible for Tax Credits, which help meet the cost of childcare if you qualify. The two information sites below can give more advice.
GOV.UK
www.gov.uk/browse/benefits/tax-credits
Citizens Advice Cambridge
www.cambridgecab.org.uk

Children's Centres in Cambridge

childrenscentres@cambridgeshire.gov.uk.
www.cambridgeshirechildrenscentres.org.uk
Sure Start is a Government project to help give children a good start in life. It has funded Children's Centre's which are open to parents and carers of children from 0-5 years. They vary but usually offer support, advice and activities for chldren such as drop-in sessions. Many of the services are free.

ArC Children's Centre
82 Akeman Street, Cambridge, CB4 3HG
Tel: 01223 703828
joanna.maxwell@cambridgeshire.gov.uk

Bottisham/Burwell/Chevely Children's Centre
Bottisham Village College, Bottisham, CB25 9DL Tel: 01223 507152
mary.barnes@cambridgeshire.gov.uk

Cambourne Children's Centre
Sackville House, Cambourne, CB23 6HL
Tel: 01954 284672
linda.henderson@cambridgeshire.gov.uk

Cherry Hinton Children's Centre
Bridge Community Primary School, Fulbourn Old Drift, Cambridge, CB1 9ND
Tel: 01223 712082
helen.freeman@cambridgeshire.gov.uk
Bumps to babies group for new borns up to 18 months.

PLAYGROUPS, CHILDCARE & SCHOOLS
IN CAMBRIDGE

'Stay and play' for toddlers every Friday.

Chesterton Children's Centre
Shirley Primary School , Nuffield Road, Cambridge CB4 1TF
Tel: 01223 729081

Conkers Children's Centre
Linton Library, Linton, CB21 4JT
Tel: 01223 893594
theresa.bateman@cambridgeshire.gov.uk

Dolphin Children's Centre
Waterbeach Community Primary School, Waterbeach, CB25 9JU
Tel: 01223 472791
kath.doyle@cambridgeshire.gov.uk

Fawcett Children's Centre
Fawcett Primary School, Alpha Terrace, Cambridge CB2 9FS
Tel: 01223 840258
cwilkinson@fawcett.cambs.sch.uk

Homerton Children's Centre
Holbrook Road, Cambridge, CB1 7ST
Tel: 01223 508766
head@homerton.cambs.sch.uk
For the families of Trumpington, Newnham and Hauxton.
Baby massage with a trained instructor for parents and babies up to crawling. Messy play is a group for children under 5. Sat Dads is a supportive group for children under 6 and their dads or male carers.

Histon Children's Centre
Histon Early Years Centre, New School Road, Histon, Cambridgeshire, CB24 9LL
Tel: 01223 712075 head@histon.cambs.sch.uk

Little Footsteps Children's Centre
Caldecote Primary School, Caldecote, CB23 7NX Tel: 01954 214444
linda.henderson@cambridgeshire.gov.uk

North Cambridge Children's Centre
Colleges Nursery and Family Centre, Cambridge , CB4 2LD
Tel: 01223 712172
joanne.maxwell@cambridgeshire.gov.uk

Romsey Children's Centre
Romsey Mill, Hemingford Road, Cambridge, Cambridgeshire, CB1 3BZ
Tel: 01223 566102
Rachel.Benntt@romseymill.org

Ofsted

www.ofsted.gov.uk

Ofsted is the Office for Standards in Education, Children's Services and Skills. It inspects and regulates services which care for children, such as child minders, nurseries and schools. You can find an inspection report by looking on their website.

You may also want to look at the history of providers who previously operated from the same site. These closed providers may or may not have a relationship with the current provision in terms of management or ownership. Providers cannot start caring for children until they have a certificate of registration.

The Young Parents Programme offers tailored ante- and post-natal support to young mothers and fathers (usually under-21). Playgroup on Mon/Wed/Fri Pre-school group. Toddler group for under 5's Weds 10.00am-11.30

Seedlings Children's Centre
Bellbird Primary School, Link Road, Sawston, CB22 3GB
Tel: 01223 706373
theresa.bateman@cambridgeshire.gov.uk

Starship Children's Centre
Barhill Primary School, Gladeside, Bar Hill, Cambridge, CB23 8DY
Tel: 01954 200473
Kath.doyle@cambridgeshire.gov.uk
Bar Hill and the surrounding villages Boxworth, Dry Drayton, Lolworth, Longstanton, Swavesey, Willingham, and Over.

The Fields Children's Centre
The Fields Early Years Centre, Galfrid Road, Cambridge, Cambridgeshire, CB5 8ND
Tel: 01223 518333
head@thefields.cambs.sch.uk
Play session for children 0-4 years.

Au Pairs

The au pair programme is a cultural exchange where a person from abroad is expected to be welcomed as a member your family and be given their own room. Traditionally, an au pair would be 18 to 27 years old, and can be on duty from 25-35 hours per week. The au pair would be given an allowance, minimum £75 per week.

There is an expectation that the au pair would attend language lessons and time off. This is in addition to light housework and helping with children and they are not permitted to have continuous sole charge of children under 2. The British Au Pair Agencies Association provides guidelines for employing au pairs. www.bapaa.org.uk

Childminders

They are self-employed childcare professionals who work from their own home. They care for smaller numbers, and it is more 'home from home'. Childminders who look after children under eight years for more than two hours a day have to be registered with Ofsted and hold a certificate. A list of registered childminders is available on the their website. The Family Information Directory from Cambridgeshire County Council also has a list of registered childminders:

Childcare Information Team
Tel: 0345 0454014
www.familiesandchildcare.org.uk

Professional Association for Childcare and Early Years (PACEY)
PO Box 209, Royston, Herts SG8 0AN

Tel: 01223 207984
Deborah.Townsend@pacey.org.uk
www.pacey.org.uk
Formerly known as The National
Childminding Association (NCMA))
PACEY provides information to help
find childcare.

Nannies

Nannies are employed by parents to
work in the child's own home. The
child can form a close relationship and
siblings can be looked after together.
Nannies can be flexible, possibly
offering evening babysitting and you
don't have to travel to the childcare
setting.

However, unlike childminders nannies
do not need to be registered by
Ofsted or have specific training. There
are national websites which list
individual nannies, or nanny agencies,
the local ones are listed below.

Gingham Kids Nanny Agency
Rose Cottage, Haverhill Rd, Horseheath
Cambridgeshire CB21 4QR
Tel: 01223 650980
info@ginghamkids.co.uk
www.ginghamkids.co.uk

Tinies Childcare (Cambridgeshire)
3-5 Free Church Passage, St Ives
Cambridgeshire PE27 5AY
Tel: 01480 300908
cambs@tinies.com
www.tinies.com

Playgroups

Pre-school playgroup are generally less
formal than nurseries and open for a
few hours a day rather than full time.
Usually the parent is expected to stay
with their child. It is a good
opportunity to meet other local
parents. There are groups listed in the
Ofsted and Cambridgeshire County
Council website. There are more
playgroups run by your local
Children's Centre so it is also worth
getting in touch with them if they are
near you.

North Cambridge

Arbury Community Centre Toddler Group
Tel: 01223 504406

Bar Hill Parent and Toddler Group
Octagon Centre, Bar Hill Church Centre,
Hanover Close, Bar Hill, Cambridge, CB23
8EH
Tel: 01954 200473
0-4yrs. Wed & Fri 9:45 to 11:15

Bobtails Baby and Toddler Group
Girton Pavilion, Cambridge Road CB3 0FH
Girton.bobtails@gmail.com
0-School age children.

Ladybird Play and Toddler Group
The Salvation Army Hall, Impington Lane,
Cambridge CB24 9LT
Tel: 07786 752949
www.ladybirdplaygroup.org

Little Learners Playgroup
Brownsfield Community Centre, 31a, Green
End Road, Cambs, CB4 1RU
Tel: 07808 520576

Pavilion Playgroup
Thorndown School, St Ives
Tel: 01480 462741
www.pavilionplaygroup.co.uk
Pre school and play sessions.

St Andrew's Stepping Stones
St Andrew's Church Hall Histon, School Hill,
Histon, Cambs, CB24 9JE
www.standrewssteppingstones.co.uk
Playgroup for 26 children. Mon, Wed,
Thur 9.15am-12.15. Toddler group
Tues & Fri 9.30 - 11.30. Baby Club
Tues 10.30 - 12:00. £1.

See-Saw Playgroup
East Barnwell Community Centre, Newmarket
Road, Cambridge
Tel: 01223 294736

Swaffham Prior Baby & Toddler Group
Swaffham Prior Village Hall, High Street,
Swaffham Prior Cambridgeshire CB25 0LD
Tel: 07920867209
kmart1103@hotmail.com
www.facebook.com/SwaffhamPriorPlaygroup

East Cambridge

Bumps to Babies
Cherry Hinton Children's Centre, Bewick
Bridge Community Primary School,
Teversham, Cambridge CB1 9ND
Tel: 01223 712082
Tues - 10-11.30am for those expecting
up to 18 months.

Clown Around Playgroup
St Thomas's Hall, Ancaster Way,
Cambridge, CB1 3TT
0-5yrs. Tues 9.30 to 11.30. £1.50 for
Parent/carer and child (50p for
additional child).

Little Bunnies Toddler Group
St Andrew's Church, Cherry Hinton
Tel: 01223 712082

Saplings Pre-School Playgroup
The Playhut, Beechwood Avenue, Bottisham,
Cambs, CB25 9BE
Tel: 01223 813226
2-5yrs.Mon-Fri 9.15-11.45and 13.15-
15.15 when demand allows.

Teversham Playgroup
Teversham C of E Primary School, Church
Road, Teversham, Cambridge CB1 9AZ
Tel: 01223 293357

South Cambridge

Jigsaw Playgroup - Sawston
The Bellbird Primary School, Link Road,
Sawston,Cambs, CB22 3GB
Tel: 07842 537473
2-5yrs Mon to Wed 9:00-11.30and 12.30
til 15:00 Thur & Fri 9:00-11.30 with an
optional lunchclub until 13:00

Messy Play - Cambridge & Sawston
Fawcett Primary School,
Cherry Hinton or Sawston
rhardy@fawcett.cambs.sch.uk
Tues Cambridge and Fri Sawston.

Trumpington Toddlers
Trumpington Meadows/Fawcett Primary
School, Trumpington, Cambridge CB2 9FS
Tel: 01223 840258
0-4yrs Fri 9.30-11.30 term time only.

Trumpington Pavilion
Paget Road , Trumpington, Cambridge CB2
9JF
Tel. 01223 847433
www.trumpingtonresidentsassociation.org/Pav
ilion

Family Café: 2nd and 4th Friday afternoons. Mums and Little Ones: Thursdays 9.30-11.30am Soft Play: Every 2nd and 4th Saturday mornings

West Cambridge

Baby and Me
The Hub, Great Cambourne, CB23 6ES
www.babyandme.org.uk
Free for parents/carers and babies 0-2years.

Peacehaven International Playgroup
Cambourne Community Centre, High St, Great Cambourne, CB23 6GW
Tel: 01954 710510
Weekly Wednesday after school art club/playgroup. £1.

Central Cambridge

Chatter Tots St Luke's Church
Victoria Road, Cambridge CB4 3DZ
Sharon.wilson@cambridgeshire.gov.uk
Weds 9.30-11am term time, story telling and book borrowing.

City Bus Babies & Toddlers Group
City Church Cambridge, Cheddars Lane, Cambridge CB5 8LD
Lclay@citychurchcambridge.org.uk
Weds 10-11.30am term time. £1.

Jumbo Toy Library Under 5's Playgroup
St Lukes Barn, Frenchs Road, Cambridge CB4 3JZ
Tel: 07939222774
sbailey@sjcs.co.uk
www.jumbotoylibrary.org.uk

Let's Play Toddler Group
St Paul's Centre, Hills Road, Cambridge
Tel: 01223 576899

Little Voices & Sticky Fingers
Mill Road Baptist Church, Mill Rd, Cambridge CB1 3LP
Tel: 01223 566102
Tues 2-3.30pm for 12 months plus. Fridays 10.30-12pm term time (booking essential).

Play and Learn at Brooklands Avenue
Cambridge & County Bowling Club, Brooklands Avenue, Cambridge CB2 8FG
Hprice@homerton.cambs.sch.uk
Weds 10-11.30am for under 5s.

Romsey Mill Toddler Group
Romsey Mill Centre, Cambridge
Tel: 01223 566102
0-3 years.

St Georges Prampushers
St. Georges Church, St. Georges Church Hall, Chesterfield Road, Cambridge, CB4 1LN
Tel: 01223 424043
Thurs 10.00-11.30 term time only.

Toddle-Along
St John The Evangelist Church, Hills Road, Cambridge, Cambs, CB2 8RN
Mon 10:00-11.30 - Toddle-Along - toddler service in the church followed by snacks, craft activities and singing.

Activity playgroups for pre schoolers

123 Soleil
Mill Road Baptist Church, 178, Mill Road, Cambridge CB1 3LP
123soleil.cambridge@gmail.com
0-5yrs. This group aims to maintain French culture and language amongst French speaking families.

Arthur Bear's Music Time
Chesterton Methodist Church
Tel: 01223 514725
Music sessions for babies and toddlers, nursery rhymes and games, Monday am.

Baby Massage - Homerton' Children's Centre
Holbrook Rd, Cambridge CB1 7ST
Hprice@homerton.cambs.sch.uk
Weds 1.15-2.45pm term time.

Baby Sensory
Cambridge - Ross Street Community Centre, Trumpington - Trumpington Village Hall
Tel: -7966 789785
Cambridge@babysensory.co.uk
There are different sensory activities designed to support a baby's sensory development every week.

Kids4Arts - Cottenham
Cottenham Community Centre and Cottenham Primary School
www.kids4arts.yolasite.com
Over 3s arts sessions for primary and preschool.

Little Quavers Music Group
Johnson Hall, Mingle Lane, Stapleford, Cambs, CB22 5SY
Jcairndugg@hotmail.co.uk
Singing, rhymes and movement. 0-4yrs

Melody Makers - Trumpington
The Bakehouse, next to Trumpington church, CB2 9LH
childrensworker@trumpingtonchurch.org.uk
Weds 9.30-10.30 term time. Music for babies and toddlers.

Monkey Music
Tel: 01353 668622
Catherine.clough@monkeymusic.co.uk
Monkeymusic.co.uk
Music classes 3 months to 4 yrs.

Music Time!
Arbury Community Centre, Campkin Road, Cambridge, CB4 2LD
Tel: 01223 524813
www.puladowns.com
Specialist Music Classes for babies and toddlers in 10 week sessions.

Semillitas (Spanish Speaking)
Ross Street Community Centre, Ross Street, Cambridge CB1 3UZ
Tel: 01223 503385 (Eva)

Sign and Rhyme
Fawcett Primary School, Alpha Terrace, Cambridge CB2 9FS
rhardy@fawcett.cambs.sch.uk
Drop in group; for children aged 0-3 years, nursery rhymes and songs using makaton signs.

Sing and Sign - Bar Hill, Trumpington and Histon
Tel: 07732 380191
Singandsigncambridge@yahoo.com
www.singandsign.com/classes/classes-near-you/cambridge

TinyTalk Baby Signing - Cambridge, Sawston
Mayfield Primary School or Sawston Free Church.
Tel: 0769 575680
Freyar@tinytalk.co.uk
www.tinytalk.co.uk/freyar
Communicate in sign before they can talk. Classes for 0-18 month olds. Thurs 10:45-11:45am. Cambridge.

Preschool Playgroups

Pre-schools provide play sessions for a few hours per week for children between 2 and 5 years usually, term time only. Hours are often 9am until lunchtime, or lunchtime to 3pm, depending on the school.

Coton Pre-School
The Mobile,, Coton School, Whitwell Way, Coton, Cambridge CB23 7PW
Tel: 07534 873649.
www.cotonpreschool.org.uk
2 years 6 months - 4 years 10 months.

Fulbourn Pre-School
Fulbourn Primary School, School Lane, Fulbourn,
Cambridge CB21 5BH
Tel: 07852 770796
fulbourn.preschool@googlemail.com
www.fulbournpreschool.btck.co.uk

Hardwick Pre-School
Hardwick Community Primary School, Limes Road, Hardwick, Cambridge, Cambs,
Tel: 01954 212823
www.hardwick-preschool.btck.co.uk

Hauxton Pre-School
Hauxton Primary School Site, Jopling Way, Hauxton, Cambridge CB22 5HY
Tel: 01223 870919
www.hauxtonpreschool.org.uk

Kings Hedges Primary School Nursery
Kings Hedges Primary School, Northfields Avenue, Cambridge CB4 2HU
Tel: 01223 518330

Little Warblers Pre-School
Great Wilbraham Primary School, Church Street, Great Wilbraham, Cambridge CB21 5JQ
Tel: 07546 535075
littlewarblers.gtwilbraham.net

Milton Cygnets Pre-School
Milton Community Centre, Coles Road, Milton,
Cambridge CB24 6BL
Tel: 01223862323
milton.cygnets@gmail.com
www.cygnets.org.uk

Newnham Nursery
Newnham Croft Primary School, Chedworth Street, Cambridge CB3 9JF
Tel: 01223 311437

Playlanders Playgroup & Pre-School
St George's Church Hall, Chesterfield Road, off Milton Rd, Cambridge CB4 1LN
Tel: 01223 420 954
playlanders@btinternet.com
www.playlanders.org.uk

Rainbow Pre-School
Great & Little Shelford School, Church Street, Great Shelford, Cambs CB22 5EL
Tel: 07985 216603
www.shelfordschool.org.uk/index.php/extended-services/rainbow-pre-school.

Sunnyside Pre-School Playgroup
Stapleford Community Primary School, Bar Lane,
Stapleford, Cambridge CB22 5BJ
Tel: 07804 041173
gill_sunnyside@hotmail.co.uk

Under Fives Roundabout - Toddlers & Preschool
Mayfield Primary School Hall, Warwick Road, Cambridge CB4 3HN
Tel: 01223 309066

Day Nurseries

These are childcare services which usually offer full-time care, usually from 8am to 6pm, for children from 3 months to 5 years. They usually operate all year round. Most offer the free early education places that are avvailable to all 3 and 4 year olds, and from September 2013, some two year olds. They are registered with OFSTED and you can find reports on their website.

Abacus Day Nursery
The Old Church Hall, Green End Rd, Cambridge CB4 1RW
Tel: 01223 576733
www.abacusdaynurseryltd.co.uk

ACE Day Nursery (1-3yr)
6A Priory Road, Cambridge CB5 8HT
Tel: 01223 366355
ace_daynursery@tiscali.co.uk
www.ace-nursery-school.org.uk

ACE Nursery School (2-5yr) Cambridge
37 Parkside, Cambridge CB1 1JE
Tel: 01223 357181
ace_nursery@tiscali.co.uk
www.ace-nursery-school.org.uk

Baby Unicorns
Sancton Wood School, 1-2 St. Pauls Road, Cambridge CB1 2EZ
Tel: 01223 471729

Brunswick Nursery School
Young Street, Cambridge CB1 2LZ
Tel: 01223 50870

Bumble Bears Pre-School Nursery
United Reformed Church, Cherry Hinton Road,
Cambridge CB1 7AJ
Tel: 0771 3209491

Buttercups Little Kindergarten
Cambridge Steiner School, Hinton Road, Fulbourn, Cambridge CB21 5DZ

Butterfly Day Nursery
27a Elizabeth Way, Cambridge CB4 1DD
Tel: 01223 358117
www.butterflydaynursery.co.uk
18 months to 5 years.

Cambridge Day Nursery
67a Milton Road, Cambridge, CB4 1XA
Tel: 01223 566323
www.cambridgedaynursery.co.uk

City Kids Playcentre
30 Union Road, CambridgeCB2 1HE
Tel: 01223 460486

Cambridge Kidsclub@ Queen Edith's
Queen Edith Cp School, Godwin Way, Cambridge CB1 8QP
Tel: 07960 412716

Colleges Nursery School & Family Centre
Campkin Road, Cambridge CB4 2LD
Tel: 01223 712168
Nursery school provision for 3-4 yr olds 9am-3.30pm term time only. Childcare
provision for 2-4 yr olds. Open 8.00am-6.00pm, 48 weeks per year.

Domino Nursery School
United Reform Church, Home End, Fulbourn, Cambridge CB21 5BS
Tel: 07769 625599

Edwinstowe Day Nursery (University Employees Only)
Edwinstowe Close, off Chaucer Road, Cambridge CB2 7EB
Tel: 01223 353068

Harvey Road Day Nursery
9-10 Harvey Road, Cambridge CB1 2ET
Tel: 01223 363860
www.harveyroaddaynursery.org.uk

Home From Home
Ross Street Community Centre, 75 Ross Street,
Cambridge CB1 3UZ

Joint Colleges Day Nursery
6B Chaucer Road, Cambridge CB2 7EB
1223 315084
www.jcn.org.uk
Day nursery for 57 children aged 3
months to 5 years. Mon-Fri 8.30am-
5.30pm.

Kidsunlimited Nurseries - Cambridge Science Park
319 Cambridge Science Park, Milton Road,
Cambridge CB4 0WG
www.kidsunlimited.co.uk/nurseries

Kidsunlimited Nurseries - Bunnybrookes
1st Floor, Frank Lee Centre, Addenbrookes
Hospital, Hills Road, Cambridge CB2 0QQ
www.kidsunlimited.co.uk/nurseries

Kidsunlimited Long Road
Robinson Way, Cambridge CB2 0SZ
Tel: 0845 365 2981
www.kidsunlimited.co.uk/nurseries

King Street Pre-School
Wesley Methodist Church, King Street,
Cambridge CB1 1LG
Tel: 07742 376299
www.kinstreetpreschool.org.uk

Koala - Kidz Old Butter Nursery School
16, High Street, Cambridge CB4 5ES
Tel: 01954 260046

Little Cherries
Cherry Hinton
Tel: 07725 951619
Info@littlecherries.org.uk
Littlecherries.org.uk

Millington Road Nursery School
4a Millington Road, Cambridge CB3 9HP
Tel: 01223 356565
www.millingtonroadnursery.co.uk
Over 2 years. Open 8.45am-4.30pm
plus early and late clubs. Term time
only.

Mulberry Montessori School
Royston Lane, Cambridge
Tel: 01223 263646
harltonmontessori@yahoo.co.uk
mulberrymontessori.tumblr.com

Newnham Nursery
c/o Newnham Croft Primary School,
Chedworth Street, Cambridge CB3 9JF
Tel: 01223 311437
Office@newnhamnursery.co.uk
www.newnhamnursery.co.uk

Pat-A-Cake Day Nursery
Sedley Court Office, Malta Rd, Cambridge
Cockcroft Hall, Cockcroft Place, Clarkson
Road, Cambridge CB3 0HF
Tel: 01223 411636
www.pata-cake.co.uk

Rainbow Day Nursery
Former Village School, Granchester Road,
Trumpington, Cambridge CB2 9LH
Tel: 01223 847444
Melissa@rainbowdaynursery.org
www.rainbowdaynursery.org

Rosebridge Steiner Kindergarten
Cambridge Steiner School, Hinton Road,
Fulbourn, Cambridge CB21 5DZ
Tel: 01223 3516756
3 Steiner Kindergartens for ages 3-6
years.

Smiths Children Montessori St Luke's Church
St Luke's Church (United Reformed with
Church of England), Victoria Road,
Cambridge CB4 3DZ
Admissions@smithschildren.co.uk
www.smithschldren.co.uk

Snap! 4 Kids Ltd
The Church Hall, 6A, Chapel Street,
Cambridge CB4 1DY
www.snap4kids.co.uk
3 months to 5 years old.

Sunflower Nursery
2A Stretten Avenue, Cambridge
Tel: 01223 578608

The Red House Day Nursery
90, High St, Cambridge CB25 0HD
Tel: 01638 741174

The Sunshine Club
Castle School, Courtney Way,
Cambridge CB4 2EE
Tel: 01223 718202

Under Fives Roundabout
Warwick Road, Cambridge, CB4 3HN
Tel: 01223 309066

West Cambridge Day Nursery
The University Nursery, 8 Charles Babbage
Road, Cambridge CB3 0FZ
Tel: 01223 464227

Holiday Play Schemes and After School

Arty Crafts Workshop Playscheme
The Scout Centre, Chedworth Street,
Cambridge CB3 9JF
Tel: 07980 146382
www.artycrafts.co.uk

Cambridge Kids club @ Queen Edith's
Queen Edith County Primary School, Godwin
Way, Cambridge, Cambs, CB1 8QP
Tel: 07960 412716
An after-school and school holiday
club set in Queen Edith's Primary
School. Open 3pm to 6pm term-time
and 7.45am to 6pm in the school
holidays.

Kidscape Out Of School Club
Milton Road Primary School, Ascham Road,
Cambridge, Cambridgeshire, CB4 2BD
Tel: 01223 713095

Kids R Us
St. Matthews School & Milton Community
Centre
Tel: 07920 046787
After school and holiday playscheme.
Term time 3.15pm-6.00pm. Holidays
8.00am-18.00.

Limetrees After School Club
Fulbourn CP School, School Lane, Fulbourn,
Cambridge, Cambridgeshire, CB21 5BH
Tel: 07702 949350

Super Camps
Perse Preparatory School, Trumpington Road,
Cambridge
Tel: 01235 832222,
info@supercamps..uk
www.supercamps.co.uk

TJ Kids
Ross Street Community Centre, 75 Ross Street,
Cambridge CB1 3UZ
Tel: 07787 425799
Provides out of school provision for local
schools.

Nurseries Outside Cambridge

Abington Pre-School
Great Abington Primary School, 68 High Street, Gt Abington, Cambridge
www.preschoolplaymates.com/AbingtonSchool

Babraham Nursery
17/18 The Close, Babraham, Cambridge
www.thenursery.babraham.org.uk

Beach Babies Ltd
82 Green End, Landbeach, Cambridge CB25 9FD
www.beachbabiesnursery.co.uk

Comberton Playgroup
Green End, Comberton, Cambridge
www.combertonplaygroup.co.uk

First Steps Day Nursery
31 Church Street, Great Wilbraham, Cambridge CB21 5JQ
Tel: 01223 655525
www.firststepsdaynursery.org

Happy Bunnies Nursery School
The Village Hall, 63 High Street, Barrington, Cambridge
www.happybunniesnursery.co.uk

Koala Kidz Ltd
Stanton Farm Day Nursery, Ely Road, Waterbeach Cambridgeshire, CB25 9NN
Tel: 01223 860263

Little Hands Day Nursery
Newton Hall, 1 Town Street, Newton, Cambridge
www.littlehands.co.uk

Little Hands Nursery School - Linton and Bartlow
Unit 5 Three Hills Farm, Bartlow, Cambridge
www.littlehands.co.uk

Little Hands Nursery School Bourn
Bourn Village Hall, Short Street, Bourn, Cambs
www.littlehands.co.uk/bourn

Little Legs of Lode Montessori Inspired Nursery
Fassage Hall, Station Road, Recreation Ground, Lode, Cambridgeshire CB25 9HB

Little Owls
Histon Early Years Centre, New School Road, Histon, Cambridge
www.histon.cambs.sch.uk

Mad Hatters Wrap Around Care
St Andrews Church Halls, School Hill, Histon, Cambridge CB24 9JE

The Old Buttery Nursery School
16 High Street, Willingham, Cambs
The Phoenix School Cambridge (Nursery, Pre-Prep & Prep)
Church Street, Willingham, Cambs
www.thephoenixschool.co.uk

The Red House Day Nursery
90 High Street, Burwell, Cambridge
www.redhousedaynursery.co.uk

The Wendy House Day Nursery Impington Ltd
Manor Farm, Milton Road, Impington, Cambridge CB24 9NG

Sawston Nursery
Sawston Nursery, Tannery Road, Cambridge
www.sawstonnursery.org

Scallywags Day Nursery (Girton)
48 Cambridge Road, Girton, Cambridge
Tel: 01223 277400
office@scallywagsdaynursery.com
www.scallywagsdaynursery.com

Scallywags Day Nursery (Oakington)
Westwick Hall Farm, Westwick, Oakington, Cambridge CB24 3AR
Tel: 01223 232400
office@scallywagsdaynursery.com
www.scallywagsdaynursery.com
3 months-5 years. Rural setting, with farm animals, lots of outdoor play space.

Snap! 4 Kids Ltd (SNAP! 4 Kids)
33 High Street, Hauxton, Cambridge CB2 5HW
Tel: 01223 870966
www.snap4kids.co.uk/snap_hauxton

Stanton Farm Day Nursery
Stanton Farm, Ely Road, Waterbeach, Cambs
Sunflower @ Cambourne
2 High Street, Great Cambourne, Cambs

Care of Children With Disabilities

You may need more tailored care for your child. Childminders and nannies have the advantage of being more flexible and home-based. Day Nurseries can also offer specialised care. It may be worth investigating a variety of options and talking to local support groups to find the best care for your child. You may need to work closely with your childcare provider to help them to understand your individual child's specific needs.

University of Cambridge Nurseries

The University has two workplace nurseries, the University Nursery at Edwinstowe Close and the University Nursery at West Cambridge. Students only can access the West Cambridge nursery. College staff and visiting fellows need to check the website for eligibility. These nurseries are not available for people outside of the college. There are long waiting lists for both nurseries.

The University's Childcare Information Adviser is available to help all students and staff with children with child-related matters. www.cam.ac.uk/cambuniv/childcare

Universities' Holiday Playscheme
Tel: 01223 764186
playscheme@admin.cam.ac.uk
www.admin.cam.ac.uk/univ/childcare/playscheme
Yellow Team - Fawcett Primary School, Alpha Terrace, Trumpington, CB2 9FS
Red Team- Chesterton Community College, Gilbert Road, Cambridge, CB4 3NY
This is a joint operation between the University of Cambridge and Anglia Ruskin University. For children aged rising 5 to 15 years in the state school holiday periods. You need to register for the playscheme on an annual basis. For children of the Universities staff and students, but members of the public are eligible to register if spaces are available.

Anglia Ruskin University Nursery

Cambridge Campus, East Road, Cambridge CB1 1PT
www.anglia.ac.uk/ruskin/en/home/student_essentials/childcare
For students and staff of Anglia Ruskin University.

SCHOOLS & EDUCATION

State Schools

State schools are free for children from the September after their fourth birthday. The school year begins in September and is divided into Autumn, Spring and Summer Terms. Apply for a place at the County Council. Primary education is for ages 4 to 11 years, Secondary education is for 11 to 16 yrs. Further education is provided in Sixth Form Colleges and Further Education Colleges.

Cambridgeshire County Council Admissions Team

Cambridgeshire County Council Box CC 1206, Castle Court, Castle Hill, Cambridge CB3 0AP
Tel: 01223 699200
Admissions@cambridgeshire.gov.uk
www.cambridgeshire.gov.uk/admissions

Primary Schools

Abbey Meadows Primary School
Galfrid Road, Cambridge CB5 8N
Tel: 01223 508611

Arbury Primary School
Carlton Way, Cambridge CB4 2DE
Tel: 01223 359568

Bewick Bridge Primary School
Fulbourn Old Drift, Cherry Hinton,
Cambridge CB1 9ND
Tel: 01223 508772
(formerly Cherry Hinton Community Junior School)

Colville Primary School
Colville Road, Cherry Hinton, Cambridge CB1 9EJ
Tel: 01223 576246

Fawcett Primary School
Alpha Terrace, Trumpington, Cambridge CB2 9FS
Tel: 01223 840258

Grove Primary School
Campkin Road, Cambridge CB4 2NB
Tel: 01223 577017

King's Hedges Primary School
Northfield Avenue, Cambridge CB4 2HU
Tel: 01223 518330

Mayfield Primary School
Warwick Road, Cambridge CB4 3HN
Tel: 01223 712127

Milton Road Primary School
Ascham Road, Cambridge CB4 2BD
Tel: 01223 712333

Morley Memorial Primary School
Blinco Grove, Cambridge CB1 7TX
Tel: 01223 508786

Newnham Croft Primary School
Chedworth Street, Cambridge CB3 9JF
Tel: 01223 508737

Orchard Park Primary School
Ring Fort Road, Cambridge CB4 2GR
Tel: 01223 438200

Park Street C of E Primary School
Lower Park Street, Cambridge CB5 8AR
Tel: 01223 576922

Queen Edith Primary School
Godwin Way, Cambridge CB1 8QP
Tel: 01223 712200

Queen Emma Primary School
Gunhild Way, Cambridge CB1 8QY
Tel: 01223 714300

Ridgefield Primary School
Radegund Road, Cambridge CB1 3RJ
Tel: 01223 712418

Shirley Community Nursery and Primary School
Nuffield Road, Cambridge CB4 1TF
Tel: 01223 712252

The Spinney Primary School
Hayster Drive, Cherry Hinton, Cambridge CB1 9PB
Tel: 01223 568836

St Alban's RC Primary School
Lensfield Road, Cambridge CB2 1LS
Tel: 01223 712148

St Laurence RC Primary School
Arbury Road, Cambridge CB4 2JX
Tel: 01223 712227

St Luke's C of E Primary School
French's Road, Cambridge CB4 3JZ
Tel: 01223 566879

St Matthew's Primary School
19 Norfolk Street, Cambridge CB1 2LD
Tel: 01223 568838

St Paul's C of E Primary School
Coronation Street, Cambridge CB2 1HJ
Tel: 01223 568840

St Philip's C of E Primary School
2 Vinery Way, Cambridge CB1 3DR
Tel: 01223 508707

Trumpington Meadows Primary School

Secondary Schools

Chesterton Community College Academy
Gilbert Road, Cambridge CB4 3NY www.chestoncc.org.uk
Tel: 01223 712150

The Manor
Arbury Road, Cambridge CB4 2JF
Tel: 01223 508742
www.manor-college.org.uk

The Netherhall School
Queen Edith's Way, Cambridge CB1 8NN
Tel: 01223 242931
www.netherhall.cambs.sch.uk

The Parkside Federation: Coleridge Community College
Radegund Road, Cambridge CB1 3RJ
Tel: 01223 712300
www.parksidefederation.org.uk

The Parkside Federation: Parkside Community College
Parkside, Cambridge CB1 1EH
Tel: 01223 712600
www.parksidefederation.org.uk

St Bede's Inter Church School
Birdwood Road, Cambridge CB1 3TD
Tel: 01223 568816
www.st-bedes.org.uk

Further Education Colleges

Cambridge Regional College
Kings Hedges Road, Cambridge CB4 2QT
Tel: 01223 418200
www.camre.ac.uk

Huntingdonshire Regional College
California Road, Huntingdon PE29 1BL
Tel: 01480 379106
www.huntingdon.ac.uk

The College of West Anglia
Campuses in King's Lynn, Isle, Downham Market, Cambridge
Tel: 01223 860701
www.cwa.ac.uk

Peterborough Regional College
Park Crescent, Peterborough PE1 4DZ
Tel: 0845 8728722
www.peterborough.ac.uk

University Technical College, Cambridge
c/o Cambridge Regional College, Kings Hedges Road, Cambridge CB4 2QT
Tel 01223 418502
utccambridge.co.uk

Sixth Form Colleges

Long Road Sixth Form College
Long Road, Cambridge CB2 8PX
Tel: 01223 507400
www.longroad.ac.uk

Hills Road Sixth Form College
Hills Road, Cambridge CB2 8PE.
Tel: 01223 247251
www.hillsroad.ac.uk

Independent Schools

St John's College School
Tel: 01223 353 652
www.sjcs.co.uk

St Faith's School
Tel: 01223 352 073
www.stfaiths.com

The Perse School
Hills Road, Cambridge CB2 8QF
Tel: 01223 403 800
www.perse.co.uk
This is a large and well established independent school with good facilities.

Perse School For Girls
Tel: 01223 454 700
www.spfschools.com

St Mary's School
Bateman Street, Cambridge CB2 1LY
Tel: 01223 353 253
www.stmaryscambridge.co.uk
St Mary's is a Catholic day and boarding school for girls aged 4-18.

Sancton Wood
St Pauls Road, Cambridge CB1 2EZ
www.sanctonwood.co.uk
A small, family orientated school, founded on the principle of small class sizes. For children aged 4 to 16.

The Leys
Cambridge CB2 7AD.
Tel: 01223 508900
www.theleys.cambs.sch.uk
Founded in 1875, and situated on a leafy 50 acre site, The Leys is an independent, co-educational boarding and day school for 11-18 year olds in Cambridge.

King's College School
West Road, Cambridge CB3 9DN
Tel: 01223 365 814
www.kcs.cambs.sch.uk
More than 400 boys and girls aged 4 - 13

The Perse Pelican School;
92 Glebe Road, Cambridge CB1 7TD
Tel: 01223 403940
www.perse.co.uk/pelican
Nursery and Pre-Preparatory School for children aged 3 to 7.

Madingley Pre-Preparatory School
Cambridge Road, Madingley, Cambridge CB23 8AH
Tel: 01954 210309
www.madingleyschool.co.uk
In the village of Madingley 3 miles from the centre of Cambridge for children aged 3 to 7.

Heritage school
19 Brookside, Cambridge CB2 1JE
Tel: 01223 350615
www.heritageschool.org.uk
This is a new and thriving co-educational, independ-ent day school with a Christian foundation.

The Steiner school
Hinton Road, Fulbourn, Cambridge CB21 5DZ
Tel: 01223 882 727
www.cambridge-steiner-school.co.uk
An independent school just outside Cambridge and is part of the worldwide network of Steiner Waldorf schools for ages 3 to 11 with a strong ethos promoting a lifelong love of learning.

The Phoenix
Tel: 08455 331183
www.thephoenixschool.co.uk
This opened in 2010 in Girton. It is a parent run, fully independent school for children aged 3 to 7 years with small class sizes.

Home Education

Cambridgeshire Home Educating Families
Camhomeed@googlemail.com
www.cambridgehomeeducators.org.uk
Holds weekly and monthly support meetings, and social activities.

Index

With Very Special Thanks
To my two fantastic sons who
helped me write this book
Charlie, Bethany, Jude, Patrick and Anastasia
Mum for her kindness, Dad for his endless encouragement
Ivan and Matt who are fantastic and brilliant
Rickard for being so patient and
making an excellent cup of tea
Sally, Sarah Jo, Sarah C, Ellen, Rey and Steph

5852864R00066

Printed in Great Britain
by Amazon.co.uk, Ltd.,
Marston Gate.